SINGING THE
GODDESS
INTO PLACE

SUNY series in Hindu Studies

Wendy Doniger, editor

SINGING THE GODDESS INTO PLACE

LOCALITY, MYTH, AND SOCIAL CHANGE IN *CHAMUNDI OF THE HILL*, A KANNADA FOLK BALLAD

CALEB SIMMONS

Cover painting from the Uttanahalli temple

Published by State University of New York Press, Albany

© 2022 State University of New York

All rights reserved

Printed in the United States of America

No part of this book may be used or reproduced in any manner whatsoever without written permission. No part of this book may be stored in a retrieval system or transmitted in any form or by any means including electronic, electrostatic, magnetic tape, mechanical, photocopying, recording, or otherwise without the prior permission in writing of the publisher.

For information, contact State University of New York Press, Albany, NY
www.sunypress.edu

Library of Congress Cataloging-in-Publication Data

Name: Simmons, Caleb, author.
Title: Singing the goddess into place : locality, myth, and social change in Chamundi of the Hill, a Kannada folk ballad / Caleb Simmons.
Description: Albany : State University of New York Press, [2022] | Series: SUNY series in Hindu Studies | Includes bibliographical references and index.
Identifiers: ISBN 9781438488653 (hardcover : alk. paper) | ISBN 9781438488677 (ebook) | ISBN 9781438488660 (pbk. : alk. paper)
Further information is available at the Library of Congress.

Library of Congress Control Number: 2022931951

10 9 8 7 6 5 4 3 2 1

*For all the women in my life
who have shown me what it means to be strong,
beginning, naturally, with Mama*

Contents

List of Illustrations	ix
Acknowledgments	xi
Preface	xv
Note on Transliteration	xvii
1. Introduction: Singing Place and Situating Deities in the Kannada Folksong *Chamundi of the Hill*	1
2. "She killed the buffalo demon and dwells on the middle of the hill": Myth, Locality, and Cosmological Significance	27
3. "You're the one who protects this place": Folk Perspectives on Urban History and Regional Significance	57
4. "He is from one caste; we are from another": Religion, Caste, and Social Change	85
5. "I live on the top of the hill . . . you remain near its base": "High" and "Low" in the Goddess Traditions of Southern Karnataka	109
6. *Chamundi of the Hill* Translation	125
Appendix: "Wodeyar Origin Narrative" from *Great Kings of Mysore*	181
Notes	189
Bibliography	223
Index	233

Illustrations

1.1	Chamundi	9
1.2	Nanjunda	11
1.3	Uttanahalli	14
1.4	Uttanahalli Shri Pada	15
2.1	Mahisha statue on Chamundi Hill	31
2.2	Buffalo Point with temple workers from Chamundeshwari Temple on Chamundi Hill	32
2.3	Chamundeshwari, Universal Mother road sign	37
2.4a &b	Maharaja at Chamundi Mahotsava	39
2.5	*The Goddess Ambika Leading the Eight Mother Goddesses in Battle Against the Demon Raktabija,* folio from a *Devi Mahatmya* (Glory of the Goddess), photo courtesy of Museum Associates/ LACMA	45
2.6a	Chamundi Hill from Vidaranyapura-Nanjangud Road (southeast Mysore)	53
2.6b	Same view of Chamundi Hill with superimposed buffalo	53
3.1	Scene from *Chama Cheluve*	81
3.2	Painting from Uttanahalli temple	82
4.1	Aniconic Chamunda Maramma	97

4.2	Temple workers with masks	98
4.3	Women ready to prepare food for Chamundi Maramma	98
4.4	Lingayat priest fire walk	99

Acknowledgments

This book, like most of my work, is rooted in my time in Mysore, during which I have had numerous aides, guides, informants, and friends. I remain thankful to the city of Mysore and its citizens for being such gracious hosts while I lived there from 2012 through 2014 and during my subsequent annual visits. This work would not have been possible without the help of Professor P. K. Rajashekhara. Professor Rajashekhara graciously gave me permission to utilize his work as the basis for my translation, provided me with various folksongs and performances of the Chamundi narrative in video, audio, and print format, and carefully cleared up several points from the narrative about which I was confused. I am immensely grateful to the people of Chamundi Hill, who played multiple roles as guides, informants, subjects, and friends, especially Madesha, Manjunatha, Mohan, Purushottam, Raja, Satyanarayana, and Shashi. Additionally, Shashishekhara Dikshita, the head priest of the Chamundeshwari Temple, has been so gracious in his support, giving of his time and knowledge, and allowing me special access to rituals and sacred spaces.

Many mentors and colleagues in South Asian studies have been instrumental in helping this book coming to fruition through their continued encouragement and guidance, and I owe each of them a great debt of gratitude: Raj Balkaran, Gil Ben-Herut, Bob Del Bontà, Manu Devadevan, Elaine Fisher, Ute Hüsken, Rachel Fell McDermott, Vasudha Narayanan, Leslie Orr, Indira Vishwanathan Peterson, Anna Seastrand, Michael Slouber, Travis Smith, Davesh Soneji, Valerie Stoker, Archana Venkatesh, Anna Verghese, and many more. As always, my heartfelt thanks go out to Sarah Pierce Taylor, who is one of the greatest scholars I know and an even better person. The memory of

Anne Monius and Kathleen Erndl, two brilliant scholars whose time on this earth ended far too soon, is heavily imprinted on this book. They were both selfless mentors and friends and remain models for myself and many others whom they have inspired. I'm also deeply grateful to University of Pennsylvania, Oxford University's Center for Hindu Studies, and Christ University Bangalore for inviting me to present drafts of this work in various venues and to Michael Slouber, who arranged the "Garland of Forgotten Goddesses" panel for the Religion in South Asia Section at the 2016 American Academy of Religion Annual Meeting and the panel's respondent Rachel Fell McDermott for her support and suggestions. This panel and the subsequent volume *Garland of Forgotten Goddesses: Tales of the Feminine Divine from India* (ed. Michael Slouber, Berkeley: Univeristy of Californian Press, 2020) provided me with the impetus to delve deeper into the songs of Chamundi.

I wish to thank the American Institute of Indian Studies (AIIS) for its academic and financial support, through which I learned Hindi, Kannada, and Persian. It was during my time in the year-long AIIS Kannada program in Mysore that I first encountered the songs of *Chamundi of the Hill* and began working on my translation of its lyrics with C. S. Poornima, RVS Sundaram, and Lakshminarayan Aurora. I was also privileged to receive the AIIS Daniel H. H. Ingalls Memorial Research Fellowship, which was funded through generous donations and which allowed me to conduct research in Mysore in 2013 and 2014, during which time I was able to carry out much of the preliminary research that would eventually ground this book. I am forever in the debt of AIIS, its board members, staff, language instructors, and donors, without whom the research that led to this book would not have been possible.

The University of Arizona has been extremely supportive of my research and this book. I am immensely thankful for the support of my dean in the College of Humanities, Alain-Philippe Durand, Vice Dean Kim Jones, Associate Dean Ken McAllister, and Assistant Dean Toni Alexander, who have supported this research in the form of research and travel funding, College of Humanities faculty research grants, and endless moral support and guidance. My sincerest gratitude goes out to Karen Seat, who selflessly guides the UArizona Department of Religious Studies and Classics, sacrificing herself for the betterment of our department and our students. I'm extremely blessed to be part of a great department in which I have found many of my closest friends. I'm indebted to Rob Stephan, the Five-Star Faculty member who has won every teaching award at UArizona, for always pushing me to think more deeply about pedagogy, for being a Property Professor, and for always being down for drinking a few cheap beers. Andrea McComb Sanchez and I have been through it all together. I am so thankful for her passion for our work; it is a constant reminder about its importance and its stakes. Thanks to Rob Groves for reminding me to think deeply about our roles at the university, to balance work and life, and, of course, to always consider a word's etymology. While everyone in the department deserves credit for their support, I would be remiss if I didn't specifically acknowledge Rae Dachille, Courtney Friesen, Alison Jameson, Sarah McCallum, Hester Oberman, Arum Park, Kristy Slominski, Konden Smith Hansen, Max Strassfeld, Daisy Vargas, and Philip Waddell. Richard Eaton has been an extremely gracious mentor and thoughtful interlocutor at UArizona. I greatly appreciate all of our conversations about Indian history and life in general. Special thanks to Lindsay Montgomery for always pushing me to think critically about my assumptions and for being a voice of reason when Rob and I cook up wild schemes. I am also deeply ingratiated to Sujay Idagunji for carefully combing through my translations and for helping me wade through my Kannada secondary sources (and to his mother for always being willing to help us understand the context more deeply). And thanks to my many other colleagues at UArizona who have been so immensely helpful: Lars Fogelin, Takashi Miura, Mimi Nichter, Ravi Palanivelu, Sadhana Ravishankar, Jayanti Sunder, Albert Welter, and Jiang Wu. But perhaps the most gratitude is due to the staff of UArizona's School of International Languages, Literatures, and Cultures, who schedule my courses, take care of our facilities, ensure that I get paid, and basically just keep this place running: Leonora Escobar, Stephanie Mao, Lauri Mott, Gennady Sare, Marcela Thompson, Stephanie Topete, Debbie Varelas, Frank Whitehead, Summer Witting, and all of our student workers.

I wish to thank Neelam and Gulshan Sethi, Meera Gopalan, Reema Jaggi, Seema Jha, Sreelekha Susarla, Prasad Bhamidipati, and all of the other members of the Indian Society of Southern Arizona for welcoming me into their Tucson community. Thanks also to Hector Reyes and Niko Sanchez. You both brighten every Sunday at Rillito with your sass and snark!

Many thanks are due to everyone at SUNY Press who has had a hand in making this book a reality. I'm grateful to Christopher Ahn and James Peltz for seeing something in this project, giving words of encouragement, and guiding me through the process. Thanks to Wendy Doniger for accepting this book into the Hindu Studies Series. Thanks are also due to my two anonymous reviewers for their insightful comments on the original submission of this manuscript; the book is much better as a result of their comments, suggestions, and critiques.

I am very thankful for my friends and family outside of academia. It is always refreshing to step into a world where no one cares about publications, grants, and student credit hours. I am especially grateful for my Mee-Maw (Janie Simmons), Paw-Paw (Howard Simmons, Sr.), Nanny (Hazel Jernigan), and Grandaddy (Roy Jernigan). I miss them all dearly. I am thankful for everyone in Jay for their love and support: the Boisvert, Dobson, Hendricks, Jernigan, Phillips, Simmons, and Wolfe families. I wish I could see you all more regularly. Thanks to my dearest friends Andy and Ava Coughlin and their entire family, who have always treated me as one of their own. Thanks to my fellow travelers Sandy and Jose Cañez for welcoming Meghan and me into their lives. My mother-in-law, Kathie Hughes, is a wonderful and supportive friend. Thanks to my fur babies (and hairless babies) Isis, Baghira, Chairman Meow, Dax, Mabel, Albert, and Rudy; they keep me sane and happy by showering me with love and attention. I am grateful for my brother, Howard, and his partner, Michael, who are truly courageous and brilliant. Thank you to Mama for moving out to Tucson and dealing with me and the heat every day and to Daddy for all of his encouraging words while I worked on this manuscript and for his and Maria's enthusiasm for the project. Last, I am grateful to Meghan Pontius. Your ambition and success are such an inspiration. I love you for always keeping me on my toes (and for so many other things). I love you, HB.

Preface

I originally translated the folksongs of the *Chamundi of the Hill* ballad while I was attending the American Institute of Indian Studies Kannada language program in Mysore in 2012–13. Over the years, I have often returned to the ballad, longing for its wry sense of humor and its poignant critiques of social inequalities. Through those same years, I presented papers on portions of the ballad at academic conferences and workshops. While I thought I might eventually write an article or two from the material, I would've never thought of publishing a book that contained a translation of the songs if it hadn't been for the discussions with students in my course Women, Goddesses, and Power in Hinduism, a class that I modified from a course for which I had been the teaching assistant of the late, great Kathleen M. Erndl during my time at Florida State University. In my course, we kept returning to the question about how Hindu goddesses and/or the Goddess relates to every day, real life women, particularly how the goddess can be used for upliftment and empowerment. Inevitably, I would tell the story of *Chamundi of the Hill* and the complexities of the tale that simultaneously extols the goddess as a demon-slayer and casts her as a forlorn lover. As we discussed the narratives of the ballad, it was clear that the songs provided entrée into many aspects of the class: the relationship between local and elite traditions and myths, local goddesses and regional and village identities, and, of course, social change.

Therefore, I decided to write this book, not just for academics, but I've purposefully tried to write in a style that is accessible to undergraduate readers and for classroom use. I've tried to avoid specialized jargon, diacritics, frequent use of Sanskrit or Kannada terms, except when necessary and always with translation (unless it is a proper noun). For these same reasons, the chapters are shorter and meant to be digestible for students, utilizing endnotes for academic references and for ongoing dialogue with other scholarship. As a result, some portions of analysis can be rather brief, which I hope will stimulate lively discussion. Recognizing that many instructors who might assign this for their class might only assign a chapter or two, some information that is pertinent is discussed in multiple chapters. I apologize if this is repetitive for some readers. Additionally, while the translation comes at the end of the book, some readers might find it helpful to read the translation first, before reading the analytic chapters.

Finally, the COVID-19 pandemic and the Black Lives Matter Movement (and #MeToo before it) have brought meaningful discussions of systemic inequities into broader public discourse. I encourage instructors that adopt this book to use it as an opportunity to discuss social change, a message that is embedded at the heart of the *Chamundi of the Hill* narrative. For more resources for having these discussions in courses related to South Asian religions please visit https://risa.arizona.edu/project/black-lives-matter-summer-2020/.

All royalties from the sale of this book will be donated to provide scholarships for underrepresented students to study in India.

Note on Transliteration

For the sake of my intended general audience, I have chosen not to include transliteration of Sanskrit and Kannada words in this book. Instead, I have chosen to utilize phonetic spellings. Therefore, the following conventions have been utilized (all examples for Sanskrit are given in Devanagari script):

All vowels, including long and short in both Kannada and Sanskrit, are transliterated with their corresponding nonmarked vowel in English, roman characters. For example:

> Sanskrit (IAST) अ (a) and आ (ā) and Kannada (ISO 15919) ಅ (a) ಆ (ā) are transliterated as "a"
>
> Sanskrit ए (e) and Kannada ಎ (e) and ಏ (ē) are transliterated as "e"

Since there is no English, roman equivalent for Indic retroflex vowels, Sanskrit ऋ (r̥) and Kannada ಋ (r̥) are transliterated as "ri."

Nasals, whether originally written in full form or as an *anusvara* or *chandrabindu*, are transliterated with their corresponding non-marked vowel in English, Roman characters. For example:

> Sanskrit ङ (ṅ), ञ (ñ), ण (ṇ), and न (n) and Kannada ಙ (ṅ), ಞ (ñ), ಣ (ṇ), and ನ (n) are transliterated as "n"
>
> Sanskrit म (m) and Kannada ಮ (m) are transliterated as "m"

All retroflex and dental consonants are transliterated with their corresponding non-marked vowel in English, Roman characters. For example:

> Sanskrit ट (ṭ) and त (t) and Kannada ಟ (ṭ) and ತ (t) are transliterated as "t" and Sanskrit ठ (ṭh) and थ (th) and Kannada ಠ (ṭh) and ಥ (th) are transliterated as "th"

The palatal and retroflex fricative unvoiced consonants are transliterated as "sh" and the dental fricative unvoiced consonant is transliterated as "s":

> Sanskrit श (ś) and ष (ṣ) and Kannada ಶ (ś) and ಷ (ṣ) are transliterated as "sh," and Sanskrit स (s) and Kannada ಸ (s) are transliterated as "s"

Sanskrit ल (l) and Kannada ಲ (l) and ಳ (ḷ) have been transliterated as "l"

Finally, to avoid confusion in pronunciation Sanskrit च (c) and Kannada ಚ (c) and Sanskrit छ (ch) and Kannada ಛ (ch) have been transliterated as "ch" and "chh" respectively.

Chapter One

Introduction

Singing Place and Situating Deities in the Kannada Folksong *Chamundi of the Hill*

> *Merit comes to all who have told the story of Chamundi and to all who have heard her story. Dharma should be with us.*
>
> —"Dharma Should Be With Us," *Chamundi of the Hill*

The focus of this book is the Kannada ballad *Chamundi of the Hill* (Kannada: *Bettada Chamundi*), a collection of songs that tells the stories of the gods and goddesses of the southern portion of the South Indian state of Karnataka. The ballad narrates the romantic relationship between the goddess Chamundi and her consort, Nanjunda, with Chamundi's younger sister Uttanahalli acting as their "go-between." While the story is about gods and goddesses, the lives of the deities reflect everyday life in southern Karnataka. The deities are embedded within the same social worlds in which their devotees live, work, love, and worship. The original date of this group of songs is unknown, and it is sung in its many variants throughout the region, mostly by castes that are classified as agriculturalists. The version that provides the content for this book can be dated to the late 19th or early 20th centuries and is traditionally performed outside of temples and at important village festivals throughout southern Karnataka by Kamsales, traditional performers from the Devaragudda subcaste of the Kuruba caste. The ballad, therefore, is situated within and preserves their specific local system of knowledge. By delving into the world of *Chamundi of the Hill*, we can begin to better understand how the physical environment is transformed through people's relationship with it and how this relationship helps build meaning for the communities that call it home.

The narratives of the ballad are quite novel within the broader genre of Indian mythology as they focus not only on three deities but the identities of those deities are tied to specific places and their local temples: Chamundi is the city deity of Mysore, her consort Nanjunda is the city deity of nearby Nanjangudu, and Uttanahalli is the goddess of Uttanahalli, whose name literally means the "in-between village." Consequently, through the performance of these songs, the balladeers sing the goddesses and gods into the region, situating the deities within a local religious and social landscape and creating a local sacred history or *sthalapurana* of the region. The ballad *Chamundi of the Hill* is not only a mythology of the place, but it places myth, actively transforming southern Karnataka into a land where gods and goddesses live and remapping the region into a sacred geography where temples, deities, villages, and cities are connected through networks of devotion and pilgrimage.

The Story of Chamundi

In order for us to understand the significance of the narrative, it is first important that we introduce the ballad itself. This section is meant to serve this purpose. It begins with a brief introduction to the style and structure of the ballad before summarizing its central plot. This summary is intentionally laconic since the narrative is discussed in greater detail in the chapters of this book and the full translation of the story is provided in the final chapter.

The Form and Style of *Chamundi of the Hill*

The form and style of the songs in *Chamundi of the Hill* reflects its broad applicability and appeal. The ballad is comprised of ten songs, two frame hymns and eight narrative songs. The two hymns provide the anchors for the narrative, directly addressing the goddess Chamundi. The opening hymn asks the goddess for a boon or wish, and the concluding hymn restates the wish and describes the merits of singing and listening to the story contained in the ballad. The interior narrative songs tell the story about the goddess's establishment in Mysore and how her romance with Nanjunda unfolded.

Chamundi of the Hill has been described as a "mythic ballad" and a work of "natural poetry" (Kannada: *naisargika kavya*), both of which help us to understand its form and function.[1] These folksongs easily fall into the layperson's definition of "myth" because they are songs about deities or what some have called "casually effective divine personalities."[2] However, as a mythic ballad, *Chamundi of the Hill* does so much more than just tell a story about gods, goddesses, and demons. It is a story "about something significant;" that is, its effectiveness lies in its ability to make sense of the complex modern physical and social worlds of southern Karnataka through the subjectivity of their divine protagonists.[3] The worlds that it creates with its stories about the goddess and her lover reflect the same world in which its performers and audiences live. By singing the goddess into the places that they all live, work, play, and worship, the balladeers ground the region's institutions (and their critique of these institutions) within a worldview of broader significance that is rooted in the divine past but uniquely situated in the local present.[4]

The composition of *Chamundi of the Hill* is a simple narration, "natural poetry," that is primarily prose with the occasional insertion of verse, a style that in Kannada is called *janapada champu*, a folk version of the traditional Indian literary genre of *champu* that consists of mixed prose and verse. The prose portions occupy a space somewhere between prose and poetry, the form of which has been compared by some Kannadiga scholars to the famous *vachanas* or spoken word poems of the Shaiva Sharana saints (c. 12th–13th centuries CE) of medieval Karnataka.[5] The lines of the songs do not rhyme, nor do they adhere to traditional Indian rules of poetic meter, neither in length (*jati*) nor in sequences (*vritta*) of syllables. Instead, the lyrics of *Chamundi of the Hill* are sung to a tune that mixes several *ragas* (melodies), a style known as *ragamalika* or "garland of melodies" in Carnatic music. Within the melodies, there is a great deal of space for improvisation, and performers do not strictly adhere to traditional melodies, nor can it be said that there is a standard tune for the songs.[6]

While the narrative certainly evokes emotions of devotion (*bhakti*) within Chamundi's devotees, I would not classify *Chamundi of the Hill* only as a collection of devotional songs or as *bhakti* poetry.[7] Instead, the ballad also serves as a *mahatmya* (glorification text) of the goddess Chamundi and a *sthalapurana* (local sacred history) of the region with a narrative that functions like any Sanskrit or vernacular Purana (ancient mythic story) upholding a religious and ideological position.[8] To put it another way, *Chamundi of the Hill*, like all Puranas, operates within what Madeleine Biardeau has called "the universe of *bhakti*."[9] The songs and their lyrics assume a theological position, in this case devotion and ritual practice to the goddesses Chamundi and Uttanahalli, and, to a lesser extent in this collection of songs, Nanjunda. That said, within the ballad, there are instances in which the performers and certain characters express themselves in forms that are very closely aligned with *bhakti* devotional songs (e.g., "Mother, Grant Me a Wish" or Uttanahalli's words to Nanjunda in the song "Have You Lost Interest in Your Wife?"). Therefore, while *Chamundi of the Hill* might not be classified as a devotional ballad, devotion to these deities and the networks that support that devotion is taken for granted within its lyrics.

Summary of *Chamundi of the Hill*'s Narrative

The story begins on top of Chamundi Hill outside of the city of Mysore, as the goddess Chamundi fights the buffalo demon Mahisha. After slaying the mighty demon, Mahisha's brother, Aisu, appears and challenges the goddess. Chamundi quickly becomes overwhelmed fighting Aisu because of his supernatural power that produces demons from his blood; however, as she wipes the sweat from her brow and slings it to the ground, her sister, Uttanahalli, is born from Chamundi's perspiration. Together they are able to defeat the demon foe, confirming Chamundi's place on the hill as the protector of Mysore and establishing the goddess Uttanahalli in the village of Uttanahalli at the base of her hill.

After the battle, Chamundi goes to the confluence of the Kapini and Kaveri Rivers to bathe, and, as luck would have it, Nanjunda, a local form of Shiva, had also come to the rivers to worship. Spotting the lovely young goddess, the deity Nanjunda approaches her. After some negotiation, Nanjunda, despite already having two wives, convinces Chamundi to join him in a love marriage, which they consummate there on the riverbank. For several weeks after their marriage, Nanjunda and Chamundi enjoy their honeymoon in Chamundi's temple on Chamundi Hill. As the festival season approaches, Nanjunda has to take leave of Chamundi to attend to the needs of his devotees; he forgets about Chamundi and returns home to Nanjangudu and his two other wives, Deviri and Somaji.

Missing her husband and feeling like he had tricked her into a fleeting romantic tryst, Chamundi calls upon her sister, Uttanahalli, to go to the homeland of Nanjunda and his wives and bring her husband back to Chamundi Hill. In order to convince Uttanahalli to go on this seeming suicide mission, Chamundi describes a horrific dream wherein bloodthirsty goddesses attacked Mysore, the Sharana poet Channabasava married a tribal woman and performed a ritual animal slaughter, and her husband's wives mourned, having become widows. Uttanahalli is convinced and goes to fetch Nanjunda for her sister.

In the middle of the night, Nanjunda hears Uttanahalli's calls to return to Chamundi. He is eager to return but has to manage to free himself from his wives with whom he is sharing a bed. After tricking his wives by using a log in his stead, Nanjunda goes to join his new lover. After borrowing money from his brother-in-law Kalinga, a local serpent deity, and a brief run-in with Nandi, his other brother-in-law, Nanjunda reaches Chamundi, who immediately welcomes him back into her bed. As the couple lies in postcoital bliss, Deviri and Somaji arrive at Chamundi's temple and catch Nanjunda red-handed. As Deviri hurls insults at Chamundi, Nanjunda sneaks back home hoping to avoid a fight; however, when his elder co-wives returned home, Deviri stripped him naked and kicked him out of their home.

Naked and homeless, Nanjunda devises a plan to not only get Deviri and Somaji to accept Chamundi as their younger co-wife but to beg her to join their union. First, Nanjunda goes to the divine abode of Brahma and instructs him to go the Nanjangudu to give Deviri and Somaji a false *shastra* or incantation that is made entirely of gibberish. Next, Nanjunda goes to Chamundi and tells her to take the form of a fortune-teller and to go by his home claiming to have the power to use any *shastra* to raise the dead. Finally, he goes home and pretends to be dead. Brahma comes by shortly thereafter and gives Deviri and Somaji the false incantation. Not long after, the co-wives hear Chamundi in the guise of the fortune-teller on the streets proclaiming her gift of necromancy and run to inquire about her services. The fortune-teller, however, explains that the incantation will not work because they have cursed the goddess Chamundi.

Immediately, Deviri and Somaji repent of their maltreatment of Chamundi and resolve that she must be their co-wife and that

Nanjunda can live with her six months out of the year. With that, Chamundi-as-fortune-teller leaves, and Nanjunda opens his eyes. Deviri and Somaji give Nanjunda their jewels and instruct him to give them to Chamundi. Then, all three deities go to Chamundi Hill and convince Chamundi to join their family, splitting time between Chamundi Hill and Nanjangudu.

Place and Locality in *Chamundi of the Hill*

Place-Making and Locality Production

As can be seen even within this short summary of the story of *Chamundi of the Hill*, its events, themes, and deities are intimately tied to specific sites of the region of southern Karnataka, especially Mysore, Uttanahalli, and Nanjangudu. This ballad does the work of both making place and producing locality for the community that performs these songs and the common folk who are its usual and intended audience. It is this commitment to place-making and locality that ties this book together. When I say that the songs make place and produce locality, I am using both terms in a technical and theoretical sense. By "place," I refer not to physical environments but the result of when these environments have been transformed through people's "perception, attitude, value, and world view."[10] Place is space that has been overlaid with meaning. Place, therefore, is not naturally occurring, but it is made by and reflected through those whose identities are linked to that particular environment.[11] Locality, on the other hand, is more relational and more agentive.[12] Locality is an expression of a community's perception of place that can be part of a broader negotiation of multiple and, perhaps, competing perspectives on one particular space.[13] Therefore, while place is made and perpetuated within local communities and their social systems and rituals, locality is produced and exhibited through "performance, representation, and action."[14] To put it another way, place builds the community; locality is the demarcation of its boundaries.

The stories of *Chamundi of the Hill* that are discussed in this book are primarily intended for an internal audience as they are typically sung by the Kamsale performers outside of temples (but not as part of any sanctioned ritual and not by another of the brahmin priests) and for functions within the community Devaragudda and Kuruba communities.[15] They are reflective of the society in which they were created and in which they continue to be performed. They assume shared values and culture, including social organization, attire, food, beliefs, and religious practices. The songs come alive as the deities are placed within this world view. Chamundi, Uttanahalli, and Nanjunda become members of the community. They are part of the same kinship groups. They follow the same customs. They dress the same. They eat the same foods, have the same arguments, and share the same anxieties. The deities are not abstracted but are intimately connected to specific sites throughout the region. The deities live amongst the people. They walk the same roads, go to the same festivals, and visit the same temples. The important devotional and pilgrimage sites aren't portrayed as sites of royalty or brahminical authority. Instead, they are reinterpreted as sites of the folk (see below for further discussion about this term), as they are enlivened by their divine residents who uphold the same values as the community of performers. By situating their deities within the landscape, *Chamundi of the Hill* situates the community there. It makes the spaces and sites of the Mysore region meaningful to the community and the community meaningful to the space. From the very first song, *Chamundi of the Hill* is not only singing the goddess into place, but it is also placing the folk community at the heart of the region, making it their place.

Along with making the space meaningful for its own community, *Chamundi of the Hill* also does the work of negotiating the sacred spaces of the region and promoting their interpretation of its social worlds. This is particularly clear in the case of Chamundi and her temple on Chamundi Hill. The Chamundeshwari temple is now overseen and officiated by a brahmin priest whose lineage originated outside the region in what is now the modern state of Tamil Nadu. The brahminical portrayal of the goddess of the temple aligns with other elite interpretations as Chamundi is equated to the universal Goddess, who manifests throughout India in different temples. As even the title of the ballad indicates, *Chamundi of the Hill* presents the goddess as a singular local deity that resides on Chamundi Hill and who can live at only one place at a time. While at first these positions seem irreconcilable, the ballad acknowledges its own positionality and that of the elite traditions and uses the story as an occasion to carve out space for a folk locality within the site. For the folk raconteurs, this negotiation of the space is not about exclusivity, and they present Chamundi Hill and Chamundi herself as capable of supporting both the folk tradition and the elite traditions. This theme of plurality and inclusivity in religious and ritual practice is carried throughout the entire ballad as it uses the relationships of the deities as an opportunity to critique normative social hierarchies, particularly associated with caste and ritual practice, narratively demonstrating that they are parallel traditions that ought to coexist without discrimination.

As a negotiation of place and locality, the stories and songs of *Chamundi of the Hill* constructs a network of peoples, gods, goddesses, and sites and binds them all together into a larger place or region made up of smaller connected places.[16] At its heart, the tale told in the songs is about the lives of important regional deities and the negotiation of their identities as members of different elite and nonelite communities. Therefore, it is necessary at this point to briefly introduce the places and their deities about whose tradition many readers will undoubtedly be unfamiliar.

Deities of *Chamundi of the Hill* and Their Places

CHAMUNDI AND MYSORE

In many parts of India, Chamundi, or Chamunda as she is more often called, is a fierce hag-like goddess, emaciated and fond of blood rituals. In Mysore, however, Chamundi is a regal goddess who rides solo atop her lion vehicle following the iconographic conventions of the Pan-Indian goddess Durga in popular devotional art (figure 1.1). She is described as "sweet" and "beautiful" and as the "Queen of the Universe." In popular mythology, she is said to be the slayer of the buffalo demon Mahisha and her hill, Chamundi Hill, the physical site where she defeated the demon king, and her primary stone image depicts a powerful warrior goddess slaying the buffalo demon.[17] As is explored in subsequent chapters, it is this identity of the goddess that binds the various parallel traditions that worship Chamundi, though most of them conceptualize her in related but ultimately very different ways. For the royal tradition, Chamundi is an independent, powerful, and regal warrior goddess who sits on her lion vehicle with her weapons ready to take on her enemies and to grant sovereignty and ruling power to the kings of Mysore. In the Sanskritic/brahminic tradition of Mysore, she is the mother goddess who accepts vegetarian offerings and is the most efficient path to prosperity and to *moksha/mukti* or liberation. In the folk traditions captured in *Chamundi of the*

Figure 1.1. Chamundi.

Hill, Chamundi is a martial goddess and a (sometimes virgin) mother goddess, but she is also invested in the trappings of regular, everyday life. The Chamundi of the folk traditions blends the more divine and supernatural aspects of her royal and Sanskritic/brahminic depictions with one that reflects the more quotidian, mundane concerns of the common folk of the region. For the folk traditions, Chamundi is embedded within the social and cultural worlds of domestic life in southern Karnataka, struggling through many of the this-worldly issues with which her devotees have or will struggle themselves. In *Chamundi of the Hill*, Chamundi becomes a much more immanent goddess, one in whom a devotee can see themselves.

Chamundi's primary temple in the region is the Chamundeshwari temple, located on top of Chamundi Hill a few kilometers from the center of the "Royal City" of Mysore. Mysore is a city of roughly one million inhabitants in the southern portion of the state of Karnataka, about 90 miles southwest of Bangalore, the large cosmopolitan city commonly called India's Silicon Valley. Mysore is a popular site for tourists within India who come to the city for its moderate climate and to visit its many exquisite palaces, including the world-renowned Amba Vilas or Mysore Palace. The Chamundeshwari temple overlooks the city and is also a popular tourist destination, one of the most important pilgrimage sites in Karnataka, and, as a sign on the road up the hill boasts, "one of the 18 most holy sites in South India." On top of the hill the rather quaint but attractive temple with large seven-tiered tower shares its position as the highest point in the area with the Ram Vilas palace and a series of television and cell phone towers. The village that surrounds the temple is equally charming. It is populated by no more than a few hundred people and has until recently resisted commercial interests and state-funded construction.[18] The relatively simple site completely masks the importance of this temple in local devotional practice and regional pilgrimage networks. The temple is presided over by Dikshita brahmins who were brought to serve in the temple in by Krishnaraja Wodeyar III between 1819–1848 as part of his larger program of incorporating forms of Hindu ritual and devotion that were recognized throughout India as elite forms of belief and practice.[19] These brahmin priests displaced the previous officiants of the temple from the agricultural Tammadi (also Tomadi) caste who are commonly referred to as Shivarchakas (lit. "those who perform rituals to Shiva") and introduced *agamic* brahminic rituals into the temple.[20]

Also at the top of the hill are the Satyanarayana (Vishnu) temple and the Mahabaleshwara (Shiva) temple. The oldest temple of the hill is the Mahahaleshwara temple, and until the rise of the Wodeyar king of Mysore in the 17th century, Chamundi Hill was known as Mahabalachala or the "Mountain of Mahabala (Shiva)." I mention this here because the earlier preeminence of the Shiva temple provides clues to the rise of the deity Chamundi in the area. As far back as the 8th century on the northern portion of Shaiva temple complexes of South India, subsidiary shrines were regularly installed to a group of fierce but powerful goddesses called the *saptamatrikas* or "seven little mothers." These shrines were frequented by practitioners who needed the help of the goddess with issues like conceiving children or to alleviate disease. The cult of the seven little mothers was very popular throughout the southern portions of India, including southern Karnataka. The last of the seven, who was the eldest and often considered the most powerful,

Introduction

was the emaciated goddess Chamunda/Chamundi, whose own cult continued to grow due to its efficacy in helping petitioners overcome their issues and often resulted in standalone shrines to Chamundi.[21] While there is no concrete historical evidence to confirm this theory, it is very likely that the Chamundi temple on Chamundi Hill, which is located close to the Mahabaleshwara temple on its northern side, was originally connected to the Shiva temple and the cult of the seven little mothers, elements of which continue in folk religious rituals to Chamundi.

NANJUNDA AND NANJANGUDU

Nanjunda is the love interest of Chamundi and the ballad's second protagonist. He is the deity of Nanjangudu, a smaller city with a population of approximately 50,000 located about 15 miles south of

Figure 1.2. Nanjunda.

Mysore. Nanjunda is commonly associated with the Pan-Indian deity Shiva, and Nanjangudu is known in the region as Southern Kailasa, a reference to the Shiva's divine abode in the Himalayan mountains. Nanjunda, whose name is a compound of *nanju* (poison) + *unda* (having consumed), is connected to Shiva specifically through the story of cosmic creation when Shiva saves the gods by consuming the poison that emerges as the gods churn the ocean of milk in pursuit of the nectar of immortality (*amrita*). From this story in the Sanskritic tradition, Shiva receives the nickname Nilakantha or the "one with blue throat." The Nanjunda's temple in Nanjangudu also references both the local and the Sanskritic traditions in its two names, Nanjundeshwaraswamy and Shri Kantheshwara Temple. The temple's dual identity possibly stems from a similar shift as took place in Chamundeshwari, when in the 19th century the local Kannada Tammadi (also Tomadi; Shivarchaka) priests were displaced by Tamil brahmins who inaugurated *agamic* rituals.

Because of his power over poison, in the local tradition, Nanjunda is considered a deity who is particularly adept at healing petitioners. Devotees who are suffering from sickness, pain, or disease make religious vows and offer small Nanjunda votive charms fabricated out of silver representing the part of the body afflicted with the disease.[22] Devotees also perform acts of penance, such as circumambulation around his temple while rolling their bodies on the ground (*uruluseve*), shaving all their hair (*mudikoduvudu*), or prostrating fully every step as they go to the temple (*hejje namaskara*). Another common practice is the offering of *kambis* or iron bars during his annual festivals. Particularly, during his annual chariot or *ratha* festival, nearby villages offer Nanjunda these iron bars from which they hang earthen pots full of juices and jaggery (a type of unrefined cane sugar). Another healing tradition centered around Nanjunda that is rapidly fading is the practice of alternate insemination in which married couples would perform various rituals (*holekere, terina pattadi, talemele*) during which the women would be impregnated by another man.[23] Historically, he has been an important deity for the kings of Mysore. In 1845 CE, Krishnaraja Wodeyar III commissioned the construction of the temple *gopura* or tower, and nine years later constructed subsidiary shrines for various goddesses in honor of his queens. Before him, the Muslim ruler Tipu Sultan gave the deity, whom the king called "Hakeem Nanjunda," a garland of emeralds and a solid emerald *linga* (an aniconic representation of Shiva) in gratitude for Nanjunda restoring the eyesight of Tipu Sultan's favorite royal elephant.[24] Because of his

Introduction

healing abilities, Nanjunda is also considered a gift-giving deity or *phaladevate* and is known as "Enjoyment" or *bhoga* Nanjunda.

Locally, many people claim that Nanjunda was a historical person who was a contemporary of both Chamundi and Male Madeshwara, another important regional deity/saint. According to folklorist P. K. Rajashekhara, Nanjunda was the brother of Madeshwara, both of whom studied at the Kunturu Matha before becoming leaders at the Virashaiva Sutturu Matha, a religious institution that traces its foundations to the tenth century and the Chola empire and bases its teachings on the philosophy of the 12th-century Sharana poet Basava.[25] Rajashekhara, therefore, suggests that Nanjunda was probably a historical physician from the Chola period who practiced Persian Unani medicine and became the adjudicator of regional disputes; over time, Nanjunda's legend grew, and he became known as a manifestation of the deity Shiva.[26] While this is an interesting theory, there is no historical data that supports this claim.

Chamundi of the Hill, however, gives us another glimpse into Nanjunda's identity. One of which he is a cunning, conniving character, almost a trickster. This local version is similar to other depictions of Shiva in local and regional songs, including those from the goddess devotional songs of Bengal.[27] Along with Nanjunda, his family includes several supporting characters in the *Chamundi of the Hill* narrative. In the ballad, before meeting Chamundi, Nanjunda already has two wives: Deviri, his eldest wife, and Somaji, the younger.[28] Additionally, the serpent deity Kalinga, and Nandi (called Basavanna in the ballad), Shiva's vehicle, are both introduced in the ballad as the brothers of Deviri and Nanjunda's brothers-in-law.

UTTANAHALLI AND UTTANAHALLI

The last of the three main characters of *Chamundi of the Hill* is Uttanahalli. Uttanahalli is the sister of Chamundi and is, out of the three leads, the deity that is least well known outside of the region of southern Karnataka. Uttanahalli is not only the goddess's name, but it is also the name of the village wherein she resides. As will be discussed in several chapters, the goddess's name suggests her function as a village deity or *gramadevate* as she is both the goddess of Uttanahalli and the protector of her eponymous village. Uttanahalli, the village, is very small, with a population of only 1,325 per the 2011 census. The village's name is a combination of *halli*, the Kannada term for "village," and *utta*

Figure 1.3. Uttanahalli.

(+*na*), which would best be translated as "middle" or "in-between." Its name denotes its location between the popular pilgrimage sites of Chamundi Hill and Nanjangudu. In *Chamundi of the Hill*, Uttanahalli, the goddess, also embodies this "in-between-ness" as she serves as the go-between for the lovers Chamundi and Nanjunda, going back and forth delivering messages from/to the goddess and god.

In addition to (and perhaps because of) her identity as an intermediary, Uttanahalli is one of the most popular and powerful goddesses of the region, with a robust devotional and pilgrimage network. As we see in the first narrative song of *Chamundi of the Hill*, Uttanahalli is a fierce goddess who comes to the aid of Chamundi as she fights the gargantuan demon Aisu, who self-replicates from every drop of blood that hits the ground. While Chamundi is overwhelmed by the deity, Uttanahalli extends her tongue over the battlefield, absorbing all the blood before it can mingle with the earth. Perhaps because of the similarities between this story and the story of Raktabija (for more, see chapter 2), Uttanahalli is commonly associated with the Sanskritic Pan-Indian deity Kali. As a result of the emphasis on her tongue in this myth, at least since the 19th century, Uttanahallii has also been linked to Jwalamukhi, the important pilgrimage goddess with a tongue of fire whose temple in Himachal Pradesh is considered a seat of the goddess (*shakti pitha*) that manifested after the goddess Sati's tongue fell there after Sati's self-immolation.[29] In the local tradition of Jwalamukhi in Himachal Pradesh in northwest India, the goddess is one among a group of seven sister goddesses, as is Chamundi.[30]

The fierce and powerful nature of Uttanahalli is also reflected in the rituals performed to her at her temple. Regularly, devotees offer the goddess flesh-offerings of chickens and goats, walking them up to the temple entrance to be presented to the goddess before ritually slaughtering the animals and preparing and cooking their meat for distribution as *prasad* or "blessed" leftovers to her devotees at a nearby rest-house. The blood and flesh offerings have clearly been a part of Uttanahalli's ritual complex for a while, as even the temple's ritual image of the feet of the goddess (*shri pada*) are surrounded by carvings of devotees beheading themselves as an offering to the goddess (figure 1.4).[31]

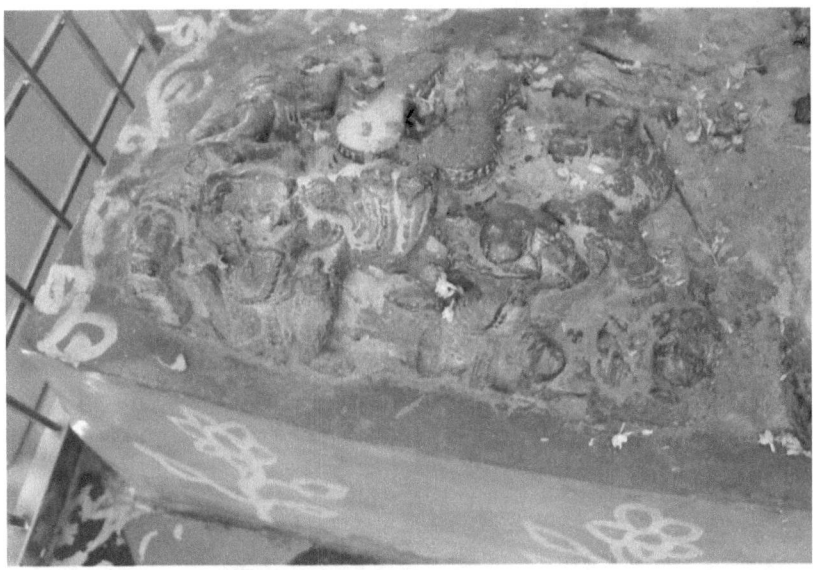

Figure 1.4. Uttanahalli Shri Pada.

Chamundi of the Hill, Folksongs, and Orality

In July of 2012, while I was living in Mysore studying Kannada through the American Institute of Indian Studies Language Program, I attended the opening night of a drama titled *Chama Cheluve,* the performance that introduced me to the folksongs of Chamundi.[32] I had been to several dramatic performances during my time in Mysore, and most were usually well attended but usually nothing that would require special notice. *Chama Cheluve,* however, was different. The large open-air theater was packed. As I watched, I could see why people had come out in droves to see the performance. The story had it all: action, suspense, romance, comedy. One time wasn't enough. I had to see it again. I returned the next night. So had everyone else, and more had come with them. *Chama Cheluve* would become a sensation that year, extending beyond the original week-long schedule for months to consistently packed crowds before moving on to Bangalore. I was unaware that the subject of the play was not a novel one, and the story of Chamundi was one that was well known in the region through folksongs, songs of which different iterations could be heard in folk performances in the yards surrounding temples, on the radio, and even on reality television competitions. The songs and the story they tell are a ubiquitous part of life in southern Karnataka, and they have mass appeal. As the director of *Chama Cheluve,* Mandya Ramesh, would say, "People are beginning to pay attention to styles of folk performance: Yakshagana, Veeraghase, and Kamsale."[33]

It seems, however, that people had been paying attention all along. The story of the romance between Chamundi and Nanjunda and the songs that tell these stories have been part of oral and folk traditions for at least a century (probably much longer) and are sung by a wide variety of traditional performers, including performance-based castes, like the Kamsale, Nilagara, Helava, Tambure, and Manteswa, and are commonly sung by rural village women.[34] In each context and in the different districts of southern Karnataka, the stories are told slightly differently, with additions and deletions and embellishments that suit the specific local context, audience, and religious traditions. The larger tradition of telling and singing about Chamundi is dynamic and ever-evolving, something that can never be captured in a translation of one telling of its story; therefore, in this section, I discuss my source for the translation of *Chamundi of the Hill* and the community that performs this ballad, the categorization of the songs as folk, and finally the relationship between scholarship and the creative and performing traditions that create and recreate the songs of Chamundi.

Chamundi of the Hill, a Kamsale Ballad

Years before the popular performance of the story of Chamundi in *Chama Cheluve*, renowned Kannada folklorist P. K. Rajashekara published *Bettada Chamundi* (translated as *Chamundi of the Hill*) that recorded the songs of the folksong master and guru Kamsale Mahadevayya, as performed by K. B. Shivamudrappa and Shrimathi Kalamma.[35] Due to the popularity of the folksongs, Rajashekara subsequently published a prose rendition of the ballad and performed a dramatic rendering on radio and television that was eventually published in 2012, the same year that *Chama Cheluve* opened, leading to a controversy over oral traditions and ownership to which I return below.[36] So, when I decided to write this book in 2017, I met with Rajashekara to get his advice on distilling the many variants of this song into one digestible volume. As it turned out, this was the same question with which Rajashekhara had struggled for almost 50 years ago.[37] In the end, he decided to select the songs of Kamsale Mahadevayya because of his renown and the complexities and poetry captured within his telling of *Chamundi of the Hill*. In addition to consulting notes from live performances by itinerant Kamsale bards outside the Chamundeshwari Temple on Chamundi Hill and Uttanahalli's temple in Uttanahalli, a variety of modern media, such as CD and MP3 recordings, and the dramatic performances of *Chama Cheluve*, with his permission, my translation of these stories is based on the Kamsale Mahadevayya version of the story that was collected and recorded by P. K. Rajashekara. Indeed, his *Bettada Chamundi*, remains the most thorough documentation of the ballad to date.[38]

The Kamsales, who are discussed in greater length in chapter 4, are traditional performers from the Devaragudda or Siridevaragudda subcaste (*upajati*) of the Kuruba caste (*jati*) who have been initiated into the tradition by a guru. Their name comes from their identity as performers and refers to the small cymbals, called *kamsale*, with which they perform. Traditionally, the community sings a variety of songs whereby they maintain much of the oral histories of the region. Most of their songs focus on mythological and devotional themes; however, some are historical in nature, including a heroic song about the battle of Piriyapattana and Tipu Sultan.[39] Even though the songs translated here are about Chamundi and Nanjunda, the Kamsales' traditional home is Male Madeshwara Hills, and they are devotees of the local Kannada deity/saint Madeshwara, whose temple is located there.

Despite their important role as the keepers and performers of the region's religious and oral histories and its remembered pasts, the Kamsales are categorized within the Indian government's list of "Other Backward Castes" or OBC. This designation of OBC was established in the Indian Constitution (Article 340) as a means to safeguard "socially and educationally backward classes" from discrimination based on the hegemonic traditional system of social stratification and hierarchy commonly referred to as "caste." As an OBC, within the normative hierarchy of commensality and ritual purity and pollution according to caste, Kamsales are generally considered a "low caste." As a result of centuries of caste discrimination, many Kamsales (and Devaraguddas more generally) have converted to Lingayatism (for more see chapter 4). Lingayatism, which collectively constitutes approximately 20% of the population of Karnataka, is a tradition of devotion to the deity Shiva that is multivalent in its identities and diverse in its composition, as groups from various caste backgrounds have converted into the religion, and, like the Kamsales, some have maintained the ritual and social practices associated with their caste identity.[40] Generally speaking, Lingayatism arose from a movement led by a collection of 12th and 13th century Shaiva saints known as Sharanas. The Sharanas are best known for their devotional poetry that took the form of poignant yet folksy aphorisms called *vachanas* that praise the local deities of the Kannada-speaking world. The Shaiva Sharanas' poetry has garnered much attention because of their strong reform message that critiques ritualism and caste hierarchy, leading many in the West to draw comparisons with Christian Protestant movements.[41] In this regard, the Kamsales carry on the tradition of the Sharanas, not only in the style of their songs, but also in their message. As is seen in *Chamundi of the Hill*, the songs of the Kamsales include a strong anti-caste-discrimination message and advocate for social change.[42]

Chamundi of the Hill, a Folk Ballad

At the onset of this section, I must admit that "folk" is a loaded term. Outside of academic studies of folklore, the term "folk" can be and has often been interpreted as a pejorative classification. When I ask my students the meaning of folk, most respond with references to folk music, by which they often refer to musical genres, like bluegrass, related to the rural southeastern United States. Others associate the term with noneducated and/or working-class groups of people. When pushed to dive deeper, most eventually form some sort of contradistinction (often a hierarchy) between "high"/elite, mainstream, and folk cultures, with a casual assumption that folk represents the lowest forms of culture. On the other end of the spectrum, inspired by romantic sentiments, historically, some, including scholars, have turned to folk culture to excavate and recover purer, more natural forms of art that contrast the banality and artificial (re)productions of industrial and technological life; indeed, the Romantic era was the context in which the academic discipline of folklore studies began.[43] While these two perspectives seem inherently at odds, they, in fact, produce the same divisions of culture that are linked to hierarchical systems of valuation, only inverting what is "high" and what is "low." In this book, I do not intend on reifying either of these positions; that is, my goal is neither to uphold the naïve perspective that folk culture is "lower" nor to validate folk culture as natural or somehow a corrective for society.

Instead, I use the term "folk" in its most generic sense, and, like the German *volk*, in this book, "folk" simply refers to ordinary people, as in the general population. In the case of southern Karnataka, at least, this does have some affinities with the assumptions held by many of my students. Most people in this region live in rural areas and villages and are part of working-class, agricultural demographics, though this is rapidly changing due to increased urbanization and an expansion of the professional middle class. The culture of the folk is also often in contrast to the brahminic and royal culture and its hierarchical hegemony. Hesitatingly, throughout this book, I refer to the brahminic and royal traditions as "elite," not because of any inherent valuation, but because these traditions, while representing a smaller percentage of the population, promote their communities as the top of the social hierarchy, a position that is widely accepted across the populace. Though not created in a vacuum, folk narratives are creative expressions that reflect the outlook of a large but overlooked demographic, a demographic that is being increasingly marginalized as people move into cities and large towns and their art forms are occluded through a homogenization of Indian culture through mainstream digital media and mass reproduction. As I hope is demonstrated in the pages to follow, the folk ballad of *Chamundi of the Hill* is a rich piece of literature that records the significance of its local place, the remembered pasts of its people, and attempts to promote its own value system.[44] While I've tried to ensure that these stories are presented on their own terms, in order to elucidate the positionality of *Chamundi of the Hill*, I provide similar stories from elite royal and Sanskritic traditions. These are meant as helpful comparisons, not as sources from which the folk tales are derived.[45] In this way, specifically because it comes from the folk tradition, *Chamundi of the Hill* encapsulates a perspective that runs parallel to and, often, in competition with the elite culture that also exists in the region.

Of equal importance for understanding this book's approach to *Chamundi of the Hill* is the underlying assumptions of the inherent value of knowledge systems contained in oral folk traditions and orality as a valid and important means of recording and transmitting this knowledge. Building on the recent work of literary theorists Chamberlin and Chamberlain, throughout this book, the oral folksongs of *Chamundi of the Hill* are treated as meaningful contributions to the literature of Mysore and of India that open our understanding of South Asian literary production to include forms and stories through which a great number of people make sense of their world.[46] Orality presumes listeners who hear the songs as they are performed. In the performance of the narratives, the audiences are part of the generative process and help to shape and/or perpetuate the stories as the storytellers improvise for the context.[47] As such, built into oral traditions is a sort-of real time peer review, and, unlike written material, orality assumes some semblance of community consensus around the given narrative and its themes. The dynamic and changeable media of orality and performance provides means whereby local religious and social issues can be worked out in a public forum. Therefore, the songs and stories from oral folk traditions act as reliable archives in which we can see the values and social concerns of the local population reflected.

Songs and Scholarship

I've had to ask myself repeatedly how one can write a scholarly book, especially one that contains a translation, while still being true to the tradition of *Chamundi of the Hill* and to the people who sing its songs. I recognize this book—and much of Indological research—is a form of coloniality: a white man goes to India, collects a valuable resource, repackages and distributes it for profit.[48] This is an uncomfortable reality in the field of South Asian studies, a field that is slowly changing and becoming increasingly more diverse but that still has a long way to go. Acknowledging the significant drawbacks of this form of knowledge production (is that enough?), I hope that what follows does more good than harm in helping us to understand the rich perspective of the local folk tradition of Mysore.

Another question that comes to mind regarding a scholarly work of this sort is the relationship between this translation of the ballad and the many tellings and iterations that have come before it and will assuredly come after it. Given the local nature of the ballad, one must recognize that capturing these songs in print necessarily stifles their dynamicity and creativity and removes them from the context that gives them so much power and meaning.[49] To put it another way, how does this version of *Chamundi of the Hill* fit into the ocean of *Chamundis of the Hill*?

To answer this question, let us return to 2012 and the controversy that surrounded the drama *Chama Cheluve*. As discussed above, the drama *Chama Cheluve* opened to great critical and commercial success, garnering the attention of the entire region of southern Karnataka. While for some the drama served as a refreshing addition to the world of Kannada-speaking theater, for others, like folklorist P. K. Rajashekhara, the story was not new. As an academic and professor of folklore studies, in 1972 Rajashekhara had collected and published *Bettada Chamundi*, a scholarly monograph that contained a version of the narrative as told by Kamsale Mahadevayya. As a poet, however, Rajashekhara also created several versions of *Chamundi of the Hill*. First, he wrote and performed a radio broadcast of the narrative in dramatic form for the Mysore Radio Broadcasting network in 1992 that was revised and rebroadcast during Dasara of 1993, both of which integrated the folk ballad's mix of *vachana* spoken word and choral verse. The radio drama was again revised and published in a prose version of the story titled *Chamundi Siri Chamundi* in 1994. As the attention around *Chama Cheluve* began to grow, Rajashekhara couldn't help but notice the similarities between the dramatic telling of the story Sujatha Akki, the author of *Chama Cheluve* who also holds a PhD in Kannada folklore studies, and his work both as a scholar and as a poet. In this context, Rajashekhara republished *Chamundi Siri Chamundi* in its *vachana* and choral verse format and sought litigation against Akki. which was eventually dismissed. This controversy surrounding the stories of Chamundi provides us an opportunity to think about the relationship between scholarship and oral folk narratives.

I don't wish to get into the well-theorized methodological implications of ethnographic research. I leave it to those better suited than me to reflect on that. Instead, my question is more basic: How does one capture an oral tradition rooted in improvisation and retelling in a medium that is so rigid and singular? One of the most important sources for thinking about the relationship between the interrelated fields of scholarship and oral performance has been the early work of Rajashekhara himself, as he at times identifies with both the scholarly and performative perspectives.[50] Rajashekhara suggests that in the case of folksongs, "the ballad is important, not the poet. A ballad written by a single poet becomes the ballad of a community and grows like a river. When sung by many, it is refined and perfected. When the same ballad is sung by the different artists, it takes on different forms and shapes, and in the end, it reaches to such a height that the original ballad is now engrained as part of local memory."[51] The origin of a folksong is less important than its repetition. For it is within that repetition, the creativity of the performers, and the interaction with the community the story that the songs are refined, intimately shaped within its context and now reflect a shared communal identity. Indeed, it is at this point that "this music does not belong to some people, but it is meant to entertain all."[52] Given this perspective, it might be difficult to understand why Rajashekhara would pursue litigation against Akki and *Chama Cheluve*.

However, even in the introduction to *Bettada Chamundi*, 40 years before any controversy, he recognizes that publication necessarily changes the tradition, shifting it from folklore to scholarship: "The 'folklore' tradition is created by the common people, but 'booklore' is the creation of scholars. They do not grow independently. They grow hand in hand. Poets and artists are inspired by folklore. Scholars are no exception to this. They too are inspired by folklore. Through give and take, they are both transformed."[53] Rajashekhara is acknowledging that, though they might tell the same story, poets, artists, and scholars, specifically because they participate in "booklore," are inherently different from the folklore performers from whom they take their inspiration. Therefore, while a plurality exists in the world of the folk tradition, once published, new rules, including intellectual property laws, begin to apply. Whether or not you agree with Rajashekhara's conclusion, he poignantly gets to the heart of the issue: this ballad ceases to be the same when it is published. Instead, it takes on the shape, form, and media of different traditions, either that of copywritten poetics or academic studies (also copywritten).

For Rajashekhara, the process of containing the tradition of *Chamundi of the Hill* in one book was one that could never truly be reconciled. In the introduction to *Bettada Chamundi*, he lamented, "Singers are not researchers. So, it is surprising that the same songs can be sung the same way in different places. At the same time, the same song might be sung by the same artist different ways at different times. The challenge of a folk scholar is this [to capture only one of these]."[54] Even 40 years later, in 2012, he continued to regret this aspect of scholarship: "I am still very sad that I had only published one version of the many versions that I had collected."[55] I also keenly feel the resignation that Rajashekhara has described. However, acknowledging that this version is inspired by the folk tradition, I hope it will lead to an increased recognition of the folksongs and open them up to a wider audience. Therefore, I offer the version of *Chamundi of the Hill* translated in chapter 6 as a subsidiary of the original folk tradition performances, a less dynamic, different type altogether.

Layout of the Book

Singing the Goddess into Place is meant to introduce the *Chamundi of the Hill* ballad and how it functions as a means to both ground and shape local identity. It is divided into six chapters, with this introduction being the first. In the second chapter "She killed the buffalo demon and dwells on the middle of the hill": Myth, Locality, and Cosmological Significance" examines the first narrative song of the ballad that tells the story of the goddess Chamundi killing the buffalo demon Mahisha.

In this chapter, I argue that *Chamundi of the Hill* uses this story to construct a foundational myth of the region, one that shapes the space to reflect a distinctive local perspective, presenting an intimate vision that places the local deities within the topography of Mysore and its surrounding region. The foundational myth that appears in *Chamundi of the Hill* is compared to other myths from elite traditions (namely, royal and Sanskrit) that share some details. Instead of viewing the myths from the folk ballad as derivative of these myths, this chapter argues that they are meaningful productions in their own right, and, therefore, they ought to be understood within their own context. In doing so, the chapter demonstrates how the myth of the goddess and the buffalo in *Chamundi of the Hill* constructs a unique vision of the foundations of its sacred geography and its goddesses that is reflective of the beliefs and practices of the common folk.

In chapter 3, "You're the one who protects this place": Folk Perspectives on Urban History and Regional Significance," *Chamundi of the Hill* is examined as an archive of urban history. The ballad is read as a means to recover and preserve a history of the Mysore region that has been overlooked in contrast to the well-known history of the region from the perspective of the kingdom of Mysore. Particularly, when we examine *Chamundi of the Hill* as a repository for a folk history of the place, we find that the ballad contains a complex and sophisticated history of the region that documents local festivals and deities. Through this unique perspective, *Chamundi of the Hill* frames the region, not as a royal center, but as a devotional and pilgrimage network through which its different villages and cities are connected.

The next chapter "He is from one caste; we are from another": Religion, Caste, and Social Change" examines the love story between Chamundi and Nanjunda as a treatise on social change, particularly one that argues against discrimination based on caste and ritual/religious tradition. Reading the narrative through the lens of a modern romantic comedy, this chapter demonstrates how the narrative places the deities within the social worlds of southern Karnataka, simultaneously making the deities reflect the lives of their devotees and allowing them to speak out against its ills. I suggest that the embedded and mundane nature of the deities in *Chamundi of the Hill* allows for it to make poignant critiques of local culture.

Chapter 5, "I live on the top of the hill . . . you remain near its base": 'High' and 'Low' in the Goddess Traditions of Southern Karnataka," continues the inquiry into issues of hierarchy. Particularly, I reflect on the designations of "high" and "low" as they are applied to the ritual worlds of goddess traditions. Using the spatial approach to the study of religion, in this chapter, I argue that the goddess traditions of southern Karnataka have an indigenous understanding of "high" and "low" rituals that can be seen in *Chamundi of the Hills*. These labels, however, do not reflect assessments of inherent value; instead, they present complementary practices that relate to the desired results, some more immediate and material, some more abstract and spiritual, that ultimately reflect the plurality of the goddess traditions encapsulated by the epithet Bhuktimuktipradayani, the giver of enjoyment and liberation.

The book concludes with a final chapter that contains a translation of Kamsale Mahadevayya's rendition of the ballad that was first recorded by Rajashekhara in *Bettada Chamundi*.

Singing the Goddess into Place seeks to demonstrate how *Chamundi of the Hill* is a uniquely situated narrative that reflects local folk knowledge of southern Karnataka. In doing so, it also constructs a history of the place and its people and simultaneously critiques its social structures that reify discrimination against certain communities and religious practices. All the while, the ballad also tells a story of romance, kinship, and family, themes with which many of us can also identify.

Chapter Two

"She killed the buffalo demon and dwells on the middle of the hill"

Myth, Locality, and Cosmological Significance

From the very beginning of the Kannada folk ballad *Chamundi of the Hill*, space is the central, grounding theme. The first narrative song "Sister, Stand on My Tongue and Fight" functions as a foundational myth, positioning the goddess Chamundi and her sister Uttanahalli within the broader Indian mythological context while simultaneously and specifically situating them within the local religious and devotional context. The focus of this chapter is local foundations, which for *Chamundi of the Hill* can be found in the first song of the ballad. The myth contained in this first song tells about the epic battle between the goddess and the buffalo demon. While this song has characters that parallel more well-known Pan-Indian myths, this chapter highlights that this myth simultaneously establishes the cosmic importance of Mysore's religious landscape, is uniquely formed within the context of southern Karnataka, and reflects particularly local concerns. Therefore, the mythological opening of the *Chamundi of the Hill* story serves not only as an epic opening to the romantic ballad, but it establishes its narrative as an oral local sacred history (*sthalapurana*) of Mysore. Therefore, it speaks to both the cosmological importance of the region, locating the city as the epicenter of divine power (*shakti*) and action, and the situatedness of the goddess, focusing the results of her efforts within the local milieu.

The mythological narrative contained within *Chamundi of the Hill* provides a unique local story, the details of which deserve our full attention and consideration beyond a mere comparison to the Pan-Indian myth with which it shares some details. Therefore, before moving into the analysis of the folk narrative, it is necessary that the reader be familiar with the details of the mythological context of Mysore and the specifics of the local myth. In the following section, therefore, I briefly discuss Mysore and its relationship to the buffalo, summarize the narrative of the slaying of the buffalo demon as told in *Chamundi of the Hill*, and provide a brief analysis of its mythological tropes as it relates to the broader themes of the ballad as a whole, namely, the situatedness of its narratives and its critique of normative social roles. Some readers might find it helpful to read the translation of the first song in its entirety in chapter 6 before continuing with this chapter. After this brief introduction to the mythic context and summary of its story, this chapter demonstrates how the deities and their epic deeds are fully localized within the context of Mysore and how they produce a unique local myth that reflects regional religious practice, giving us a glimpse into how local (religious) history is understood by the common folk.

In order to demonstrate how the buffalo-slaying myth in *Chamundi of the Hill* reflects the concerns and identities of the folk, the narrative of the folk ballad is compared with parallel Sanskritic myths and with the elite royal ritual practice of the Mysore kings. Therefore, the second section of this chapter titled "Royal and Local Goddesses" compares *Chamundi of the Hill* with the analogous royal history of the city and the elite royal ritual context from which it comes. Particularly, it highlights the tension between the local focus of the folk ballad and the decentering effect of its royal counterparts, which shift importance from Mysore to outside of the region. Similarly, the final section, "Resisting Pan-Indianization (Sanskritization, Brahminization, and Sanitization)," compares the myth from *Chamundi of the Hill* with Sanskritic narratives of the slaying of the buffalo demon (Mahisha) and the blood-seed demon (Raktabija), both of which share certain characters and motifs with the folk ballad from Mysore. By comparing the local myth with the royal and broader Pan-Indian narratives, the ballad's emphasis on spatiality becomes clearer, demonstrating the local situatedness of the myths.

Together, then, the goal of this chapter is to show that *Chamundi of the Hill* provides a specific and local perspective on the foundation of the city's deities and local religious practices. As a foundational myth, *Chamundi of the Hill* provides a story of Mysore and its goddess that is unique to its context and reflects local concerns of its broader non-elite population, namely the folk. Now, however, let us turn to the mythic establishment of the goddesses in Mysore, the land of the buffalo.

Establishing the Goddesses of Mysore:
The Demon-Slayer Folk Myth in *Chamundi of the Hill*

The first narrative song of *Chamundi of the Hill* "Sister, Stand on My Tongue and Fight" begins the foundational myth of Chamundi and Mysore. Using devices of oral and performing cultures, the narrator begins by praising the goddess for her "annihilation" of the buffalo demon Mahisha, as the listener is quickly informed that Chamundi's renown is a result of this victory (see below). Through this simple acclamation, the episode immediately transitions from general honorifics to a specific local history, situating the mythology of the buffalo demon that has perpetuated in the South Asian subcontinent for millenia firmly within the local goddess tradition of Mysore and its surrounding areas. While the explicit connection of the local network of deities and their attendant practices with the myth of the buffalo demon are certainly a novel aspect of the narrative, the connection between Mysore and the great buffalo demon has existed for quite some time.

"Mysore" is an anglicized name for the city/region from the colonial period that was derived from its original Kannada name "Mysuru" (also spelled "Maisuru" or less commonly "Maysuru"). The common and popular etymology of Maisuru is that it too is a derivation but from the Sanskrit term *mahisha* or "buffalo" that was combined with the Kannada term for city or "native place" *uru*: *mahisha* + *uru* = *mahishuru* or "native place of the buffalo." Over time Mahishuru was truncated to Maisuru within the local language. The connection between the buffalo and the name of the region dates back to at least the 5th century CE, and, by the 10th century "buffalo," in some form or another, was frequently included in names for the region surrounding Mysore City (e.g., Mahishavishya).[1] In 1128, however, the city that is now Mysore—and more specifically its Chamundi Hill—was explicitly associated with the buffalo in an inscription from the reign of the great Hoysala king Vishnuvardana.[2] After the 12th century, records that called the Mysore region "buffalo country" became sparse and did not resume with any consistency until a few decades after the Wodeyar kings of Mysore emerged onto the political scene in 1610. It was at this point in 1639 that Kanthirava Narasaraja Wodeyar (r. 1638–1659 CE) associated the goddess of the hill with the slaying of the buffalo demon Mahisha a royal inscription.[3] Since the rule of Kanthirava Narasaraja, the myth of the local goddess and the buffalo demon has been engrained into the local psyche.[4]

As alluded to but not fully explored in "Sister, Stand on My Tongue and Fight," the popular etymology of Mysore as the "native place of the buffalo" is reflected in both the folk and elite mythological history of the city. Throughout the region, it is popularly believed that the buffalo demon formerly ruled over the region and that Mysore was his capital.[5] Even today, as pilgrims reach the top of Chamundi Hill, they are greeted by a larger-than-life sculpture of the demon in his anthropomorphic form (figure 2.1). The battle between the goddess and the buffalo demon is also stamped into the landscape of Chamundi Hill and local collective memory at what is called "Buffalo Point" (*kona mule*). This site is located in the protected forest lands of Chamundi Hill not far from the colossal image of Shiva's bull-vehicle Nandi that was installed midway up the footpath leading up the hill. The site, at first, seems like a rather unremarkable geological formation that provides a decent vista of Mysore. When in the presence of learned local guides, however, the site comes alive with the movements of the epic mythological battle. The cracks and divots in the face of the hill's rock are imprinted with memories of the footsteps of the goddess, the paws of her lion vehicle, the hooves of the buffalo demon, and the blows directed at Chamundi and those absorbed by Mahisha (figure 2.2). Expertly, the workers from the temple use these features to recreate the entire battle even down to the massive crack where the hill was split by the force of the goddess's trident. Interestingly, the name of the site—"Buffalo Point" or *kona mule*—suggests that the origins of this myth are indeed local since the Kannada term *kona* is used in reference to the buffalo demon instead of the Sanskrit *mahisha*.

"She killed the buffalo demon and dwells on the middle of the hill" 31

Figure 2.1. Mahisha statue on Chamundi Hill.

While the context for *Chamundi of the Hill* is certainly framed against the backdrop of the goddess slaying the buffalo demon, the actual focus of the song is on another battle waged by the goddess against Mahisha's younger brother Aisu ("Many").[6] According to the song, after Chamundi kills Mahisha, Aisu emerges on the scene and grabs the forearm of the goddess. As we will see in other portions of the overall ballad that focus on the romantic relationship between Chamundi and Nanjunda, the action of grabbing the forearm is symbolically loaded as it suggests that the demon was attempting to take Chamundi as his wife against her will, what *dharmashastra* (legal) literature would call a *rakshasa* or "demonic" marriage.[7] The goddess, however, withstands this forceful proposal, and with another of her four arms, she grabs the hilt of her sword, and with yet another takes

Figure 2.2. Buffalo Point with temple workers from Chamundeshwari Temple on Chamundi Hill.

hold of the nape of the demon's neck, as she thrusts her sword into the demon. Instead of bringing about instant death, as the blood gushes out of Aisu, from every drop that hits the ground another demon is born, producing an enumerable demonic army in the process. As his blood produces more and more demons, the clever Aisu hides in the belly of his deceased elder brother, the buffalo demon Mahisha, knowing that the goddess would not be able to overcome the demons that he is miraculously producing.[8]

Chamundi, despite her best efforts, cannot overcome the exponentially increasing number of foes. This leaves the goddess both exhausted and bewildered. As she looks around for someone to ask for help, she wipes the sweat that is pouring all over her body and flings it to the ground. In this moment, as her frustration reaches its limits, the narrative breaks from the action and leaves Mysore, only to relocate the scene within the divine ranch (*gokula*) of the god Krishna. Krishna at once realizes that Chamundi is fighting a losing battle. So, the god leaves his divine abode and travels to Mysore to give Chamundi aid. Immediately, the narrative focuses back on the goddess, as she slings "rivers of sweat" unto the ground. Then in an action that mirrors the blood-reproduction of Aisu, another goddess, named Uttanahalli ("[Goddess of the] In-Between Village"), emerges from Chamundi's sweat, spreading her seven hoods and her seven tongues. Upon seeing Uttanahalli, Chamundi is confused because she doesn't know who the new goddess is or where she has come from. But after hearing that Uttanahalli had been born from her own sweat, Chamundi becomes overjoyed and welcomes the goddess as her younger sister.

Then, Chamundi quickly relates the impossible situation to her new sister, explaining that she had successfully killed the great buffalo demon but is unable to thwart his younger brother because of his magical reproductive blood. Luckily, Uttanahalli does not share her elder sister's pessimism. Uttanahalli, instead, quickly spreads her seven tongues, covering the entire hill, and says to Chamundi, "Sister, stand on my tongue and fight!" The fight, then, resumes, on Uttanahalli's tongue, which absorbs all of Aisu's blood before it can reach the earth. Now with no further reproduction, Chamundi quickly defeats all the replica Aisu(s), but there is no sign of their source, the original Aisu. So, the elder goddess stands on the corpse of Mahisha and looks all around the hill for the buffalo demon's brother. Uttanahalli, however, realizes that he must be hiding inside the buffalo's body, and Chamundi thrusts her trident into the corpse, splitting it in half. From the carcass, the real Aisu emerges far more formidable and monstrous than his elder brother.[9]

At the sight of this hideous demon, Chamundi once again becomes overwhelmed. As tears come to her eyes, she meditates on Shiva. Through this meditation the deity Brahma becomes aware of Chamundi's situation and his responsibility to intervene. As it turns out, it was Brahma who had given Aisu his powers of blood reproduction. To undo the unfortunate effects of his shortsighted boon, Brahma sends the goddess a lion to serve as her vehicle and companion. With the aid of her lion, she quickly defeats Aisu, and the song ends with the goddess victorious and seated on her lion, a lyrical reference to her standard contemporary iconography.

If the local emphasis was not clear at this point, the conclusion of "Sister, Stand on My Tongue and Fight" makes explicit Chamundi's and Uttanahalli's roles within the local religious networks. This is most clearly and explicitly related as the two goddesses discuss the division of divine responsibilities and devotion that ties them to the city of Mysore. After Aisu's death is confirmed, Uttanahalli opines that she will not always be around to help when her sister is in danger and then realizes that since she was only just manifested and that she is homeless with no place to go and no place to call her own. Chamundi, however, explains that as the divine protector of the city she must reside on the top of the hill. Additionally, she serves as the house deity (*mane-devaru*) of Chamaraja, the Wodeyar king, and as part of their relationship every year she leaves her hill for her annual worship (*puja*).[10] She asks Uttanahalli, however, to stay close by, and that if she does, the elder goddess promises that the local people will have a great annual festival in Uttanahalli's honor, during which they will prepare and give Uttanahalli all her favorite foods.

While the theme of royal patronage and the relationship between the Wodeyar king and Chamundi is alluded to several times in its verses, *Chamundi of the Hill* presents royal devotion and patronage as a different tradition that is secondary for Chamundi and not within the ritual or devotional worlds of Uttanahalli. Therefore, it is important to understand the relationship between the local and royal traditions and the tensions between the two. So, let us now turn our attention to another aspect of Mysore's legendary history and compare the parallel traditions of royal and local goddess traditions.

Royal and Local Goddesses

The history of Mysore as a site of royal importance, like its mythological significance described above, is well engrained in popular imagination; however, the royal stories of the city's foundation provide a very different scope for the region, inverting the focus of its identity from situated to dislocated. Most modern popular, courtly, and academic histories rehearse the same story concerning the rise of the Wodeyar kings at the end of the fourteenth century (for more see chapter 3 and the appendix).[11] As the story goes, per instructions from the deity Krishna given in a dream, two Wodeyar brothers, Yaduraya and Krishnaraya, migrated from the kingdom of Dwaraka, located in the modern state of Gujarat in northwest India, in search of a place that would become their kingdom. Before coming to Mysore, the brothers passed through the popular mountainous pilgrimage site of the goddess Vindhyavasini (She Who Dwells in the Vindhya Mountains), who directed them to Mysore, which she says was the kingdom promised to them by Krishna. Once they arrived in Mysore, they worshipped the goddess Chamundi, after which she appeared before the brothers, giving them instructions whereby they could defeat the tyrant who ruled the region and become kings themselves. As part of this alliance with the goddess, the brothers accepted Chamundi as their house deity, taking the privileges of kingship along with the responsibilities of providing proper ritual sustenance to the goddess.[12]

This narrative appears in its final form in the *Great Kings of Mysore* (*Maisurina Shriman Maharajavara Vamshavali*), a text that was composed during the reign of Krishnaraja Wodeyar III (r.1799–1868) to whom its authorship is attributed. As a product of the Mysore royal court during the British colonial period, the *Great Kings of Mysore* provides an elite version of the founding of the city and the establishment of the Wodeyar kingdom of Mysore and cements the Wodeyar rulers' relationship with Chamundi (a translation of this story has been provided in the appendix). As will be the topic of the next chapter of this book, both the local folk ballad and the royal history use narrative as a means to establish their protagonists in Mysore. Perhaps surprising given the different emphases of the two narratives, the Wodeyar foundation myth suggests that the kings went to Mysore because of Chamundi, while the myth of the folk songs relates that Chamundi stays there, at least in part, because of her obligations to the Wodeyar kings.

In both narratives, however, the relationship between the goddess and the kings is grounded in the reciprocity of ritual, though the ritual context is conceived of differently. In the lines of "Sister, Stand on My Tongue and Fight," Chamundi highlights that once every year she must fulfill her obligations as the deity of the royal family:

> I live in the midst of this hill.
> I am the house god of Chamaraja Wodeyar.
> Once a year I take worship,
> but I live on top of the hill.

The reciprocal exchange is further alluded to later in the ballad in the song titled "Go, Give My Love to Your Brother-in-law Nanjunda, and Tell Him to Return," which provides an example of the exchange:

> Chamundi must remain
> in her place in Mysore.
> Since she was the house god of Chamaraja,
> she gave him twelve lakh rupees.
> So Chamaraja built a twelve-tiered temple
> for her with his own hands.
> On the temple, he carved an elaborate tower.

In the lines of *Chamundi of the Hill*, we see the relationship between the goddess and the king is intimately linked to her specific abode on Chamundi Hill, where she resides and that was built and renovated by the Wodeyar kings.

The *Great Kings of Mysore*, however, depicts the goddess, located not only in Mysore but connects her to other goddesses throughout the subcontinent, extending her identity to align with the entire Hindu Goddess tradition that views all goddesses as manifestations of the Great Goddess (*Mahadevi*) or primordial Goddess (*adishakti*):

> While [Yaduraya] performed austerities there, Vindhyavasini, was pleased and said, "I have lived on the Mahabala Mountain [another name for Chamundi Hill], which is between the Kaveri and Kapila, and there I'm called Chamundeshwari [Lady Chamundi]. If you go to Mahabala Mountain and worship me, you will marry the daughter of the king of the city named Mysore, which is next to the mountain, and this city will become yours."

In these lines of the *Great Kings of Mysore*, Chamundi is directly connected with Vindhyavasini, a goddess whose temple in the Vindya mountains is a popular pilgrimage site for many Hindus. After the brothers reach the hill, the text confirms that the goddess in Mysore is in fact the Great primordial Goddess, *adishakti*:

> After crossing the Kaveri River and climbing the Mahabala Mountain, he worshipped the goddess Chamundi, who is *adishakti* [primordial power], the mother of the universe, and dwells on the mountain. He bowed with devotion to Shri Kantheshwara [Shiva], who is the lord of Bhukailasa [Nanjangud], which is 20 miles from the mountain. That

night Yaduraya slept peacefully, meditating on the feet of the goddess.

Through this explicit connection between the Great Goddess tradition and Chamundi, the *Great Kings of Mysore*, a royal text, is intentionally attempting to make the case that that goddess who lives on Chamundi Hill is not just a goddess but *the* Goddess. This rhetoric continues today and can be seen on road signs leading to the temple even today (figure 2.3).

Chamundi of the Hill seems to acknowledge, at least partially, Chamundi's service in elite traditions. While the ritual for which she leaves her hill in the folk song is not explicitly named, the details that the goddess provides gives us clues through which we can decipher which festival it is that requires her to descend from her hill as part of her responsibilities to Mysore and its Wodeyar rulers. Throughout the ritual calendar cycle, there are several important events for Chamundi. The first of these, Chamundi's birthday festival, takes place in on the seventh day of dark fortnight in the summer month of Ashada (typically June/July) according to the Kannada calendar. While this is a day of revelry with royal participation—the Wodeyar royal family provides the silver palanquin that carries the festival image on procession—the festivities are isolated to the top of the hill, and

Figure 2.3. Chamundeshwari, Universal Mother road sign.

the rituals more closely reflect the practices of the folk (see chapter 4). Likewise, Chamundi's "Great Festival" (*mahotsava*), which takes place at the end of the autumnal month of Ashwin, is replete with royal participation—the chariot festival is inaugurated by the Mysore maharaja with a *puja* ritual and the ceremonial "pulling" of her large wooden chariot (figures 2.4a & 2.4b), and the royal family's attendance at major events like the boat festival are expected; however, this festival is also conducted entirely on top of the goddess's sacred hill.

Between these two festivals, however, is the great Mysore celebration of Dasara (lit. "Tenth"). Dasara is the culmination of the festival of Navaratri (lit. "Nine Nights"), which celebrates the goddess and her many forms and feats, including her victory over the buffalo demon. Nowadays, Dasara is a large pageant of Kannadiga (Kannada-speaking peoples of Karnataka) and Indian cultural pride, but the festival is rooted in a long history of goddess devotion.[13] In contemporary practice of the Dasara festival in Mysore that takes place outside of the public eye and inside the religious spaces, we can still see aspects of the rituals to which the bards' songs refer. At the beginning of Navaratri in Mysore, a festival image of Chamundi that is kept in the Mysore Palace is sent to the Chamundeshwari temple on top of Chamundi Hill and is installed in one of the side shrines of the temple to receive daily *puja* throughout the ten-day festival. By receiving *puja* in her primary temple, the festival image is imbued with the divine power (*shakti*) from the goddess's primary image (*mula murti*) in the temple's main chancel (*garbha*). On the final day of the celebration— the "tenth" day or "Dasara"—the image is taken on procession from the hill temple to the palace wherein a special *puja* is performed by the king and the goddess's priests. Traditionally, this would be the moment when the power of the goddess was transferred to the king, after which the king would leave the palace on a procession that commenced his annual military expeditions. In contemporary India, however, since the nation is a secular republic and the maharaja is without military power, the image of the goddess has replaced the king on procession, and the image newly invigorated by the goddess is taken on a procession throughout the city.[14] In the song "Sister, Stand on My Tongue and Fight," the bards, through the words of the goddess, confirm the royal importance of this ritual alluding to this *puja* as a significant annual event for which she temporarily leaves

Figure 2.4a&b. Maharaja at Chamundi Mahotsava.

the hill, demonstrating that the broader population recognized the importance of this courtly ritual of the transference of power within the broader historical apparatus of the festival.

While Chamundi is depicted as a royal goddess, *Chamundi of the Hill* is equally transparent about the role of her sister Uttanahalli. If Chamundi is to serve the kings, Uttanahalli must remain there for her sister and for the people. Instead of remaining on the top of the hill, Uttanahalli is told to go below to the base of the hill to her eponymous village Uttanahalli ("in-between village," i.e., geographically located between Chamundi Hill and Nanjangudu). There, Chamundi promises that the goddess Uttanahalli will regularly receive *puja*, homemade offerings, and *tambittu* (sweet made from rice flour and jaggery). To the careful reader, distinct formulations concerning the ritual and devotional apparatuses of the two goddesses are clear: Chamundi's ritual imbues power to the royal family, but Uttanahalli is a goddess for everyone and is particularly partial to homemade things and inexpensive treats.[15] These details, along with her epithet of Mariamma, are reflective of Uttanahalli's role as a South Indian village goddess or *gramadevate* (Sanskrit: *gramadevata*), an identity that we find later in the ballad is shared by both sister-goddesses (see chapter 4).[16]

Gramadevates (lit. "goddesses of village") are common phenomena in South India and are situated within and on the outskirts of villages, towns, and cities, where they rule the metaphysical and physical space under their purview.[17] They are responsible for warding off evil beings, providing good health for the villagers, and invigorating their territory and the human ruler through their powerful energy (*shakti*). These deities, however, can also be temperamental and require the village to pay their respects through sacrifice, or their benevolent protection and blessing can turn into destruction and malevolence. The practical and devotional lives of these goddess traditions focus on the goddesses' relationship to specific situated spaces, and their devotion is often connected with blood sacrifices and flesh offerings. Though they are often incorporated into the ritual worlds of brahminic culture, the cults of these local village deities originate in local (typically nonbrahminic) context and persist in their practice of nonstandardized (nonagamic) rituals and practices that have developed outside the Sanskritic and brahminic Mahadevi Shakta tradition or the Shaiva traditions.[18]

The details from the entire *Chamundi of the Hill* collection provide further evidence of the nonbrahminic village-deity identity of Uttanahalli, including one major topic of the overall ballad, ritual offerings of flesh. While Chamundi never speaks directly about blood rites, they are brought to the forefront repeatedly by Uttanahalli, as the goddess overtly rejects incorporation into the brahminical world of vegetarian ritual. Indeed, the goddess repeatedly identifies herself as both a meat eater and as being from a caste that is typically considered "low" on the normative ritual hierarchy as a result of her ritual appetite. The nonconformity expressed by Uttanahalli in *Chamundi of the Hill* sheds light on underlying tensions between the local traditions and the elite ritual world that often subsumes these smaller traditions. In the royal *Great Kings of Mysore*, we also see an attempt made in the text to disconnect Uttanahalli from her small eponymous village through a process of renaming:

> *At daybreak the goddess [Chamundi] came in the form of a woman and said "Go to the southeastern portion of my mountain first thing tomorrow morning, and just as you have worshipped me, do* puja *to the goddess who killed Raktabija and became known as Jwalajjihva and now resides there . . . In accordance to the words of the goddess, [Yaduraya] joyously performed puja to the goddess Jwalamukhi.*

Here Uttanahalli's place at the base of the hill is alluded to, but its/ her name is not given. Instead, she is called Jwalajjihva and Jwalamukhi, Sanskritic names and also the names of a goddess whose temple in Himachal Pradesh is a popular Pan-Hindu pilgrimage site. Additionally, the text glosses Uttanahalli as Kali, the Pan-Indian Hindu goddess from the myth of the slaying of the demon Raktabija in the *Devi Mahatmya* (see below). In both instances, the *Great Kings of Mysore* works to decenter Uttanahalli from her village. Though the village goddess Uttanahalli is sometimes homogenized and homologized with Pan-Indic goddesses like Jwalamukhi or Kali in contemporary discourse, as we see in *Chamundi of the Hill*, she has continued to resist homogeneity through the persistence of local practice and ritual and her connection with the village of Uttanahalli.

From the details given later in *Chamundi of the Hill*, it seems that Chamundi partially shares the local *gramadevate* identity with Uttanahalli. In several other songs in the overall ballad, there are extended conversations in which Chamundi is reminded about her station with specific references to the food that she eats, that is, what ritual offerings she accepts. When questioning Chamundi about her love marriage with Nanjunda, Uttanahalli reminds her sister that Shiva is "high caste" and wears a *linga* and ochre robes (signs of Lingayat ascetic identity) but that they—the two goddesses—both eat chickens and goats. At one point, Shiva's two elder wives even insult Chamundi by saying that she enjoys eating cats. While Uttanahalli retains her meat-eating identity, the songs resolve this tension for Chamundi by repeatedly but obliquely suggesting that eating meat is what makes her compatible with the kings. At one point, one of Shiva's elder wives makes this quite explicit when she says that Chamundi "eats buffaloes and sheep like they do in the palace."

There is a tension within Chamundi's identity as fierce, independent goddess and one who wishes to marry a Lingayat *jangama* (wandering ascetic). Indeed, her identity seems to be shaped by both local and elite concerns. This strain has also shaped the structure of the Chamundeshwari temple on Chamundi Hill whose traditionally nonbrahmin agricultural Shivarchaka priests (also known as Tomadi or Tammadi), a caste found in the Mysore district, were replaced by several brahmin castes and *sampradaya*s (sects), including the Dikshita head priests who were imported from Tamil Nadu by the Wodeyar rulers between 1819 and 1848.[19] It was at this point that the non-Sanskritic, nonagamic rites at the temple began to dwindle.[20] Additionally, at this point, the elite interpretation of Chamundi took hold, as she became associated with the Pan-Indian goddess Durga, the slayer of the buffalo demon Mahisha, who played a prominent role in the *Devi Mahatmya* and the *Devi Bhagavata Purana*.[21]

Scholars like Thomas Coburn have argued that the incorporation of a plethora of goddesses under the rubric of the Great Goddess is foundational to the Great Goddess tradition.[22] Additionally, Sree Padma has demonstrated that within modernity, the identities of village goddesses tend to be subsumed by the larger goddess traditions as, particularly, "the famous Hindu deities Durga and Kali . . . have grown to encompass many *gramadevata* cults."[23] Indeed, the diversiform nature of the goddess is a common motif in her Pan-Indian, Sanskritic mythology. Therefore, let us now analyze the foundational myths of the goddesses of *Chamundi of the Hill* with the Pan-Indian stories of the goddesses with which they are often compared.

Resisting Pan-Indianization
(Sanskritization, Brahminization, and Sanitization)

The mythological narratives of Chamundi and Uttanahalli found in *Chamundi of the Hill* share affinity with material found in broader Indian mythological contexts, particularly, the well-known Puranic battles between the Goddess and the demons Mahisha and Raktabija. I have intentionally only gestured to the Sanskrit iterations of these narratives up to now because it is important that we don't simply consider local or folk narratives as derivatives of these Pan-Indic stories but as meaningful creations of their own merit. Therefore, I hesitate to compare the local Kannada songs with these more well-known myths lest I unintentionally reinforce the too-simplistic theory that local myth is only derivative of the broader mythic corpus. I proceed, however, because through the process of comparison the complexity that exists within the songs of southern Karnataka can demonstrate how they function as important contributions to regional memory and history.

The complicated relationship between the local and the Sanskritic, Pan-Indic traditions begins with the name Chamundi itself. Though the name Chamundi and/or Chamunda is commonly found in Sanskrit sources, like the Puranas, most scholars believe that the name has a complicated history that demonstrates the fluidity of traditions in India and how theories like Sanskritization and Brahminization (see below) can often be misleading and are unhelpful because they attempt metatheorization of all local goddess traditions.

The first major inclusion of Chamunda within the Sanskritic mythological tradition is found in the third episode of the Puranic *Devi Mahatmya*.[24] Like in the text's previous episode, the gods had been overtaken by demons (Shumbha and Nishumbha), who had stolen their portion of the Vedic sacrifice.[25] The gods, however, remember the promise, which had been made to them by the Goddess at the end of the previous chapter and the conclusion of the second (Mahisha) episode of the text and call to her for help. Two of Shumbha and Nishumbha's spies, Chanda and Munda, see the beautiful Goddess and return to tell their kings about this great jewel. After several attempts to seize the goddess, during which she defeats several of Shumba and Nishumba's lesser generals, the demon-lord Shumbha orders Chanda and Munda to go and violently bring her to him, dragging her by her hair. Chanda and Munda attack the Goddess on the highest mountain with four legions of demons (*asuras*). The Goddess sees the oncoming armies and lets out an angry cry that caused her face to become black as ink. Then, from her, Kali ("black one") emerges with sword, noose, skull-staff, necklace made of severed heads, and a tiger skin skirt. With her mouth wide, tongue lolling, and deep red eyes, Kali lets out a mighty roar and devours all the demon armies. Chanda and Munda, then, begin to assail her with an onslaught of arrows and *cakra*s (discus) that vanish into Kali's mouth like the sun enveloped by a black cloud. Amused by the futility of her enemy's tactics, the hag goddess Kali "cackles," bears her terrible teeth for all to see, and mounts the lion. Then she grabs Chanda by the hair and decapitates him. Munda, seeing Chanda dead, runs at her but is immediately felled by her sword. Carrying the heads of Chanda and Munda, Kali approaches the Goddess (called "Chandika" here) and playfully says, "From me, the great sacrificial animals (*mahapashu*) Chanda and Munda, your portion of the battle-sacrifice (*yuddhayajna*). [Now] you will kill Shumbha and Nishumbha."[26] Pleased with Kali's offering, the Goddess replies, "Because you have taken hold of Chanda and Munda and brought them (to me), you will be called 'Chamunda.'"[27]

In the remainder of the episode, Kali is called Chamunda several more times but only in the context of the Goddess's battle with the demon Raktabija ("blood-seed").[28] In this battle, which shares similarities with the story of Uttanahalli and Aisu, Kali/Chamunda was forced to drink the blood of the demon who was overwhelming the "band of mothers" (*matrigana*).[29] In the *Devi Mahatmya's* story, the Goddess and the *matrigana* were overwhelmed in their fight with Raktabija since every time the goddesses struck him each droplet of his blood spawned another Raktabija—the more they fought the greater the opponent becomes. Realizing the futility of their methods (and the humor of the gods' fear), the Goddess commands Kali, who is explicitly called Chamunda at this point in the text, to open her mouth and drink the blood of the demon as it fell from her sword and then to eat all of the demons that had been previously produced by Raktabija's reproduction. Proceeding with this new strategy, the goddesses promptly defeat their demon foe. While not explicit in the verses of the text, many illustrated manuscripts of the *Devi Mahatmya*—similar to the narrative in *Chamundi of the Hill*—have envisioned Chamunda extending her tongue across the battlefield to protect it from Raktabija's gushing blood, as depicted in a 18th-century Nepalese manuscript from LACMA (figure 2.5). Like the episode in which Chanda and Munda were defeated, Chamunda was immediately efficacious because of her fierce nature and bloodlust. Chamunda and Kali are grouped together because of their similar thirst for violence and their nonnormative appearance and actions.[30] In fact, historically, the iconography of Kali and Chamunda—emaciated hag goddesses seated or standing on a corpse—was virtually identical during the medieval period, except for Chamunda's fondness for her owl companion and Kali's predilection for copulation.[31] They are the fiercest of all the goddesses (Chamunda, though, seems to be the fiercer of the two) that the author(s)/editor(s) had incorporated into the narrative.

The *Devi Mahatmya* also contains the story of the Goddess and the buffalo demon. As alluded to above, the narrative of the buffalo demon is one of the most well-known stories in India and is central in the Pan-Indian festival of Navaratri and Vijayadashami, or Dasara, as it is known in Mysore. The Goddess and the buffalo-demon myth appears to predate its literary tradition and can be seen in numerous images, especially from Mathura, where a female figure snaps the neck

Figure 2.5. *The Goddess Ambika Leading the Eight Mother Goddesses in Battle against the Demon Raktabija,* Folio from a *Devi Mahatmya* (Glory of the Goddess), photo courtesy of Museum Associates/ LACMA.

of the theriomorphic buffalo.[32] The *Devi Mahatmya*, however, provides the first literary narrative of the Goddess (instead of Skanda) killing the buffalo demon. Thereafter, the slaying of the buffalo demon became a common story within Goddess-oriented texts or in Goddess-oriented portions of larger Puranic works. In subsequent tellings of the myth, however, additional narrative details were added including the story of the Goddess granting Mahisha liberation or *moksha* through his self-sacrifice (e.g., *Kalika Purana* 60.101–102).

In the *Devi Mahatmya*'s telling of the story, the Goddess (here called "Ambika") materializes from the collective energies (*tejas*) of the male deities to combat the demon king, who has stolen their portion of the Vedic sacrificial offering, destabilizing cosmic administration. Upon seeing this divine figure manifested, the gods rejoice and offer her their primary war implements to the Goddess.[33] After being properly outfitted for battle, she, along with her army and lion mount, go out to battle Mahisha and his army of demons. The Goddess and her army easily win the first round of battles and kill numerous hordes of demons. However, when Mahisha joins the battle, it quickly turns the tide against the Goddess's army. But, when the demon king turns his sights toward her lion, the Goddess becomes infuriated and resolute on his destruction, catching the buffalo demon in a snare. Mahisha promptly frees himself by changing into the form of a lion. As soon as he shape-shifts, Ambika beheads him, but Mahisha emerges as a man. The Goddess, then, hits the demon with a flurry of arrows, but he resists the onslaught by taking the form of an elephant. After she is able to cut off his trunk, Mahisha once again resumes his buffalo form and roars at the Goddess. Amused by his performance, the Goddess downs an intoxicating beverage, lets out a loud laugh, and says, "Roar now, you fool, while I drink this wine, but after I kill you, only the gods will roar!" Then, the Goddess leaps upon the demon kicking and striking him with her spear. Trying to escape from the blows dealt by the Goddess, Mahisha begins to morph into another form; however, as he emerges from the head of the buffalo, the Goddess decapitates the *asura* killing him on the spot. The gods were so overwhelmed by the power and majesty of the Goddess that they praise her as the creator, the Vedas incarnate, the Vedic sacrifice, and the root of all existence (*prakriti*), amongst many other adulations. Moved by their exaltations, the Goddess offers the gods a boon. Sensing her unlimited power, the gods ask her to come to the aid of her devotees whenever they call upon her. It is this boon that is remembered in the Shumbha and Nishumbha episode and is perhaps invoked by millennia of goddess worshipers since the origination of the tale.

Scholars like Thomas Coburn have argued that the narratives contained within the *Devi Mahatmya* were the first attempt to subdue these gruesome, bloodthirsty, independent, and overwhelmingly powerful goddesses within the brahminic pantheon under the umbrella of the Great Goddess tradition.[34] The connection that the text makes between the Great Goddess (*Mahadevi*) and Kali/Chamunda seems to support Thomas Coburn's theory of the "crystallization" of the Goddess tradition in which he argues that the *Devi Mahatmya* was the first systematized attempt to reconcile the various goddesses of South Asia into one large tradition by ordering various local, regional, non-Sanskritic, and Sanskritic goddesses into one comprehensive entity: Mahadevi, the Great Goddess. A crucial process for making sense of Coburn's thesis of the crystallization of Shakta tradition is "Sanskritization."

Sanskritization theory was made popular by Indian sociologist M. N. Srinivas in a modern study of the castes of the Coorgs (Kannada: *Kodagu*) in what was the princely state of Mysore. Srinivas used the term to describe a means of social mobility in which castes that were considered "lower" or "ritually polluting" adopted the "Sanskrit Hinduism" of castes that were "higher" within the hierarchy of normative Sanskritic rites.[35] He suggested that Sanskrit rituals spread to all levels of society through similar processes of adoption at various times throughout India, during which the non-Sanskritic tradition was gradually lost. Over time, usage of the theory of Sanskritization has broadened and is often used as shorthand for the process of evolution within local traditions in which Sanskrit rituals and practices were implemented and Sanskritized names were adopted for local deities. J. Fritz Staal was one of the first scholars to critique Srinivas's implementation of the term, which he claimed was riddled with inconsistencies and unknowable assumptions about the loss and gains of the traditions. He suggested that the process was not a one-way emulation or imitation of another tradition. Instead, at all points in time, ranging from the Vedic to the modern, the relationship was always dialectical in which Sanskritic traditions influenced regional cultures and regional cultures influenced the Sanskrit traditions.[36] Perhaps as a result of these critiques, the term "Brahminization" became more fashionable in describing these processes. Instead of theorizing that nonbrahmin castes mimicked the elite Sanskritic ritual and cultural world, "Brahminization" points to the agency of brahmins in proselytizing their ritual and mythic worldview, slowly integrating it into most levels of Hindu practice.

Both terms—"Sanskritization" and "Brahminization"—and the processes that they theorize can be seen in portions of the history of Mysore and its surrounding deities, Chamundi, Uttanahalli, and Nanjunda. In the religious and devotional proliferation of the 19th-century court of Krishnaraja Wodeyar III, Sanskrit increasingly replaced Kannada in local temple inscriptions, and the names of the local deities were altered to include Sanskrit honorifics and to reference Pan-Indic myth. Chamundi's and Najunda's names were supplemented with the feminine and masculine forms of the Sanskrit term *ishwara* (lord), and they became known in official documentation as Chamundeshwari and Nanjundeshwara and were connected to Durga and Shiva, respectively. These Sanskritic suffixes are frequently used in the songs of *Chamundi of the Hill*. Uttanahalli's local identity, as we have seen, was also masked through her name change, and official records and inscriptions began to refer to her as Jwalamukhi ("The Tongue-Flamed"), a famed manifestation of the goddess who was formed from the tongue of the goddess Sati after her self-immolation in Daksha's fire ritual. Additionally, the Tamil brahmins, who were invited by the same king, Krishnaraja Wodeyar III, introduced the ritual programs of the Shaiva *agamas* (ritual handbooks). So, in the case of Mysore's local tradition, there is evidence of processes similar to Sanskritization and Brahminization taking place. However, this is only part of the story, and neither can make sense of the totality of the developments within the local tradition. While incorporating these changes, local practices continue alongside and together with the newly introduced names, priests, and rituals. Therefore, as discussed above, while the processes described as Sanskritization and Brahminization have certainly occurred within both the elite and folk traditions of Mysore (the association of the local goddesses with the Pan-Indian goddesses Durga and Kali, the adoption of ritual calendars, etc.), the narrative and ritual details of *Chamundi of the Hill* resist these forces and act as an archive for local traditions.

The tense relationships between elite Sanskritic/brahminic traditions and nonbrahminic traditions is not a recent phenomenon. Indeed, goddesses, like Chamundi or Chamunda as she is more often referred to in Sanskrit sources, have always had a complicated insider/outsider relationship with elite traditions. Though the goddess Chamunda was introduced into the Sanskritic tradition in the *Devi Mahatmya* during the 6th or 7th century, in *Malatimadhava* (ca. 7th–8th century CE) of Bhavabhuti, Chamunda devotion is shown to be at odds with and threatening to the *agamic* ritual culture of the court.[37] In the text, the devotees of Chamunda are referred to as Kapalikas, who are depicted as practicing their rituals in cremation grounds and abducting young virgins in order to sacrifice them to the goddess.[38] As the story goes, a female Kapalika, named Kapalakundala, who has the ability to fly through the air because of her perfection (*siddha*) of *yoga*, discovers Malati (the daughter of the minister Bhurivasu) who has smitten the hero Madhava (the son of Devarata, minister of Kundinapura) with her beauty and modesty. For these same reasons, Malati is the perfect specimen for Kapalakundala's *gurudiksha* sacrifice required by her teacher Aghoraghanta—in this case, the sacrifice of a virgin to the goddess Chamunda.[39] When act 5, scene 2 begins, the Kapalikas have captured Malati and have taken her to Chamunda's temple for the sacrifice. They begin their ritual by incanting the name of the fierce goddess: "Devi Camunde namaste namaste."[40] The hymn continues:

> O Goddess, your prideful, destructive, rumbling, confusion[-producing] dance, which is the manifested power of the entourage of Shiva that causes the egg of Brahma to be destroyed because [it] presses down the earth-ball and submerges the shaking tortoise shell, causing the churning seven seas to be thrown into your gaping mouth (*gallavivara*) that rivals hell.

The hymn goes on to describe the ornaments worn by the goddess, which include an elephant hide robe, necklace of skulls, and crescent moon in her hair.[41] Written from the perspective of the medieval court, Bhavabhuti associates devotion to Chamunda with the nonbrahminic practice of human sacrifice and clearly demonstrates a distrust of the goddess's devotees.[42] The text also praises Chamunda's ability to provide magical powers (*siddhi*s) but shows that these powers are harnessed by her devotees for evil and disreputable worldly achievement, not for a higher goal such as *moksha* or *kshatriya* dharma. Perhaps these rituals were allusion to local fierce goddess practice, like those to the goddess Aiyai described in the 5th century Tamil *Cilappatikaram* or even human sacrifices that supposedly took place on Chamundi Hill prior to the 19th century.[43]

While the *Devimahatmya* (ca. 6th–7th CE) and *Malatimadhava* (ca.6th–8th CE) are very different in their perspectives on fierce goddesses, both are united in that they depict goddesses who were terrifying and craved blood and flesh. The *Devi Bhagavata Purana* (ca. 12th century), however, constructed a different image of the Goddess even within the same narratives. The *Devi Bhagavata Purana* emerged from a context of sectarian and communal chaos as a reaffirmation of the Shakta theological stance in the *Devi Mahatmya* and as a response to the Vaishnava *Bhagavata Purana*.[44] According to C. Mackenzie Brown, the composer(s) of the *Devi Bhagavata Purana* had two theological goals: "to demonstrate the superiority of the Devi to all other deities, especially Vishnu; and to articulate in new ways the manifold nature of the Goddess and her supernatural powers as they are manifested in the historical process."[45] This new "articulation" within the *Devi Bhagavata Purana* shifts the militant identity of the Goddess of the *Devi Mahatmya* to the focus on the Goddess as Mother and materiality (*prakriti*). To accomplish the transition to Mother, the composer(s) sought to "sanitize" the older martial and erotic myths of the Goddess, especially those contained within the *Devi Mahatmya*, replacing them with a new vision of the Goddess as a "mother of infinite compassion."[46] As part of the reworking of the Goddess tradition in the *Devi Bhagavata Purana*, two new "Devi Mahatmyas" were created. These new *mahatmya*s were modeled on the *Bhagavad Gita* and the *Bhagavata Purana*, and focused only on the path to liberation, opposed to the dual path of spiritual and immediate earthly boons promised in the *Devi Mahatmya*. The *Devi Bhagavata Purana* reinterpreted the Goddess's previous nature that was "somehow dark, malevolent, sinister, and only when appeased become[s] benevolent" to "stress to a greater degree the supremely compassionate nature of the Goddess."[47] The stories of the Goddess that were previously so raw, visceral, and powerful were transformed into transcendent metaphysical lore, and fierce goddesses such as Chamunda were pushed further to the periphery of mainstream elite/refined religious culture.

Therefore, even within the elite Sanskritic tradition, the Goddess and goddesses are not stagnant characters, but they inhabit a range of identities depending on perspective, rhetorical strategy, and time period. Indeed, as Kathleen M. Erndl and Lynn Foulston demonstrated several decades ago and recent work on the Himalayan goddess Hidimba by Ehud Halperin has thoroughly corroborated, individual goddesses can occupy multiple positions on any spectrum of ferocity-docility and/or malevolent-benevolent through cycles in their ritual lives and through the perception of those observing them and manipulating their identities.[48] Therefore, these theories that put the two traditions at odds—elite versus folk or regional versus Pan-Indian—are too limiting in their binaries, doing little to help us to understand the form and function of the songs under discussion, much less how they serve as sites for the construction of local meaning.

Instead of traditions-at-odds, comparing the similar but ultimately very different narratives as stories on equal footing, we can see how the particular details reflect the context of the stories and the agency of those that tell them. For instance, in "Sister, Stand on My Tongue and Fight," the victory over both demons occurs in one epic battle. With both the shape-shifting buffalo demon and the producer of "blood-seed," the Kannada songs describe a more difficult conflict that not only demonstrates the goddesses' extreme power but also reflects the two-brother trope found in foundational narratives of local dynasties, including the Wodeyar origin story from the *Great Kings of Mysore*.[49] Moreover, the protagonist goddesses in the *Devi Mahatmya* and *Chamundi of the Hill* both produce their helper goddesses from within themselves, but they do so in different ways. Whereas the Goddess produces Kali from her angry facial expression, Uttanahalli comes to life from the waters produced by Chamundi's perspiration. Certainly, this small diversion is meaningful as it relates the wrath of the Goddess on one hand and has implications for water resources and life-affirmation on the other. Additionally in the Puranic tale, the protagonist goddess is extremely self-assured, laughing at the demon while she orders Kali to drink his blood. In the Kannada episode, Chamundi is scared and overwhelmed as she looks around for help with tears welling in her eyes, and it is Uttanahalli who comes to her aid, tells her not to fear, and offers to drink the demon's blood.

Additionally, when we dive deeper into the interpretation of the myths, we can see how those contained in *Chamundi of the Hill* construct their own theology that is as equally complex as the elite traditions. Indeed, the myth of Chamundi and Aisu from Mysore seems to reflect some of same commentary on gender norms and reproduction that has been observed by scholars of the Sanskritic narrative.[50] However, in *Chamundi of the Hill*, the narrative is much more assertive in its inversion of normative understandings of reproduction, establishing one of the major themes of the overall *Chamundi of the Hill* ballad that critiques a variety of prohibitive social norms. Through the tale of their battle, there is clear symmetry between the virility of Aisu and Chamundi and even a transposition of the normative, gendered sexual roles within the reproductive process. In the narrative, Aisu and Chamundi undergo similar reproductive processes, but ultimately Chamundi proves to be more virile. Indeed, in every aspect of the process, the goddess is more auspicious and more powerful: the source of her power is from Krishna, Aisu's is Brahma; Chamundi produces the powerful goddess Uttanahalli, Aisu less powerful, replicas of himself; while both their reproductive fluids are polluting, sweat is far higher on the purity scale than blood (table 2.1).

The narrative's focus on reproduction also firmly entrenches the situated and local nature of the story. The battle is not a war for cosmic domination or to restore the cosmic realms to the Vedic deities. It is a battle over Mysore, a battle to be the master of this specific place on earth. There have long been rituals that linked the virility (*virya*) of a ruler with the fecundity (*prasavana*) of the earth over which the king rules. As far back as the Vedas, rituals have connected the male king's virility to the fertility of the ground as a basis for the king's sovereignty and right to rule.[51] However, in *this* narrative, after the death of the king (Mahisha) at the hands of the goddess, Chamundi challenges the virility of the rightful successor, the younger brother, Aisu. Through the birth of Uttanahalli, the product of the mixing of Chamundi's reproductive fluid (sweat) and the earth, she produces greater offspring, thereby demonstrating her power as the proper ruler of the Mysore domain. This was further realized when she was able to use her superior virility to best the demon in combat.

Table 2.1. Comparison of Aisu and Chamundi

	Aisu	Chamundi
Source of Reproductive Power	Brahma	Krishna
Product of Reproduction	Demon replicas	Goddess Uttanahalli
Reproductive Fluid	Blood	Sweat

The myth is further linked to the locality of Mysore through local geological knowledge of the hill itself. While the hill is called Chamundi Hill, another folk history of the geological formation says that it was formed from the carcass of the massive buffalo demon itself (figure 2.6). The massive carcass is also critical to song's ongoing inversion of gendered reproductive assumptions. After the death of Mahisha, the demon Aisu hides in the belly of the demon. The belly of Mahisha in this case also acts as a metaphorical womb from

Figure 2.6a. Chamundi Hill from Vidaranyapura-Nanjangud Road (southeast Mysore).

Figure 2.6b. Same view of Chamundi Hill with superimposed buffalo.

which Aisu is born after Chamundi thrusts her trident into the buffalo demon. Mahisha's corpse, then, produces the true form of Aisu who looks "like a huge hillock." I do not wish to push this metaphorical reading too far, but it is important to note this inversion of Chamundi's normative gendered expectations here as the song emphasizes her virility in what can be read as "masculine" reproductive tropes [i.e., her reproductive fluid impregnates the earth and her thrust into the belly of Mahisha leads to the production of Aisu]. This theme, however, is overshadowed with the third song and, perhaps the overall ballad, which often downplay Chamundi's virility and ferocity in favor of a more domesticated version of the goddess, though as we will see toward the end of *Chamundi of the Hill*, her wild and unruly nature is the source of her power and appeal for both Nanjunda and Chamundi's (future) co-wives Deviri and Somaji.

There is so much that can be said of the local implications of these narratives—social expectations of women and potential wives, the wrath of a goddess, and so on—but for now suffice it to say that the local perspective creates its own novel tradition that runs parallel with (i.e., not contrary to) Pan-Indian myth, presenting a history of the goddess for the area that happened in the not-so-distant mythic cycle of time.[52]

Conclusion

As a local myth, the narrative provides a history of the temple and its foundation that is rooted in the deeds and actions of the deities, grounding local landscape within the field of cosmic significance but significance that is tied to this specific place. The city and her temple on Chamundi Hill are given primacy in the song because the deity chooses to stay there after the battle.[53] The narrative also provides a background to explain the relationship between the goddess on the top of the hill (Chamundi) and the goddess at its base (Uttanahalli), building a devotional, ritual, and spatial relationship between the two that is subsequently extended to include Nanjunda in later songs. The song references the goddess's journey down to the city during Dasara.[54] It also describes the establishment of Uttanahalli's ritual worship, which is promised to the goddess by Chamundi.[55]

In doing so, these songs—and the overall ballad—describe the foundation of these temples, provide narrative justification for the expense of festivals, and promise that deities will remain local if these rituals are continued. The entire devotional landscape and ritual calendar are simultaneously placed within significant space and time, while the deities are made extremely immanent, with the gods and goddesses traveling the same roads, climbing the same hills, and bathing in the same rivers as their devotees.

Chapter Three

"You're the one who protects this place"

Folk Perspectives on Urban History and Regional Significance

Urban histories provide important glimpses into the ways in which meaning is constructed for cities and their inhabitants. They also help us to understand how cities are formed, how they continue to operate, and perhaps most importantly (for our purposes, at least) how place and social identity are intertwined in a reciprocal relationship that shapes peoples, landscapes, and cityscapes. While one narrative might become the dominant, well-known history, multiple visions of urban spaces and city-regions can also be present that articulate different perspectives about how place is situated in the world/cosmos. Through an analysis of these alternate narratives, we can begin to understand how the stories that are told about cities reflect the concerns of the communities that tell them. This is certainly the case in Mysore in South India. The dominant history of the city comes from the royal histories and can be found in every media from internet sites to tourist brochures at roadside book stalls. As one might expect, this history of the city reflects the imperial and colonial concerns of the ruling family that sought to connect its rulers with Pan-Indian royalty, who resided throughout the South Asian subcontinent. There are, however, concurrent histories of Mysore told in media generally outside the purview of the mainstream, namely, the folk traditions. This is certainly the case for the folk ballad *Chamundi of the Hill*. The narratives contained in these songs not only provide mythological and cosmological significance that was explored in the previous chapter, but they also contain a history of the region, detailing important temples, deities, and networks between urban centers, villages, and the communities that live in and between these sites. These narratives, unlike those from the royal court, reflect a radically different set of concerns that focus on grounding the city's significance in its locality. After discussing the aforementioned royal history of the city through an excerpt translated from its most important source, this chapter closely examines the collection of Kannada folk songs to highlight its vision of the history of Mysore and its people. By looking at the folk songs sung about the goddess Chamundi and her lover Nanjunda, we can see a vision of Mysore and its surrounding cities that reflects a history in which the dynamic of local devotional geography and its networks of pilgrimage are paramount within its identity.

Folk Ballad as Urban History: Recovery and Preservation

The stories of cities more often than not have been told from the perspective of the elite. The histories of important places and regions are replete with tales of kings and rich merchants, battles and patronage, detailed within archives written by court poets and historians or literate religious professionals who were often embedded within courtly culture. It should, therefore, be no surprise that the focus of these histories often reflects the perspectives of the authors and their benefactors, obscuring the everyday lives of the vast majority of populations. When these sources do offer insights into the common folk, they are inflected with the goals and concerns of the elite and are often unreliable in understanding the variegated pasts of urban and village spaces and the various networks that create webs of meaning for different segments of society. Indeed, the act of writing the story of a city—or any history for that matter—is not an apolitical reconstruction of earlier events or descriptions of culture; urban history is the act of choosing a city's past, a political act that highlights certain data and demographics while obfuscating others.[1] Over the past few decades, historians have begun to look more closely at life throughout the various rungs of society to gain a fuller picture of our pasts and the pasts of the spaces in which we live, work, play, and worship.[2] Urban history provides one of the most compelling methodologies for its ability to recover the stories of diverse segments of society because of the ways that place is embedded and encoded with the social lives of people that inhabit the space and how space is configured to reflect the needs of both the folk and the elite.[3] Cities, villages, and the networks that form around the full spectrum of society are public performances of collective memories that provide us with information about their pasts and present.

For millenia, textual and literary traditions have labored to define the roles that space and place play in religious and social lives within South Asian religions. In Vedic corpus, certain space is delineated as noble (*aryavarsha*) and contrasted with the lands of the ignoble peoples (*anaryan*). The epic Ramayana and Mahabharata and the Buddhist Pali canon give great attention to movement through space and the importance of religious sites and boundaries of kingdoms. Cankam poetry from the Tamil-speaking South intimately connected landscape with religious and secular sentiments while developing a network of important public sites throughout the region. Many puranas (literally "ancient;" encyclopedic collections of myths) contain *mahatmyas* or glorification texts that praise the spiritual power of particular sites, often associating the physical space with a metaphysical, supernatural event or action by a deity from the brahminic Hindu pantheon. With the rise of the regional vernacular *bhakti* devotional movement in the 6th to 9th centuries and its subsequent spread throughout India, however, the emphasis on the histories of specific local sites surged. Due to their emphasis on specific deities at specific locations, art historian Anna Lise Seastrand notes, "bhakti poems are noted for their role in developing regional consciousness, laying the ground for patterns of pilgrimage and the construction of large temples, as well as for the strong sense of devotion they convey."[4] By the 13th century, the genre of local vernacular *sthalapurana*, "sacred geographies" or "local mythic histories," that told the mythic histories of religious and pilgrimage sites of local and regional importance began to proliferate.[5] While these texts were rooted in local concerns, they, more often than not, asserted hegemonic and monolithic identities onto the spaces that they described. The *sthalapuranas* not only promoted these specific sacred sites from a particular perspective, but they inherently reflected the broader popularity of the places as pilgrimage sites that were part of expanding networks of religious practice and movement. Ranjeeta Dutta, historian of the South India Tamil Shrivaishnava community, suggests:

While a continuum was acknowledged between the texts and practice, the idea of pilgrimage in the case of the latter provided a single context for the assertion of multiple identities within the community paradigm. Further, these identities were always fluid and underwent constant reconfigurations under the influence of the pilgrimage network, which provided a space for a continuous interface between various social and political groups, ideas and cultural values.[6]

The interfaces of these different social and political groups also shaped the landscape and the infrastructure that supported them. Kanchipuram in Tamil Nadu is an excellent example of how cities develop around their designation as a sacred site and as part of networks of worship and pilgrimage. Emma Stein has recently shown that the streets of Kanchipuram bear witness to the past and are designed to accommodate the flow of devotees from one temple to the next, as well as to house different communities of various caste backgrounds and their associated deities.[7]

Chamundi of the Hill, likewise, is a repository that contains a history of local sacred space, as it provides yet another portion of the story. It tells a local sacred history, grounding the city through its mythological origins, sacred pilgrimage networks, and provides details of the development of its infrastructure, including roads and temples.

Kingship, Migration, and Conquest in Courtly Urban Histories of Mysore City

Beginning in 1610 CE, Mysore City served as a cultural outpost of the Wodeyar rulers whose political capital and palace were located in nearby Shrirangapattana, a former seat of power for the great Vijayanagara Empire (1336–1646 CE). At the height of their power under powerful kings like Kanthirava Narasaraj Wodeyar (r. 1638–1659) and Chikkadevaraja Wodeyar (r. 1673–1704), the Mysore kingdom challenged its neighboring states for supremacy as the successor of Vijayanagara and for dominance of South India and encompassed most of the modern state of Karnataka. The Mysore kingdom is most well-known for its sultanate period, when Tipu Sultan and his father Haidar Ali resisted the insurgency of British colonialism in four successive Anglo-Mysore wars (1767–1799). After the defeat of Tipu Sultan and his forces in 1799, the British reinstalled the Wodeyar lineage of the Mysore kingdom, placing 4-year-old Krishnaraja Wodeyar III (r. 1799–1868) on the throne and installing their resident in his court to educate and advise the young king. Additionally, they took Shrirangapattana for themselves, moving the Mysore capital to Mysore City. By 1831, however, administrative and military powers were taken from Krishnaraja Wodeyar III and granted to a series of British commissioners who oversaw administration of the kingdom until the king's death in 1868 when direct rule was restored to Krishnaraja Wodeyar III's adopted son, Chamaraja Wodeyar X (r. 1868–1894).[8]

Since its colonial days under the British resident, Mysore has been styled a royal city or the "City of Palaces." Though the colonial princely state never received the highest honor afforded to its neighbor in Hyderabad, it was granted a 21-gun salute throughout India, an honor granted to only five Indian states. Additionally, Mysore was commonly referred to by the epithet the "model princely state" because of its cooperation with the British administrators, which led to the city developing modern technological infrastructure more rapidly than many of their neighboring states.[9] Due to their success in the colonial framework, many European and Indian historians writing during the colonial period took special interest in Mysore and devoted much time and effort to examining the history of the city, particularly in reconstructing the establishment and birth of the city through positivist historiography. These histories tended to focus on what they considered to be reliable and verifiable evidence that was archived in courtly documents and regional epigraphy and only briefly alluded to the mythological history of the city and the goddess's adversary Mahisha, who was said to have formerly ruled the region that, as we will see, is central in many local histories.[10] As a result, the majority of these histories replicated royal interpretations of Mysore's past and incorporated the dominant narrative of its origins from genealogies produced by the Mysore court.[11] These episodes of the establishment of the kingdom, which can be found within many epigraphic *prashasti*s (royal praises) and most literary genealogical texts dating back to 1639 CE, however, demonstrate the preoccupation of the Mysore court to tell, not only the history of their kings, but the history of the city from which they hailed. The details contained within the narratives differ in the various tellings;[12] however, there are two common tropes that appear to be mostly ubiquitous among the different versions: that the Mysore kings descend from *yadu vamsha* or "the lineage of the Yadus" and that their line was established in Mysore after their progenitors immigrated from a foreign land. From these details, we can see the preoccupation of the court to establish the kingdom through external Pan-Indian elite imperial concerns that were connected with the Pan-Indian epic genre.

While the royal history of Mysore has varied considerably in its different iterations, since the colonial period the version of the kingdom's origin narrative found in a text titled *Maisurina Shriman Maharajavara Vamshavali* or *The Great Kings of Mysore* (ca. 1860s) has become the principle account in modern histories and in popular imagination.[13] *The Great Kings of Mysore* was first composed in Kannada during the middle of the nineteenth century and is attributed to the Mysore king Krishnaraja Wodeyar III (r. 1799–1868) and retold the story of the origins of his kingdom in a way that helped re-establish his sovereignty as it waned vis-à-vis British colonial hegemonic rule.[14] As new technologies of print reproduction were made available in Mysore, these narratives spread widely throughout the kingdom and in England, solidifying this account as *the* history of Mysore and its kings and has often been repeated as the authentic history in historical scholarship.[15] Therefore, the history of Mysore articulated in *The Great Kings of Mysore* provides a source of comparison for the urban history found in *Chamundi of the Hill*.

The account contained in *The Great Kings of Mysore* like *Chamundi of the Hill* begins with a focus on deities. *The Great Kings of Mysore*, however, commences with an allusion to the story of creation that is part of the puranic tradition in which the deity Brahma emerges from the navel of the Vishnu and speaks the cosmos into existence. In *The Great Kings of Mysore*, however, the story is not framed as a creation story, but it is the beginning of a long family tree, a genealogy that begins with Vishnu and his progeny Brahma and descends through the legendary Yadava line that includes the deity Krishna and his son Pradyumna and finally to a great king named Rajadeva who rules in the 14th century. Rajadeva does not, however, rule in Mysore, but he is the king of Dwaraka, the former kingdom of the Krishna in the *Mahabharata* that is located over 1,000 miles away in northwestern India. According to this history, Rajadeva had two sons named Yaduraya and Krishnaraya. These two sons are the progenitors of the Wodeyar line of Mysore kings. Because there is so much overlap in the overall structure and the characters between *The Great Kings of Mysore* and *Chamundi of the Hill*, I think it would be helpful to reproduce the story of the foundation of the Wodeyar Mysore kingdom in its entirety in order to allow a meaningful comparison (this translation is replicated in the appendix):[16]

Yaduraya comes from Dwaraka and the details of his dream

According to instructions received from Shri Krishna in a dream, Yaduraya left the borders of Dwaraka. He reached the goddess, who dwells in the Vindhya mountains. While he performed austerities there, Vindhyavasini, was pleased and said, "I have lived on the Mahabala mountain [another name for Chamundi Hill], which is between the Kaveri and Kapila and there I'm called Chamundeshwari [Lady Chamundi]. If you go to Mahabala mountain and worship me, you will marry the daughter of the king of the city named Mysore, which is next to the mountain, and this city will become yours." After the goddess's command, Yaduraya awoke happy, and he, along with his younger brother, Krishnaraya, left for the Vindhya mountains. They came through Vijayanagara to Yadavagiri [Melukote]. They bathed in the temple tank and took *darshana* of many gods, including Yoga Narasimha, Lord Narayana, and Lord Cheluva Narayana, who was the god of the great king Yadu Shekhara's family. After crossing the Kaveri River and climbing the Mahabala mountain, he worshipped the goddess Chamundi who is *adishakti* [primordial power], the mother of the universe, and dwells on the mountain. He bowed with devotion to Shri Kantheshwara [Shiva], who is the lord of Bhukailasa [Nanjangudu], which is 20 miles from the mountain. That night, Yaduraya slept peacefully meditating on the feet of the goddess.

At daybreak, the goddess came in the form of a woman and said, "Go to the southeastern portion of my mountain first thing tomorrow morning. Just as you have worshipped me, worship the goddess Jwalajjihwa [Uttanahalli], who killed Raktabija and resides there. Then, go to the Kodibhairava shrine beside the temple tank inside the Shiva temple worshipped by the Sage Trinabindu, that is on the east side of Mysore City and stay there. At that time, a man wearing the robes of a *jangama* and a linga will come. When he sees you, he will say a few words. If you do as he says, everything I promised you in the Vindhya mountains will become yours." After she said this, Chamundeshwari vanished.

The Blessing of Shri Shri Kantheshwara

Yaduraya awoke and told his brother about the dream. Following the instructions of the goddess, he joyously worshipped Jwalamukhi [Uttanahalli]. Then after breakfast, they left and waited at the Kodibhairava shrine near the tank behind Mysore's Trineshwara temple. A great *jangama*, who was wearing a saffron robe and a linga, came just as the goddess Chamundeshwari had told in the vision. When he saw the *jangama*, Yaduraya joyously arose and honored the ascetic by touching his lotus feet. He sat down and thought, "The words spoken by the Goddess in the dream are coming true." Then the great *jangama* asked in the words of the ordinary folk, "Prince, who are you? Where are you from? What are your intentions?" Then Yaduraya told him his own history and said, "I have been expecting the *darshana* of your feet as was prophesied by the goddess Chamundeshwari. I will follow your every command."

Upon hearing Yaduraya's words, the great *jangama* said, "Prince, I will tell you a secret. Previously, a valiant, brave, and wealthy king named Shuradevaraya was born in the lineage of Bhoja from the Gautama gotra in the city of Mathura. He, along with his family, left that city and came to Karnataka, gained wealth and the kingdom of Mysore, and lived happily because of the blessings of Shri Chamundeshwari. In the lineage of Shuradevaraya, a king named Chamaraya was born and ruled the kingdom. He had a jewel of a daughter, but he died without a son.

The city was without a king. Now, an evil general named Maranayaka is threatening Devajammani, the wife of the deceased king. With my blessings, you will gain the power to kill that wicked man. Another great *jangama* will come and give you all the instructions in detail. If you follow this, not only will you marry the king's daughter, but you will obtain kingship and your lineage will prosper eternally (literally: "will become like the sun and the moon"). You will live happily. If you do whatever that great *jangama* requests, I will be very happy." After saying this, he vanished. When Yaduraya and Krishnaraya saw this, they were astonished and determined "Shri Kantheshwara, who lives in Nanjangudu, just came here to this hill in the form of this great *jangama*). If we fulfill these commands given by the goddess then just like the goddess Shri Chamundeshwari is our family goddess, Nanjunda Kantheshwara will become our family god." And they worshipped him.

The Dream of the Devajammanni, the wife of the king of Mysore

At daybreak Parameshvara [Shiva] came to the suffering wife of Chamaraja in a dream because she could not bear the troubles caused by Maranayaka. He said, "O Queen, don't worry. Calm your mind and listen to my words of comfort. Two princes, brothers born into the lineage of Yadu and the Atreya *gotra* have come to the Kodibhairava shrine of Mysore City. The eldest prince is a suitable match to marry your daughter. Send a wise and friendly man to them to tell them about all the things that have happened here. Have him bring them to the city. Give your daughter to the eldest prince. If you do this, you will have great peace. He will kill all of your enemies with his martial prowess. He will rule your kingdom with righteousness. He will have many descendants." After he said this, he vanished. The queen immediately arose and was happy. She woke up her daughter and told her the events of the dream. The two called a man, who, as had been described in the dream, had a peaceful countenance and wore a *linga*. They told him what was said in the dream and sent him to the princes. Excited, she called two more servants and said, "Servants, immediately go to the Bhairava temple, which is beside the tank of the city. Go so that no one knows and find out physical features, intellect, and qualities of the men who are there and tell us with whom they speak and events about which they speak." Then, she sent them away. As they had been commanded, the servants went immediately. They heard the words that the two princes spoke to the *jangama*. They observed their youthful form and beautiful qualities until they became tired. Then, they quickly returned. The servants properly and secretively narrated all these observations to the queen, and she was immensely happy. Meanwhile, the great *jangama* enquired about the *gotra*, culture, and family of the princes. He asked about their health and wealth. The *jangama*, then, in a condensed manner, told them about the event that had transpired in the city, the queen's heartfelt desires, and the brave deeds that need to be done, saying, "I will come again and take you inside the fort." Then he came to the palace, and as the *jangama* was narrating all the events that took place, Queen Devajammanni thought, "All the prophesies that were made by Parameshwara are true." They were confirmed by the great *jangama*, and she was happy. In order to find out the next thing to do, she called the two scribes, named Timmarasayya and Naranayya, who had been very close to her for a long time. She told them all these events in detail. She told them, "I will make whatever arrangements are necessary in order for you, with your intelligence, to bring the princes here." Then she sent them away.

Yaduraya enters the city

The two scribes received the command of the queen, and they convinced a few brave men to sign a treaty of peace and became enemies of the general Maranayaka. Secretly, these people, who were now close to them, were stationed with weapons near the guards at the palace gate. Then Timmarasayya and Naranayya, along with the one who wore the *linga* went to the Bhairava temple to talk with the princes. They conversed about all the events with the princes and told them, "Kill your enemies either by your strength or by deceit. If you do this, all of us will be happy." Having heard those words, the princes excitedly joined the three men from the palace. When they entered the city, the gatekeepers, who were allied with Maranayaka, attempted to stop them from entering the gates of the city; however, the gatekeepers were quickly killed, and the brothers entered the city and arrived in the courtyard of the palace per the queen's command.

The assassination of Maranayaka

Maranayaka heard what happened and, along with this army, came and confronted the brothers. Maranayaka, holding a sword, shouted, "Who are you? Where are you from? Why have you killed my men? You've made a big mistake, and, now, I will kill you both." But Yaduraya and brave men who were installed in secret by the scribes engaged their enemy. The brothers' coalition quickly killed Maranayaka and his allies. They had obtained the goddess of wealth. Then they remembered Shri Chamundeshwari and Shri Kantheshwara and prayed. When they entered the city, as the two scribes proclaimed their victory in battle to their leader, queen Devajammanni. They were then commanded to bring Yaduraya into the royal court of the palace with the honor worthy of a king.

The marriage of Yaduraya

Yaduraya honored his soldiers and then sent them away. He called the two scribes, the linga-wearing *jangama*, and his younger brother. He bowed to the queen, who was behind the curtain in her inner chamber, and sat down and crossed his arms. The queen looked at that prince and was pleased. She lovingly said, "Prince, you with the blessing of Shri Chamundeshwari were the answer to all my problems. Aou have obtained the goddess of kingship without obstacles, according to the scriptures take the hand of my daugher Devajammanni. Be happy and stay here protecting this kingdom." She gave him clothes and flower and leaf ornaments and ordered the scribes and other people to follow the orders of Yaduraya. She decorated the city, erected many canopies, prepared all the things that were necessary for marriage—clothes, ornaments, etc.—and called everyone, including their relatives. At the time that the astrologer had said was auspicious, according to the tradition of the palace, she worshipped Shri Kantheshwara and Shri Chamundeshwari, who were the family gods. The bride worshipped Indra's wife, Sachidevi, and queen Devajammanni fulfilled her vow, and, through her cousin, Kenchalagudu Nanjarajayya, gave her daughter, who looked like Krishna's wife, Rukmani, to Yaduraya. Yaduraya after completing a pilgrimage to Kashi (Benares), put on all the ornaments looking like Shri Krishna, and they celebrated the marriage festival.

The royal coronation of Yaduraya

In the auspicious time on Monday the 5th day of the waxing moon in the month of Vaishakha in the year Pramathi, which happened in 1322 of the Shalivahana *shaka*, Yaduraya was crowned king of Mysore. Having been offered the regions, the treasury, and the royal signet ring, Yaduraya doubled in brilliance. When he was ruling the kingdom, he appointed the work of the palace correspondence to the two scribes, who had done the highly secret work. Having made it their family tradition as requested by the *jangama*, who had been pleased by these actions, they commanded that all the rulers who had the royal coronation be called by the name Wodeyar, and that saffron cloth, which is symbol of the *jangamas* be included in their flag. Having come to know that his father-in-law's cousin, named Karagalli Shantarajayya would oppose him, he curbed him. He married his younger brother Krishnaraya to Shantarajayya's daughter, and Krishnaraya became the ruler of the village of Karagalli.

In this story of the foundation of the kingdom of Mysore, one can see many of the same features that are similar in form to regional *sthalapuranas*: there is divine presence and intervention that highlights the sacrality and importance of the site; Mysore is placed within a broader network of local and regional pilgrimage sites, like Melukote, Nanjangudu, and Uttanahalli; and marriage is invoked as a means to join peoples and cities. Additionally, the foundational narrative involves many of the same characters and places as are found in *Chamundi of the Hill*: the goddess Chamundi plays a central role in the narrative, Shiva manifests as his form from Nanjangudu as a *jangama*; Chamundi ensures that Uttanahalli, who is credited with drinking the blood of a demon, receives her fair share of worship.

While these features confirm that the origin story found in *The Great Kings of Mysore* are embedded within the same social context as *Chamundi of the Hill*, other aspects belie its function as a text that affirms Wodeyar claims to sovereignty in the region. Particularly, the narrative of the migration of Yaduraya and Krishnaraya follows established motives found in dynastic royal lineage texts in the region that date back to at least the 12th century in inscriptions from the western Ganga kingdom of Talakadu.[17] In this royal trope, two brothers from kingdoms in northern India, who are said to come from legendary dynastic lineages, travel south to a kingdom that has been promised to them by a deity. The narrative functions to give a proper lineage to local rulers by connecting them to kings from the great Sanskrit epics and to give the rulers a history that is grander than their own local history. Additionally, the kings win the kingdom through the right of conquest by defeating the would-be ruler Maranayaka and marrying the daughter of the former ruler. There is, of course, similarity here with *Chamundi of the Hill*, where Chamundi defeats the demon brothers, Mahisha and Aisu, and is ultimately established in the region through her marriage to Nanjunda.[18] The local deities, in the case of the courtly history, are connected to Pan-Indian deities, which does the work of extending their influence and glossing over their local identity. This process of obscuring the local identity of deities was also accomplished by the same king who authored *The Great Kings of Mysore* as he displaced the local nonbrahmin priests of Mysore's temples with brahmin priests from nearby Tamil Nadu. In *The Great Kings of* Mysore, the city, its kings, and their deities are important not because of their roots in the specific location but because their identities lie outside of the region.

This idealization of the nonnative lineage of kings still continues within the rhetoric of the royal family. In my conversation with the late maharaja of Mysore, Shri Kanthadatta Narasimharaja Wodeyar (1953–2013), he suggested that my examination of Kannada materials was not necessary for understanding his family, lineage, and Mysore kingship in general. Instead, he instructed me to look to the Rajput kings of northwestern India—the kings from which the Wodeyars insisted his family had descended.[19] The pervading ethos for the elite histories of the Mysore court is the valorization of the external that connects this kingdom in south central India with Pan-Indian concerns of kingship and its relationship with the Sanskrit epic corpus. As we turn our gaze toward other, local sources for the urban history of Mysore, however, we see that the emphases turn toward autochthonous, resident characters and the importance and construction of locality.

Situatedness and Significance in *Chamundi of the Hill's* Folk History of Mysore

The history contained within *Chamundi of the Hill*, however, provides an alternate view in which the city is part of a local devotional tradition that gains its power and significance from the situatedness of its deities, temples, and customs. In these songs of balladeers of southern Karnataka, we see that Mysore, the city/region of Nanjangudu, and the village Uttanahalli form a network of important devotional sites in which powerful deities physically reside and provide protection and wealth for the region and its inhabitants.

As we have already seen, the songs that make up the total ballad of *Chamundi of the Hill* relate different scenes in the mythological past of Mysore. The ballad starts with the slaying of Mahisha and Aisu by Chamundi and culminates in the acceptance of the love marriage between the goddess and Shiva's manifestation as Nanjunda from nearby Nanjangudu. The songs take us through their courtship, their secret marriage, Shiva's absence due to his other wives' anger that he took another (younger and more attractive) lover, and their eventual reunion after some trickery from the newlyweds. While the songs relate a narrative focused on the love story between two deities, this collection also demonstrates a different vision of Mysore's history in which the primary actors are not the ruling elite but local folk, albeit divine local folk.

As discussed in the previous chapter, the first song relates the epic battle between the goddess and the buffalo demon Mahisha—a story central within Mysorean mythological lore—and his fiercer brother, Aisu. The battle narrated in the song, however, does not unfold as do similar narratives of the goddess and buffalo demon found in Sanskrit texts, such as the *Devi Mahatmya* or the *Devi Bhagavata Purana*. In this folk narrative, the goddess Chamundi is approached by the demon king on the top of her hill (Chamundi Hill). The demon grabs her forearm (an action that is paralleled with her marriage to Nanjunda later in the ballad), but the goddess takes offense, withdraws her sword, and thrusts it into his neck. With this act, the true demon Aisu emerges from the belly of the buffalo, and a fierce battle ensues, but from every drop of the blood that gushes forth onto the ground countless other demons spring forth. Not to be bested in the arena of magical reproduction, the goddess, exasperated, wipes the sweat from her brow and slings it to the ground. Instantly (because of a boon from the deity Krishna) the fierce goddess Uttanahalli is born from the perspiration with seven hoods and seven lolling tongues. After a brief conversation in which Uttanahalli tells Chamundi her name and the two hash out the nature of their relationship (they determine that they are indeed siblings), Uttanahalli devises the plan that she should spread out her seven tongues so Chamundi can wage war with the demon standing on this lingual battlefield with no blood hitting the earth. This strategy proves successful as the sisters are able to defeat the demon king once and for all.

Establishing Festivals

The victory, however, is bittersweet because the goddess Uttanahalli immediately realizes that she is homeless and unemployed, asking her sister, "What should I do?" and, "Where should I live?" The elder sister then explains that she, Chamundi, is the goddess of the hill and the house god of the local rulers. She also explains that she is celebrated with special *puja* once a year.[20] She urges Uttanahalli to remain nearby, promising the younger goddess that if she remains in the region, the people will also celebrate an annual *puja* in her honor, during which they will offer her all sorts of homemade goodies, including *tambittu* (a delicious rice sweet of which goddesses are particularly fond). Uttanahalli is convinced and takes up residence at the base of the hill in the village named Uttanahalli ("village in-between [Chamundi Hill and Nanjangudu]").

This narrative describes the situatedness of the goddess on the hill, her role as the protector of the people and the family deity of the kings, and her younger fiercer sister's autochonous birth and establishment in her eponymous village at the base of the hill. While the songs reference the ruling elite and their patronage, the goddess's role as the family deity of the kings is not her primary identity with the assumption that both goddesses are sustained in their locales because of the devotion and offerings given by the people. The annual *puja* to which Chamundi refers is ambiguous, and it is most likely a reference to the large celebration of Navaratri ("Nine Nights of the Goddess") or Dasara (also known as Vijayadashami; the "Tenth [Day] of Victory") (see chapter 2). From context and details of the offering, the allusion to Uttanahalli's promised *puja* introduces the milieu of folk goddess festivals that are celebrated by local nonbrahminic castes and that are shared by both goddesses. In these festivals, more commonly called Chamunda Maramma Jatre ("Fierce Mother Chamundi Festival") and Uttanahalli Maramma Jatre ("Fierce Mother Uttanahalli Festival"), the goddesses receive blood sacrifices of chickens and goats, which is also alluded to in subsequent songs. It is through the devotion of the common folk that the goddesses remain attached to the hill and the city.

Throughout the ballad, the songs continue to ground religious practice, specifically festivals, and their origins within this mythic narrative. Much later in the overall story, in the song "He Ran Tripping over Himself to the House of Chamundi of the Hill" Nanjunda is returning to Chamundi and realizes that he has no money to bring her a gift. So, he visits the temple of Kalinga, a seven-hooded serpent and the younger brother of Nanjunda's wife Deviri (or Deviramma), in order to trick him into funding his dalliance. After convincing the serpent that the money was to buy medicine for Deviri, Nanjunda takes the money from the temple's donation box and leaves to go to the market. There he is spotted by Nandi (called Basavanna), his bull attendant, who alerts Kalinga to the deception. In order to win their silence, Nanjunda appeases both deities with gifts. Nanjunda promises to give Nandi a bell for his neck, a humorous nod to the agricultural reality of a bull and to his common iconography in the region. After beating the snake deity, Nanjunda agrees to create the Subramanya Shristi festival at his brother-in-law's temple, a festival that incorporates folk practices of snake worship and establishes another node in the region's pilgrimage network.

Connecting Cityscapes and Village Landscapes as Devotional Networks

In this vein, the narrative constructs a devotional map that connects not only goddess of the hill to Nanjangudu but forms a network that includes other pilgrimage sites and their festivals that are important within the region, contrasting with the networks formed in *The Great Kings of Mysore* in which the original pilgrimage was conceived of by the Pan-Indian deity Krishna, and the goddess of the Vindhya Mountains directed the brothers to Mysore through Vijayanagara and Melkote. *Chamundi of the Hill* begins with Chamundi presiding over and protecting her hill and the establishment of her fierce younger sister in the village of Uttanahalli. From there it connects the goddess with Nanjunda through their respective pilgrimages to the sacred confluence or *triveni sangama* in Tirumakudal Narsipur, where the two deities meet for the first time. Therefore, from very early in the ballad, the narrative establishes pilgrimage networks that are for the most part only significant to the local population of the region, tying the space together with the people who move through those same networks.

Movement is an important theme for both the songs and local religious practice. It is quite common for Shaiva—relating to the deity Shiva—practitioners to move between Nanjangudu and Chamundi Hills quite regularly. Before the advent of major paved roads that easily transport pilgrims between Nanjangudu and Chamundi Hills, the trip was much more arduous. The footpath on the southern side of the hill is unlike the northern path that connects the hill to Mysore upon which the Dodda Devaraja installed 600 steps to ease the trek for devotees. Instead, the southern path is steep and winding and, even today, comes with the danger of predatory wild animals. Therefore, in premodern times many pilgrims would stop at Uttanahalli's temple at the southern base of the hill before continuing around the hill to take the northern stepped footpath. Perhaps, this is why the village is called Uttanahalli or the "In-Between Village."

The pilgrimage that connects Uttanahalli to Chamundi Hill and to Nanjangudu is documented in the *Chamundi of the Hill* in the song titled "Go Give My Love to Your Brother-in-Law Nanjunda, and Tell Him to Return." In the beginning of the song, Chamundi frantically calls her sister to come up the hill to her aid. Uttanahalli prepares as any female devotee would prepare for a pilgrimage as she begins her journey. Uttanahalli takes a ritual bath, dresses in a fine sari and blouse, parts her hair, and decorates her hair-bun with a golden ornament and jasmine flowers. She, then, grabs a staff and goes on the winding streets from Uttanahalli to the small villages of Sakkalli, Nalatadaripura, and Barighatta all the way to Mysore's Doddakere Lake before ascending the footsteps up the hill. The scene that balladeers set when describing this always gets a big laugh from the audience who can identify with Uttanahalli as she wipes beads of sweat and flips her hair out of her face as she marches up the steep steps. When Uttanahalli arrives atop the hill, she finds out that the reason that Chamundi called her was because Chamundi wanted her younger sister to go to Nanjangudu to fetch her husband. This is reminiscent of *The Great Kings of Mysore*, in which Chamudi instructs the Wodeyar progenitors to go worship Uttanahalli and then to wait for Nanjunda in the form of a *jangama*. Here, however, Uttanahalli takes on the identity of her eponymous village's situated geographic identity as she becomes the go-between in their romantic relationship, truly acting as the "In-Between" goddess.

Before her younger sister will accept her commission, Chamundi has to convince Uttanahalli of the validity of her marriage to Nanjunda and impress upon her the urgency through the details of a series of visions that foretold possible destruction and death. In her descriptions of these visions, Chamundi sees Mysore going to ruin and seven fierce goddesses on procession through the city like festival images atop a massive processional chariot (*ratha*) coming to bring about the city's destruction.[21] In Chamundi's visions, we find a reversal of the themes in the courtly urban histories. While the elite history privileges the outside and the external, as we've seen in migration/conquest narrative in *The Great Kings of Mysore* in which outsiders rulers are sent from outsider deities in order to save the region, in *Chamundi of the Hill*, Mysore is threatened by the external, foreign powers—that is, the Durgas who come from outside, from the Ujjain region—only to be saved by local and situated deities.

Through the description of the wrath of the goddesses, we are also given insight to the layout of the city, its important areas, and how they relate to different sectors of society.

> *I dreamt the little ones*
> *died on the little streets.*
> *I dreamt the big ones*
> *died in the big areas.*
> *I dreamt that in Virangere*[22]
> *they were putting the dying people outside the house.*[23]
> *I dreamt that in Bandikeri*
> *the seven Marammas*
> *were binding the death carts.*
> *I dreamt that in the clock tower street*[24]
> *there were loud screams.*
> *I dreamt that in Sunnakeri*[25]
> *they were looting.*
> *In Hallakeri*
> *they scooped up men.*
> *I dreamt that in Bandikeri*
> *they buried corpses.*
> *I dreamt that on Kalamma Road*[26]
> *all the people on the road*
> *were screaming and praying*
> *to Kalamma.*

Similar to the description of Uttanahalli's journey to Chamundi Hill, as the balladeers narrate the story, they also reconstruct the urban geography embedding it with the social life of the city. From the first lines of this selection, the words of the goddess describe the city as a place of segregation and hierarchy: *I dreamt the little ones died on the little streets. I dreamt the big ones died in the big areas.* As the selection continues, however, one notices that the emphasis is not on difference or on hierarchy, but that the goddesses are, in fact, great equalizers. All people, great and small, are subject to the horrors inflicted by these wrathful deities.

The lyrics emphasize this message even further through the contrasting language of place. In the seven Durgas portion of the vision, Chamundi mentions several specific places: Virangere, Bandikere, Sunnakere, and Hallakere. Each of these places ends with the suffix -*kere* (or -*gere*) which means that the village was built around a tank. Tanks were crucial to village life as they are man-made structures that are sources for continual water supply, sustaining life during long periods of dry weather and droughts. As will be discussed in greater detail in the next chapter, bodies of water have an important function in South Asian ritual life as they are not only sources of sustenance, but they also provide means for ritual purification, particularly after life-cycle rituals (*samskara*) relating to death and death anniversaries. By invoking the horrific images of death in contrast to the life-sustaining and purifying qualities of tank places, the song deftly highlights the precarity of life and the social institutions and rituals that support it.

The song is quite specific about the places that the goddess envisions. While the exact location of these places is not always completely clear, it provides a detailed account of the city structure and layout that can help us date this version of the ballad to the late 19th or early 20th century. The names—Virangere, Bandikere, Sunnakere, and Hallakere—are names of distinct villages in Karnataka that would have been part of the Mysore state before Indian Independence but that are spread out all over the larger Mysore region in the districts (*taluk*) of Mysore, Chamarajanagara, and Hunsuru. In conversation, my Kannadiga interlocutors explained that at least Virangere and Sunnakere are also names of neighborhoods within Mysore City. The latter interpretation of the names referencing neighborhoods in Mysore City aligns with the other details in the selection that names both the Clock Tower Street and Kalamma Road, which are both located in Mysore City. These two street names also provide clues that can help us to date *Chamundi of the Hill*, at least in this iteration. Most likely, the clock tower that is referenced here is not Mysore's large Silver Jubilee Clock Tower that was built in 1927 to commemorate the twenty-fifth anniversary of the reign of Krishnaraja Wodeyar IV (r. 1902–1940);[27] instead, it most likely refers to the small clock tower (*chikkagadiyara*) or Dufferin Clock Tower that was constructed in what is known called Devaraja Market in 1886 to commemorate Lord Dufferin, viceroy of India's visit to Mysore. There are several clues within the lyrics that help to make that conclusion. First, the songs often refer to Chamundi as the house god of the ruler named Chamaraja. Chamaraja is a frequently used name in the Wodeyar family and is also the name of the deceased king of Mysore in the origin story found in *The Great Kings of Mysore*; however, the Wodeyar who ruled during this period was Chamaraja Wodeyar X (r. 1868–1894). Second, I have been told that the reference to Kalamma Road is the old local name for what is now named Irwin Road, which received its name in commemoration of Lord Irwin, another Viceroy of India, during his visit to Mysore for the celebration of Krishnaraja Wodeyar IV's silver jubilee celebration.[28] Therefore, from the details of the urban history contained within *Chamundi of the Hill*, we can roughly date this version of the ballad between 1886 and 1927.

As the song continues, however, the narrative does not just focus on Mysore as a single locale but connects the city with a network of local pilgrimage sites wherein the deities are—or at least are supposed to be—situated. This is evident in the song "Have You Lost Interest in Your Wife?" Given Chamundi's abandonment and lovesickness, one might expect that when she sends Uttanahalli to fetch her husband, she wants him to join her on Chamundi Hill. Instead, when Uttanahalli finds Nanjunda in Mulluru, a small village about 10 miles from Chamundi Hill and 15 miles from Nanjangudu, she encourages him to return to his home in Nanjangudu (here called Nanjalagudi).

> Sir, the regal Parvati,
> whose man has gone from Nanjalagudi,
> that beautiful one has sent me.
> The beautiful one sent me because
> her man went on a quest beyond Nanjalagudi
> and hasn't returned.
> Chandrashekhara [Shiva], Nanjundappa,
> Have you lost interest in your wife?
>
> Swami Nanjunda, who dwells in the middle of the forest
> where palms grow and shake,
> there, where palms are growing and shaking,
> is a bird sanctuary, banyans, and
> jasmine fields.

While the pretext of Uttanahalli's quest is to have him remember his wife Chamundi, the lyrics reveal that his return to Nanjangudu is actually for the sake of his devotees.

> *Mount your elephant*
> *and come to Karutu street.*
> *O lover, Enamored one, please speak.*
> *Swamishekhara, Nanjundesha,*
> *Have you lost interest in your devotees?*
> *. . .*
>
> *In Nanjalagudi,*
> *there are four or five doors,*
> *five pillars and five banners.*
> *There is one pillar, five banners,*
> *and fifteen auspicious women with lamps, O Nanjunda Lingayya,*
> *Have you lost interest in your devotees?*
>
> *In Nanjalagudi, he celebrated with*
> *the image of Shri Kantha that was mounted on*
> *the dolled-up seven-axled chariots.*
> *O Shiva, while celebrating*
> *in Nanjalagudi*
> *all the people on the king's street saw him.*
> *All the people on king's street who saw Shri Kaṇṭha*
> *joined their hands and raised them up.*
> *Swami King Nanjunda, who dwells in the middle of the forest,*
> *Have you lost interest in your devotees?*
>
> *Mother Deviri, whom he calls "Big,"*
> *where has your husband gone?*
> *He went to the temple*
> *in the middle of the river, which is beyond Narasipura.*
> *He has come to the confluence of rivers*
> *beyond Narasipura.*
> *Chandrashekhara, Nanjunda Swami,*
> *Have you lost interest in your devotees?*
> *. . .*
> *You've forgotten the temple of Okuli (Holi).*
> *You've forgotten the Jangamma Matha.*

O One with the blessed throat
aren't you attracted to Chamundi of the hill?
O Creator, please speak up.
Lord Nanjunda, whose crown is the moon,
have you lost interest in your devotees?

As the song shifts its focus from Nanjunda's abandonment of Chamundi to the neglect of his devotees, however, the description of the context also changes from natural environs to urban space, contrasting the romantic beauty of the wilderness to the devotional love embodied in the city's sacred architecture and the rituals performed during the chariot procession during the celebration of the festival of Okuli. The description is quite vivid, lyrically placing the audience in the midst of the festival through its keen observations of the city's layout and the movement of its peoples and images of deities during its celebration. The song, therefore, succeeds in articulating its understanding of the city and its main street (King's Street): Nanjangudu is the city of Nanjunda; its main street and its buildings serve to unite the deity with its devotees. The city and its inhabitants, just like Chamundi, require their deity to be in his place for ritual life to continue. In the deity's absence, the sacred devotional network is fragile, and social life decays. As the song nears completion, the two spaces (i.e., natural and urban) and two foci (i.e., wife and devotee) are conflated with a natural scene connected to the devotees and a scene of the temple/city connected to the wife. The mirroring of lyrics suggests that the distinction between goddess and devotee is not only malleable but nearly synonymous.

At the conclusion of the ballad, the narrative ends by summarizing the ritual life and the benefits for the region that result from the deities maintaining their local, situated residences within the network of regional pilgrimage cities.

She killed Mahishasura
and stands on the middle of the hill.

The seven sisters met and
came to the mortal world.
They stood in the middle of the kingdom.
They were worshipped
by the communities of the borderlands.[29]
. . .

> *O Shiva, who has tied his ox to the bhuja tree.*
> *The beauty of the black-throated one,*
> *who is like a pearl,*
> *whose mouth is like a large water pot,*
> *who wears the hair bun [drawn] on her cheek,*[30]
> *the beauty, who looks in the mirror,*
> *O Mother of the golden tank in Ukkuda.*
>
> *Yadavale Banuvale*
> *On the left side of Nanjalagudi,*
> *there is the big Dundalakere*
> *very close to Chamalapura*
> *O Mother Chamundeshwari,*
> *you're the one who protects this place.*
> *. . .*
>
> *Dunda Deviramma, Little Somajamma, and*
> *Chamundeshwari of the hill*
> *dwell in Nanjalagudi.*
> *Shiva, you have married these three women, and*
> *your devotees have come.*
> *Now give a boon and*
> *give them wealth.*
>
> *Swami now dwells*
> *in Nanjalagudi.*
>
> *Merit comes to all*
> *who have told the story of Chamundi and*
> *to all who have heard her story.*
> *Dharma should be with us.*

While the primary plot line of *Chamundi of the Hill* centers around the romance between Chamundi and Nanjunda (see next chapter), as a whole, the narrative contained within the folk ballad shows that the situatedness of the deities is central. The fascinating subtext of devotional networks comes to the fore in the final song, "Dharma Should Be with Us," excerpted above. Specifically, this song summarizes the mythic establishment of Mysore and plots out the extension of her devotional network into Nanjangudu, forming multiple nuclei in its devotional map. As with many of the other examples given in this chapter, the song carefully records the layout of the city and the temples, archiving Chamundi within the core of Nanjangudu's sacred center. Mysore and Nanjangudu are important because they are the homes of the divine. Additionally, and perhaps more subtly, these lyrics—and the ballad in general—demonstrate how Chamundi, Nanjunda, Uttanahalli, Kalinga, and others are embedded within the landscape.

The situatedness of the deities within the physical landscape of the Mysore region was made explicit in a dramatic performance of the ballad *Chama Cheluve* that was performed in Mysore in September 2012 (figure 3.1). In this play, as the balladeers began the final song in a darkened outdoor theater, the lights rose on the actors positioned on a miniature recreation of the topography of Chamundi Hill and Nanjangudu. Chamundi stood at the top of the small mound that represented Chamundi Hill, Uttanahalli was at its base, and Nanjunda to the side of her. At this sight, the crowd erupted, confirming not only their pleasure from the play and their devotion to the deities but also the great significance of their location-based identities and relations. This interpretation of the importance of the deities' configuration is corroborated in a painting that hangs in the Uttanahalli temple that emphasizes the placement of the two goddesses and their temples within the local sacred topography (figure 3.2).

Figure 3.1. Scene from *Chama Cheluve*.

Conclusion

In conclusion, the standard, courtly elite narrative of Mysore is part of a larger paradigm that seeks to situate itself in the genealogy of royalty, locating the importance of the city within its association to important external sites of kingly power. The local and folk narrative turns our gaze, situating the region within its network of local pilgrimage sites and articulating its significance within the lives of common folk. By focusing on its details, we can understand the ways that *Chamundi of the Hill* functions as an urban history. As an urban history—even one based on mythic details—*Chamundi of the Hill* can articulate radically different concerns than the standard histories. This local urban history represents the region from nonelite segments of society. It provides another vision of Mysore, not as the City of Palaces,

Figure 3.2. Painting from Uttanahalli temple.

but as part of an interconnected network of pilgrimage that derives significance from the intimate system that creates place by establishing important festivals and connecting urban and village spaces, allowing devotees to engage with a variety of beloved situated deities. In the next chapter, we explore how these relationships are reflect the values of the community of balladeers and implicitly challenge social issues like caste and ritual discrimination.

Chapter Four

"He is from one caste; we are from another"

Religion, Caste, and Social Change

In the previous chapters, we explored the folk ballad *Chamundi of the Hill* both as a foundational myth and as a folk urban history of the Mysore region. From these perspectives, the ballad simultaneously generates cosmic significance by emphasizing the city and its hill as the site of the goddess killing the buffalo demon, and it also demonstrates the importance of the local devotional and pilgrimage networks, both providing local perspectives on the region's past. In this chapter, however, our attention is turned toward how the ballad engages with local traditions of more intimate concern. Particularly, this chapter focuses on the bulk of the narrative, the romance between Chamundi and Nanjunda that shifts the story, humanizing and, literally, domesticating the deities. Indeed, the entire ballad when stripped to its primary plot is a romantic comedy that follows many of the conventions that one might expect in a blockbuster "rom-com" from Hollywood, Bollywood, or Sandalwood.[1] To be true to its genre, this chapter is divided into three sections that follow the standard rom-com formula: the "meet-cute," the hurdle to the budding relationship, and the happy ending. These sections, however, do not focus on the details of the couple's romance or the zany comedic antics that ensue; instead, they focus on the lived reality of marriage and caste in southern Karnataka that is reflected in the songs and performances. As a public display of and for the society in which it is embedded, *Chamundi of the Hill* is a performed archive of marital conventions, including local customs of marriage arrangement, wedding celebrations, household configurations, and so on, all of which are directly influenced by and configured around a person's caste and religion (which are also completely interrelated). The ballad, however, not only reflects the realities of these social institutions, but it also provides an intricate and pointed critique of the discrimination that often exists in them, especially for those from castes that lack prestige within normative caste-based hierarchies.

The "Meet-Cute:" Establishing the Domesticity of Deities

The romantic and domestic emphasis of the overall ballad begins after the first two songs that focus on the mythology of the goddess Chamundi, particularly the killing of the demon brothers Mahisha and Aisu. As discussed in the first chapter, the mythic narrative opens the ballad, framing both the goddess and the region, including Mysore and Chamundi Hill, within a cosmically significant, albeit local, context. While the mythic backgrounds of the deities are certainly important for the story, to some (perhaps especially modern non-Indian readers), the divine status of its protagonists might also serve to mask the very real, mundane social institutions that are at the heart of the narrative's appeal. The ballad cleverly handles this disparity in its transition from a world occupied by gods, goddesses, and demons into the world of the quotidian through the act of bathing, which is rooted both in daily and in ritual life.

In the first song of this portion of the epic "She Bathes in the Kapini and Kaveri," the narrative picks up where the mythic battle ends. Akin to films and graphic novels like *The Watchmen* or *Who Framed Roger Rabbit,* which look at the imagined day-to-day lives of fiction characters, *Chamundi of the Hill* stays with Chamundi when "the camera isn't rolling." She stands on her hilltop, finally coming down from the epic battle and at once realizes that she needs a bath. On a common-sense level, this makes perfect sense. She just finished fighting two gargantuan demons, one of whom sprayed so much blood that armies of demons were born from it, and she got so sweaty from hacking at the hordes of demons that her own sister emerged from her perspiration. Of course, she would need a bath. So, she descends

"He is from one caste; we are from another" 87

the hill and walks to the Nanjangudu region (called Nanjalagudi) to bathe at the confluence of two rivers, the Kaveri and the Kapini.

Beyond its hygienic value, bathing is also an important act within the Hindu traditions as the religious system maintains strict guidelines for ritual purity and pollution. While cleanliness and purity do not necessarily correspond exactly, there is a great deal of overlap between the two.[2] This is especially true when the substance being washed is considered ritually impure, and blood is one of the most ritually polluting. The song hints at the ritual pollution problem as it singles out that "the stain of their blood remained on her right hand." Broadly, in Hindu culture, the right hand is considered to be the pure hand/side, while the left is considered impure. As a result, the left hand is to be used when one is forced to come into contact with polluting materials (i.e., cleaning oneself after defecation), and the right is to be used for other interactions, such as serving someone food or handing over goods or money. Since at least the Vedic period, the Hindu traditions stipulate that religious rituals are to be performed with the right hand.[3] The concept is so pervasive in Hindu thought that normative religious practice is called "right-handed," and antinomian practices, such as some forms of tantra that use polluting substances in their rituals, are called "left-handed" practices. The use of the right hand in ritual contexts reflects the same concerns as the interactions on the daily basis and those of the Vedic world: only a pure hand should handle sacred ritual implements and, perhaps more importantly, come into contact with the gods. In this vein, the song foreshadows the next one in which Chamundi meets Nanjunda as she bathes.

Additionally, her selection of the confluence of the Kapini (i.e., Kabini) and Kaveri Rivers in the Nanjangudu region (presumably at T. Narasipura) also demonstrates her intentions of a ritually purifying bath.[4] In most Hindu traditions, sites where two or more rivers converge are deemed to be of sacred importance and to be highly effective in cleansing one from ritual pollution. The most well-known example of this phenomenon is the tri-confluence (*Trivedi sangama*) of the Yamuna, Ganga, and the (metaphysical) Saraswati Rivers in Prayagraj (aka Allahabad), the site of the festival of Kumbha Mela that is held every four years.[5] A lesser-known phenomenon, the southern Kumbha Mela is held in T. Narasipura—its full name, Tirumakudalu Narasipura, is a reference to its tri-confluence of the Kabini, Kaveri, and the mythical Spatika Sarovara—every three years. Beyond the large festivals, confluences hold great theological significance because of their ability to wash away not only the physical filth but also the bad karma incurred in one's past, thus opening the way to liberation. Ritually speaking, confluences are also sites for important death and death anniversary rituals because they can purify the souls of the deceased and help to alleviate the pollution of death from the family of the departed.

While a small narrative moment, Chamundi's bath not only sets up the meeting between the goddess and Nanjunda, but it also effectively interweaves religious concerns for purity and mundane concerns of removing the filth from battle. In doing so, the goddess who kills the mighty demons becomes identifiable to the audience. She too needs to clean herself up after a long day of physically demanding labor and must undergo the same rituals of purity and pollution as everyone else. Through one simple but ingenious ritual action, the goddess becomes relatable while maintaining her status as divine.[6]

At the same time as the goddess was bathing at the confluence of the Kabini and Kaveri, Nanjunda left his home in Nanjangudu to bathe at the same confluence of rivers. After bathing, he performs ritual worship (*puja*) to a personal linga (*ishtalinga*), a smaller version of the aniconic representation of Shiva that is worn by the Shaiva Lingayat sect.[7] He completes his *puja* and looks up to see Chamundi combing the tangles from her hair. He is smitten and immediately runs over to the goddess and grabs her hand, asking for her name. His action is not well received by the goddess, who immediately pulls her hand away from Nanjunda, as she rebukes his aggressive behavior. Nanjunda's action is especially offensive in this instance because in traditional Kannada literature and popular culture, as in English, a man taking a woman by the hand is a euphemism for marriage. Chamundi is typically depicted in the iconographic style of the Pan-Hindu goddess Durga, who is an independent goddess and neither has nor desires a male consort. In fact, Nanjunda's actions mirror how Mahisha initially approached the goddess in the ballad's first narrative song, an act that ultimately led to his demise. Demonstrating her autonomous nature, Chamundi, who has already demonstrated that she does not back down from a male who has overstepped his bounds, does not answer Nanjunda with her name but fires back, "Who are you?" Only after Nanjunda gives his credentials as the deity of the city Nanjangudu

(Nanjalagudi) and slayer of the demon Nandikasura, does Chamundi reply back that she is the house deity of the kings of nearby Mysore and that she is the daughter of "Mavura Lingayya," the personification of the Himalayan mountains.[8]

Nanjunda seizes upon her familial relations. In particular, Chamundi identifies her father as Mavura Lingayya or Uncle Lingayya. Mavura is a derivation of the broader Dravidian *māma*, which refers to one's "mother's brother." Since she is his mother's brother's daughter (i.e., matrilineal cousin), a distinctive kinship connection, Nanjunda claims that the goddess is a suitable marriage match, his *salavali*.[9] While this might strike many modern Western readers as odd, this practice, which is often referred to as matrilineal "cross-cousin marriage," is a traditional marriage custom in South India and in many places throughout the world. In southern Karnataka even today, especially in rural areas, cross-cousin marriage is a common practice when arranging marriages.[10] Despite the familial match, Chamundi does not find Nanjunda to be a suitable match for herself, again replying to him with an indignant question, "aren't you already married?" Nanjunda confirms that he is indeed already married to not one but two wives, Deviri and Somaji.[11] Upon hearing his confirmation, the goddess repeats a common Kannada saying "Even a corpse will object to a proposal if there are cowives" adding that she didn't want to live with any other sister-wives.[12] Nanjunda, however, promises that he will never leave Chamundi even if it means that he has to leave his other wives. Nanjunda's promise to never leave her does the trick. The goddess consents to the match, and the two deities consummate their love marriage right there on the banks of the river. For two weeks, the couple enjoys a honeymoon period before Nanjunda returns to Nanjagudu for the full moon festival.

Even within these very first interactions between the goddess and the god, we can see both the novelty of the story and how it conforms to certain gender norms in the region. On one level, Chamundi enjoys a great amount of freedom, especially for a young unmarried woman (we find out later in the ballad that she is depicted as a young virgin who has only recently gone through puberty). She has killed mighty demons. She is out on her own late at night. She scolds an older man for his impropriety and offensive behavior and rebuffs his marriage proposal despite the suitable familial match. On another level, however, she constructs her identity not as the slayer of demons or as the protector of the city which she oversees as goddess (compare this with how Nanjunda identifies himself as slayer of Nandikasura and god of Nanjangudu), but she identifies herself through her relationship with men, as the house god of the Mysore king and as the daughter of the Himalayas, who is even called "Mavura Lingayya," Uncle Lingayya. This highlights the tension that is present in the ballad as a whole in which Chamundi is depicted as a powerful goddess but one who is also situated within the normative gendered expectations of the cultural and social context of southern Karnataka.

This romantic encounter marks a critical juncture in the ballad as the narrative becomes more directly reflective of the social and gender norms of a relatively typical traditional Kannadiga household, into which Chamundi is slowly domesticated. As the story moves forward, the mythological context fades from the forefront, and Chamundi and Nanjunda navigate the complicated networks and consequences of their love marriage. Superficially the songs continue to uphold many of the values of traditional culture, but the setting and divine nature of the characters allow the balladeers to also occasion a critique of many of the prejudices that exist in their society, particularly as the new relationship is strained due to the lovers' differences, all rooted in the overlapping institutions of caste and religious practice.

The Hurdle to the Budding Relationship: Caste and Ritual Difference[13]

As the ballad continues, it becomes evident that the marriage has turned Chamundi from a fierce, independent warrior-goddess into a woman pining for her man. While this marks a stark contrast to the character's persona at the beginning of the epic, it also provides the major conflict of the narrative arch and the opportunity for the balladeers to critique the social ills of caste discrimination through their theological perspective, a perspective that is informed by Lingayatism, a form of Shaivism that has its roots in the philosophy of the Sharanas, whose poetry often critiqued caste difference but also a perspective that critiques the Lingayat tradition for creating its own system of caste-based and ritual-based hierarchies.[14] Despite this shift from the mythological context to the domestic, over the course of the next few songs, the ballad becomes even more theological as it alludes to the religious history of the community and the tensions that persist in the social fabric of southern Karnataka.

The social issues of caste and religious practice critiqued in this ballad are pertinent to the community of the raconteurs who perform the songs. The performers, called Kamsales after the small cymbals with which they perform, are from the Devaragudda subcaste (*upajati*) of the broader Kuruba agricultural and shepherding caste (*jati*).[15] The Kuruba, or sometimes spelled Kurumba, are one of the largest communities in Karnataka. Though the community now emphasizes marriage outside the community, traditionally, the caste is endogamous, marrying between restricted subcastes. The Kuruba trace their historical lineage to the founders of the Sangama dynasty, Hakka and Bukka, the first leaders of the great Vijayanagara Empire (1336–1646 CE).[16] The caste also has various foundational myths about their origins, with many of them tracing their ancestry to progeny of the deities Shiva and Parvati.[17] The Kuruba share some religious practices and deities with the broader Hindu population, but they also have their own distinctive religious practices, deities, and institutions.[18] Despite their claims to noble and divine ancestry, the Kuruba are currently listed amongst India's "Other Backward Castes" (OBC).[19] As an OBC, the Kuruba are often considered a "low caste" within normative, hegemonic Hindu scales of ritual purity, which has led to centuries of prejudicial treatment and discrimination against the community by castes that are considered "higher" on the same scale. This treatment has led many within the community to pursue equality and social reform through both political activism and religious conversion.

Taking the latter course of action, many Kurubas, including the Devaraguddas, converted to Lingayatism.[20] Lingayatism is a form of devotion to Shiva that is based on radical reformulations of devotional practice as propagated by the eleventh- and twelfth-century poets (*vacanakaras*) known as Shaiva Sharanas, the first of which was Basava, who was a minister in the court of the Kalachuri and/or Western Chalukyan king Bijjala II of Kalyana.[21] The tradition was propagated after Basava's death by his nephew Channa Basava ("beautiful Basava"), who figures in the narrative of *Chamundi of the Hill*. The tradition was consolidated around the ethical and spiritual teachings of the Sharanas, which emphasized the supreme nature of the deity Shiva, who they believe is equivalent to ultimate reality (*parama shakti*), and his relationship with individual devotees. The strong bond between devotee and Shiva is marked by the devotee's personal linga (*isthalinga*), an aniconic representation of Shiva that is kept in a small case that is worn as a pendant at the end of a necklace. The central act of personal devotion is the worship of the *ishtalinga*, a form of Shiva *puja*.[22] For this *puja*, the small linga is removed from its case and held in the left palm and worshipped, after which the devotee meditates on becoming one with Shiva in the form of the linga.[23] This personal relationship with Shiva serves as the theological basis for the Lingayat social critique: all people come from Shiva, and caste is no bar to having a relationship with the deity or performing Shiva *puja*. The teachings of social equality amongst the devotees of Shiva were reflected in backgrounds of the Sharanas, which included men and women, as well as people from a variety of castes. Theoretically, as a religious tradition, therefore, Lingayatism rejects the concept of caste-based discrimination and accepts converts from any caste background.[24] In reality, however, caste has remained an important touchstone within the tradition, with Lingayats claiming a caste identity that was "higher" than even brahmin castes all the while maintaining social hierarchies within their own community, most visible in the social and theological position of the religious leaders, called *jangamas*, over the rest of the tradition's constituents.[25] Even within the religion, adherents are afforded varying degrees of social and political power based on their caste backgrounds with landowning castes occupying important positions within the community. These forms of more subtle caste-related discrimination can be seen in the Lingayat community's rejection of folk religion, including local deities such as those important within *Chamundi of the Hill*.[26] In its narrative, *Chamundi of the Hill* lays bare the complicated realities of the modern position of Lingayatism, including its caste and ritual diversity, and critiques the tradition for its conformity to social and religious elitism.

The influence of Lingayatism in *Chamundi of Hill* is implicit yet obvious to anyone situated within the southern Karnataka social fabric. From the first introduction to Nanjunda, the deity is called a *jangama* ("mover" or "wanderer"), which is a reference to a Lingayat ascetic, and he performs Lingayat Shiva *puja* to his personal *linga*. By doing so, *Chamundi of the Hill* creatively remakes Nanjunda, who is typically depicted as a brahmin "caste" Hindu with sacred thread and whose temple is presided over by brahmin priests into a Lingayat holy man. This adaptation of the deity reflects many of the iconographic details of the Devaraguddas' primary deity, Madeshwara, another local form of Shiva in Madeshwara Hills who is associated with Lingayats and Virashaivism, and makes the singers' social commentary possible.[27] Throughout the remainder of the songs, social critique forms the underpinning of balladeer's narrative, particularly undermining caste-based discrimination through restrictive endogamy; however, the songs serve as a critique of the incongruities between oft-cited Lingayat ideals of inclusivism pulled from the poetry of the Sharanas and the lived reality of caste and religious discrimination within the Lingayat community, which fails to live up to the paradigm of caste equality and looks down upon many forms of local lived religious practice.

The narrative conflict that serves as the setting for the anticaste critique is immediately set up at the beginning of the song "Go, Give My Love to Your Brother-in-Law Nanjunda and Tell Him to Return." It begins with Chamundi sleeping in her bed in Mysore and Nanjunda sleeping with his two other wives, Deviri and Somaji, in Nanjangudu. While Nanjunda sleeps peacefully, Chamundi has a nightmare in which she is engulfed in flames, and her marital ornaments shatter, a sign that she will soon be widowed. When she awakes from the dream, she cries for her dutiful younger sister, Uttanahalli, to come and comfort her. When the younger goddess arrives after the strenuous hike up the hill, Chamundi asks her to go fetch Nanjunda to avoid the inauspicious portents. Surprisingly Uttanahalli refuses her sister's request out of propriety. Uttanahalli's primary concern is what she'll say to Deviri and Somaji, Chamundi's co-wives, because Nanjunda's elder wives will not be happy when Uttanahalli calls for Nanjunda to join his new lover. She questions whether anyone would even acknowledge the new marriage because none of the wedding rituals that provide the social display of the legitimacy and auspiciousness of matrimony, like consulting astrologers to verify the proper match, tying of the wedding necklace (*thali*), etc., had been performed.[28] As she elaborates, however, we find that the true cause of Uttanahalli's hesitation is that the marriage would not be accepted because Chamundi and Nanjunda are from different castes and practice religion differently. That is, the sisters are from a "low" caste, and Nanjunda and his wives are "high" caste (Lingayats), so neither her co-wives nor the people would accept the legitimacy of their union.

To alleviate her sister's doubts, Chamundi carefully narrates the lovers' happenstance meeting, their impromptu love marriage,

Nanjunda's absence, and the nightmares that have roused her fears. The recounting of the marriage helps verify the validity of the union for Uttanahalli, but the dreams provide the audience with insight into Chamundi's psyche as a lovesick woman, and, most importantly, the destructive religious results of Nanjunda's absence. As we will see, in addition to the foreboding prophecies of destruction, the goddess's visions provide solutions for averting these catastrophes, namely, the adoption of Lingayat social ideals, which narratively justifies Chamundi's marriage to Nanjunda.

Chamundi's dreams begin with a vision of Mysore sinking into despair as it is attacked by seven fierce goddesses (called "Durgas" at one point and at another "Marammas") who had come from the city of Ujjain in the north. The goddesses are seated atop ritual chariots, conjuring visuals of processions that carry the goddesses on their important festival days; however, instead of being surrounded by throngs of adoring devotees, as the goddesses travel around Mysore, City they kill people and loot their belongings while the people of the city cry out to the goddesses for mercy as they shove their newborn children into anthills/snake dens to save them from the onslaught. While the ballad itself offers no interpretation of the dream, for those familiar with the ritual world of local goddess devotion, the major portents of the dream are clear as the song carefully encodes various layers of important local references that foreshadow later events and allude to historical figures, religious practice, and philosophical debates.

The attacking goddesses are identified by Chamundi as her co-wives and as the daughters of King Bijjala. Both scholars who have studied the narrative and the performers of the songs identify King Bijjala as the king of the Ujjain kingdom and not the Kalabhuri/Chalukya King Bijjala II who ruled in Kalyana.[29] This is perhaps an allusion to the Kalachuri (Haihaya) dynasty that ruled over Ujjain in the 6th and 7th centuries CE. Many believed that this older dynasty of Kalachuris ruled from the ancient city of Mahishamati that is referenced in the *Mahabharata* and many Sanskrit puranas ("encyclopedic collections of myths"), which has been inaccurately associated with the modern city of Mysore due to its mythological association with buffaloes (Sanskrit: *mahisha*) and the buffalo demon Mahisha and its traditional names (Mahishavishya and Mahishuru).[30] Additionally, the city of Ujjain is considered an important site for goddess ritual practice as a *shakti pitha* or a "seat of Goddess" in her form as Mahakali or

Chamunda. Through laconic but effective folk historiography, etymology, and geography, this song connects Chamundi and her city to a wider mythological and historical context that is grounded in specific sites of goddess devotion.

While the lyrics of *Chamundi of the Hill* provide generic names like Akkamma ("respected elder sister") or Akkaji Doddamma ("respected elder aunt") for the fierce attacking goddesses, when asked about their identities, the balladeers specifically named goddesses: Urismasani, Hunasamma, Kitturamma, Kannambadi Kalamma, Chowdamma, and Chamundi.[31] At different times, raconteur guru Kamsale Mahadevayya gave other names that included a total of twelve potential aliases: Urimasanamma, Bannuru Yamadri, Swasali Honnadevi, Naduvalu Choudeswari, Muguru Tibbadevi, Ummatturu Urikati, Akkama, Chikkama, Baddarabanamakali, Balagolada Hiridevti, Uttanalli Maramma, and Chamundi.[32] Moreover, although in the songs the goddesses are Chamundi's co-wives, the performers identify the seven goddesses as the sisters of Chamundi, which might explain why her name appears in the performers' lists of names.[33] The variety of names and the lack of specificity about their relationship might at first seem contradictory or confusing, but the variety of goddesses encapsulates a larger phenomenon of fierce goddess worship in the form of *gramadevatas* or local village goddesses in southern Karnataka that extends to religious practice throughout all of India and is particularly important in nonbrahminical or "low-caste"/tribal religious practice.

As local village goddesses, these Marammas or *gramadevatas* are mercurial goddesses of disease, namely of pox and fever, who look over their villages, providing benevolent protection when they are pleased and causing malevolence and destruction when they have not been properly propitiated.[34] Their situated identity is reflected in the list of names provided by the performers and their guru that often reference the city, town, or village where the goddess resides (e.g., Kitturamma is the "goddess of Kittur," and Ummatturu Urikati is the "Fire-Starter [goddess] of Ummatturu"). In their everyday ritual and devotional lives, these local fierce goddesses are often depicted in their shrines through aniconic images, including natural phenomena, such as stones and anthills/snakehills, perhaps because of their association with diseases, such as smallpox, and the visible similarity between the pustules of pox and ant bites. The references of people "cramming all newborns into anthills" from *Chamundi of the Hill* does not simply reflect an ill-advised camouflage, but it reflects a ritualized offering to the goddesses to abate the destruction of their disease and the calamities brought about by the goddesses' onslaught since anthills are commonly worshipped as representations of these fierce goddesses and/or associated with them in local goddess mythology. The cause of the destruction by these Marammas is not yet extremely apparent, but as the dream continues, we find that it had been foreshadowed by Uttanahalli's concerns about caste discrimination. The locality or situatedness alluded to in the names of these *gramadevate* or "village goddesses" is the central essence of these deities. The practical and devotional lives of these goddess traditions continue to focus on the goddesses' relationship to specific situated spaces despite any and all transformations from external influences (devotional, mythological, ritual, or technological). Certain elements of the village goddess tradition are altered over time, but in each case the core practices and stories about the goddesses continue to focus on their power to protect their "realm."

Many of the elements of the ritual worship of village goddesses is present within *Chamundi of the Hill* and can still be seen in rituals to Chamundi that are performed on Chamundi Hill by "lower-caste" devotes throughout the year at the small shrine that houses an aniconic image of Chamunda Maramma that is located just outside the large temple (figure 4.1). During Chamundi's birthday celebration in the spring, elements of the *gramadevate* tradition are still practiced on top of Chamundi Hill, as the ritual landscape is completely altered reflecting nonbrahminic, nonvegetarian ritual practice.[35] While the brahmin priests continue to operate within the temple, all of the temple workers and villagers of the hill prepare for the festival to "cool-off" the goddess. As promised by Chamundi in *Chamundi of the Hill*, Uttanahalli's annual village festival takes place just before Chamundi's, and the day before Chamundi's festival, the festival of her younger sister comes to a close with many of the families from Chamundi Hill descending to offer goats to her before ritually slaughtering them in front of their homes. That night, the village festival to Chamundi begins with a procession of the festival image (*utsava vigraha*) from the large brahminic Chamundeshwari temple on top of the hill. As the image circumambulates the hill, the villagers offer a large firework (*pachaki*) show to goddess from the temple.[36]

Figure 4.1. Aniconic Chamunda Maramma.

The next morning is spent preparing the afternoon offerings to the village deity. The women from the village clean the area outside the shrine, while men clean the inside and stack wood into a large pyre in front of it.[37] At the same time, two young men from the village take the metal masks (*mukha*) for the deity to the tank of the goddess (Devikere) and wash them (figure 4.2). After placing the masks up the stone image of the deity in a small shrine outside the main temple, they light a large pyre. After this, everyone leaves to finish preparing their homes and their offerings. Several hours later, the women of the village return to the space beside the shrine to cook food that is later placed before Chamundi, a sweet rice and coconut dish called *tambittu* (figure 4.3). After the cooking is finished and the food is left in vessels in front of the shrine, everyone returns home to put on new clothes. Around four p.m. everyone returns, including two Lingayat priests who conduct the opening *puja* that culminates with one of the priests fire-walking over the coals as other devotees fan the flames, confirming the relationship between these goddess rituals and Lingayats present in *Chamundi of the Hill* (figure 4.4).[38] Afterwards, devotees line up to give offerings to the goddess or to carry their children over the fire in

Figure 4.2. Temple workers with masks.

Figure 4.3. Women ready to prepare food for Chamundi Maramma.

Figure 4.4. Lingayat priest fire walk.

fulfillment of a vow (*harike*).³⁹ Finally, they all return to their homes, where they slaughter and cook chickens that are enjoyed with the rest of the *prasada* (blessed food) that had been blessed through its offerings to the goddess.

In the autumn, more local rituals are performed during the local Chamundi festival (*utsava*), a traditional non-brahminic celebration of the goddess and the ancestors that takes place at the end of the month of Bhadrapada (August/September) just before the Sanskritic and brahminic festival of Navaratri or Dasara.⁴⁰ These rituals, which are also alluded to in *Chamundi of the Hill*, mark the beginning of the sacred season for the villages around Mysore and are performed on Chamundi Hill by several local nonbrahmin castes (Shivarcaka, Vokkaliga/Gauda, and the Raja Parivara).⁴¹ The primary practice of the ritual is the procession of a temporary triangular wooden structure with a large metal disk at the center called the *pradhana kannu kannadi* (primary mirror of the eye), which is a nonanthropomorphic representation of the goddess Chamundi.[42] Six additional, albeit miniature in comparison, *kannu kannadi*s accompany the primary image on the procession. These additional images represent the six sisters of the goddess, whose shrines are all located in or around Mysore City and who wreak havoc on Mysore in Chamudi's visions.[43] On the day that has been selected, the seven *kannu kannadi*s are taken to the main hall of the Shiva temple located on Chamundi Hill.[44] The primary image of Chamundi is carried by a specially selected prepubescent girl from the Shivarcaka caste. The other six images are all carried by prepubescent boys from the same caste. After leaving the Shiva temple, they are joined by seven more prepubescent girls from the Raja Parivara caste, who carry earthen pots called *bonugudike* on their heads, before circumambulating (*pradakshina*) the Chamundeshwari temple.[45]

In her next dream, the scene moves to Kannambadi, an area just a few miles northwest of Mysore, near the modern Krishnaraja Sagar or "KRS" dam. In this vision, the goddess Chamundi sees the Sharana poet Channabasava as he falls in love with a beautiful woman. The object of his affection, however, is referred to as a *gangadakati*. The term *gangadakati* (also *gangakati* or *gangadikati*) is a multivalent term that can have many connotations, including a general term of affection.[46] Literally, however, *gangadakati* refers to a "low-caste" or tribal woman; however, several Kannadigas with whom I have translated this passage reflexively interpreted the term as a reference to a *jogamma* (also *jogati*), a "low-caste" woman (often associated with the Kuruba caste) who serves as a ritual professional and whose duties range from sexual activities to carrying an image of the goddess on top of her head during the goddess's festival or *jatre*, serving as the processional chariot like those alluded to in the first dream.[47] Whether *gangadakati* is interpreted as a "low-caste" woman or a *jogamma*, the sociological implication remains that same; Channabasava, a Lingayat from a brahmin background, falls in love with a "low-caste" woman. Their love is consummated in a (presumed) marriage ritual in which Channabasava chops the head off of a buffalo and then performs lamp worship or *arati puja* to the severed head. As we look closely, we can see that the dream-sequence love marriage is a metaphor for the marriage between Chamundi and Nanjunda that ties caste-nonconforming marriages to the Lingayat historiographical tradition.

Channabasava (12th century CE), the protagonist of the dream vision, was a great Sharana poet and nephew of Basava, the founder of the Sharana movement. After the death of Basava, Channabasava became the leader of the community and began systematizing the Sharana doctrine and the rituals of the growing community. If we are to accept that among the primary beliefs of the movement was a rejection of caste distinction, brahminical ritual, and strict vegetarianism., it makes sense that Channabasava would be invoked in this dream as Nanjunda's stand-in because the Sharana, like Nanjunda, believed that caste distinction was not important for marriage. However, this reading of the dream becomes difficult to accept when we consider the ritual sacrifice of the buffalo and its subsequent *puja* in light of Channabasava's disdain for sacrificial ritual. It is not the "low-caste" *gangadakati* who slaughters the animal, but it is Channanbasava himself who delivers the fatal blow, a scene that jars the audience by highlighting the tensions between Lingayat identity and folk religious practice. The sacrifice of the buffalo acts as a bridge between the "high-caste" Lingayat identity of Channabasava and the world of local goddess ritual that is framed as "low caste" throughout the ballad while reinforcing the mythology of Chamundi from the first song of the ballad and within Pan-Indic lore. It also displays the complexities of intercaste and intersectarian ritual life as the Sharana guru mimics rituals traditionally performed to Chamundi, especially during Navaratri, when buffaloes were commonly decapitated as offerings to the goddess.[48]

With no analysis or explanation, Chamundi immediately transitions to her final dream in which Nanjunda is carried to Hejjige Kere, a lake outside of Nanjangudu to be buried, as is the custom amongst Lingayats.[49] After his tombstone is erected, Chamundi's co-wives remove their marital ornaments with Deviri smashing her gold bangles on his grave and Somaji throwing her earrings into the nearby foliage. With this, Chamundi concludes her nightmares and asks her sister once again to go fetch Nanjunda with the promise that if Uttanahalli is successful in the task Chamundi will give her an annual festival and give her a fiery tongue.

Up to now the songs have provided little to no interpretation or analysis for the series of daunting dreams that Chamundi has just related, but when tasked to engage Nanjunda, Uttanahalli explicitly connects the visions to caste as she reads them as bad omens relating to their union:

> *He is from one caste.*
> *We are from another caste.*
> *He ties the linga.*[50]
> *He wears the jangu.*[51]
> *He wears ochre.*[52]
> *He uses the ascetic staff.*[53]
> *We, like fierce demons,*
> *eat chickens and goats.*
> *We have nothing in common*
> *with that place or the lord who resides there.*

In this moment, the underlying anxiety about caste-mixing and intersectarian/interreligious marriage that "high castes," here particularly "high-caste" Lingayats, are "polluted" or subsumed into the "lesser" ritual world of the "low castes" is on full display to the audience as they are reflected in Uttanahalli's own concerns. She casts both Nanjunda and Chamundi through their castes' ritual lives. Nanjunda is depicted as a "high-caste" Lingayat *jangama*. He wears the personal *linga*. He wears the ochre robes of asceticism and carries the *jangu*, a small brass ritual bell, and the *kamundu* staff, both carried by Lingayat ascetics. The goddesses, however, are compared to demons, who accept chickens and goats in their rituals. Uttanahalli, perhaps like most of the audience unfamiliar with the full narrative, believes that the mixing of caste and ritual practice is the impetus for the unleashing of calamities, the death of Nanjunda, and the overall breakdown in society. Despite her concerns and against her better judgment, Uttanahalli gives in to her elder sister's request and leaves to fetch her brother-in-law, Nanjunda.

Chamundi of the Hill has effectively set the conflict for the young couple that the remainder of the ballad will seek to resolve. It follows many of the familiar tropes of romantic comedies in which socioeconomic and cultural backgrounds create obstacles to a happy relationship and causes the temporary (though we aren't supposed to know that) separation of the lovers that seems insurmountable. While this in-and-of itself is a remarkable aspect of a folk ballad that has themes that remain important in contemporary India, as will be discussed in the next section, the resolution of the conflict turns the audience's expectations on its head by not only dismissing the concerns about caste- and ritual-mixing but also showing how the union between the deities from such different backgrounds produces powerful results.

The Happy Ending: Overcoming Caste through Ritual

When Uttanahalli leaves to retrieve Nanjunda, the audience is left to assume that the younger goddess is correct and that the visions tell a foreboding tale of the evils that will befall the deities and the region because of the intercaste marriage. As the story unfolds, however, we find that the visions are a prophecy not of death and destruction but of how Chamundi and Nanjunda prove that their marriage is powerful and auspicious. The resolution is rooted in the melding of local ritual practice with Lingayat principles with the primary message of rejecting caste distinction.

After Uttanahalli finally reaches and breaks through to Nanjunda, convincing him that he ought to return to Chamundi ("Have you lost interest in your wife?"[54]), the ballad follows the comedic exploits of Nanjunda and the scheme devised by the new husband and wife to have their union not only acknowledged but also celebrated. The scene is primed for comedy as Nanjunda hears Uttanahalli's call to remember Chamundi while he cuddles in bed with his two elder wives. In order to sneak away to visit his new lover, the deity pretends to be bitten by mosquitoes and bed bugs so that his wives roll away from him. Now with a little space, Nanjunda places a large pillow in his stead, which his wives affectionately cuddle, thinking the pillow is their husband.[55] On his way to see Chamundi, Nanjunda encounters his brothers-in-law Kalinga, the serpent, and Basavanna (aka Shiva's bull-vehicle Nandi). After comical verbal exchanges and outlandish attempts to fool his brothers-in-law, Najunda is forced to bribe them for their silence, offering Kalinga an annual festival and Nandi a bell for his neck. Finally, Nanjunda arrives at Chamundi's house for reconciliation. All of this, however, had taken time, and Deviri and Somaji in the meanwhile had awakened to discover Nanjunda's trickery. They surmised that their husband had gone to Chamundi's house and immediately left to confront the god and his mistress. Like an episode of *Cheaters* or a tawdry daytime talk show, Deviri peeps through the temple windows and finds postcoital Nanjunda and Chamundi discussing their hopes and dreams. Infuriated, the elder goddess berates Chamundi. A Jerry Springer–style physical altercation—perhaps a fulfillment of Chamundi's vision that angry goddesses would descend on Mysore—breaks out between the two goddesses, at which point Nanjunda sneaks out and returns home to Nanjangudu.[56]

Later in the evening, after Deviri returns home to confront Nanjunda, we see again the issue of caste- and ritual-mixing that had been foreshadowed in the visions of Chamundi.

> *You went to the home*
> *Of that terrible buffalo- and cat-eating demoness*
> *And now you come back?*
> *Stop! Just stop outside!*

As a result of his presumed infidelity, Deviri strips Nanjunda of the markers of his religious identity, his *rudraraksha* necklace that also held his personal *ishtalinga,* and kicked him out of the house "as naked as the day he was born."[57] As Uttanahalli had feared and as Chamundi's vision foretold, Deviri takes exception to his dalliance with Chamundi because of her caste (she calls her a "demoness") and ritual practice (she refers to her ritual consumption of meat as "buffalo- and cat-eating").[58] The social anxiety of losing one's caste identity as a result of caste-mixing is embodied in the actions of Deviri, who is the personification of the normative adoption of caste regulations. This anxiety reaches its apex as the wife literally strips Nanjunda of the outer markings of his Lingayat identity as he is cast out without his ochre robes and personal *linga.*

While the story continues in *Chamundi of the Hill*, in the other versions of the story collected from the Oddas of Madhugiri and women in Bellary by Kannada folklore scholars KR Krishnaswami and G. S. Paramashiva, respectively, Nanjunda returning home provides the conclusion of the tale. In these versions, there is no confrontation between the co-wives in Mysore; instead, much to the chagrin of Chamundi, Nanjunda leaves her bed of his own accord the morning after.[59] As he tries to leave, Chamundi begs him to think about her marriage necklace (*korala padakava*) and to think about their lineage connections. He, however, leaves anyway. Once he completes his walk of shame, his elder co-wives scold him for having slept with a "low-caste" woman who "eats cocks and goats."[60] But after performing rituals to purify Nanjunda from his contact with this woman, he is allowed back into the home. Fade to black. The end. The resolution clearly reflects different concerns than those of the Kamsale community's *Bettada Chamundi*. In the Odda and women's songs, the resolution is the return to normative marital life, the status quo, if you will. For the women of Bellary, the final scene underscores the, perhaps unfortunate, reality of a husband's infidelity but provides a means to reconcile, albeit through verbal abuse and ritual expiation. The Odda's case by comparison highlights the broader emphasis on social change in the Kamsale version. While they consider themselves a Kshatriya or warrior caste, the Odda (also spelled Wadar or Vodda) are traditionally stone sculptors and masons and are listed among Schedule Castes in Karnataka. Additionally, most Oddas in Karnataka are devotees of Yellamma, a local goddess who accepts goats and roosters as sacrificial offerings. However, because they have been ostracized by most "high-caste" Hindus, Oddas have rejected Hindu marriage customs, renaming their rituals using Urdu names.[61] Some of their lineages are exogamous; however, the broader caste (*jati*) and even most subcastes (*upajati*) maintain strict endogamy.[62] Their version of the story, then, seems to reflect generations of pain from the rejection of normative "high-caste" Hinduism. They associated themselves with the scorned Chamundi whose love is unrequited as the "high-caste" Nanjunda returns to his wives and expunges his contact with Chamundi through rituals of expiation. There seems to be no hope for change.

Within the Kamsale *Chamundi of the Hill*, however, the story continues in order to show Deviri's epiphany that the "low-caste" Chamundi is a worthy wife for Nanjunda. After being kicked out of his home, Najunda goes to the celestial world of the deity Brahma. Nanjunda tells Brahma to go visit Deviri and Somaji and give them a false incantation (*shastra*) made of gibberish sounds. Then, Nanjunda goes to Chamundi and tells her to dress like a fortune-teller and to visit Nanjangudu. Finally, he returns home where he lies down pretending to be dead. Thinking they are now widows, Deviri and Somaji burst into tears, fulfilling the final element of Chamundi's prophecy. As they are crying and lamenting their new status as widows, Brahma arrives and gives them the gibberish incantation and vanishes. At this very moment, they hear Chamundi, who is disguised as a fortune-teller, exclaiming in the streets that if she has a magical incantation, then she can raise people from the dead. Of course, Deviri and Somaji run to fetch the young fortune-teller. When they give Chamundi-in-disguise the spell that they received from Brahma, however, they are told that it can't work because of they have cursed the goddess Chamundi (of course, they don't realize that it is Chamundi telling them this). Chamundi's words here again are telling because she uses the Kannada idiom "You put it in the belly of a Holeya after taking it from the belly of a Madiga." Both the Holeya and Madiga are considered very "low" in the hegemonic and traditional system of social stratification and are considered to be "outcastes" in Karnataka.[63] Therefore, the saying expresses debasement through allusion to restrictions against caste commensality. Immediately, Deviri understands the error of her ways and repents, offering expiation for her sin of degrading Chamundi's caste and ritual practice and vowing to accept Chamundi as their equal. With that, Nanjunda arises and tells by Deviri and Somaji that he needs to go back to Chamundi.

The balladeers drive home the point that caste- and ritual-difference were no longer a bar for Nanjunda's co-wives. After he is told to go to Chamundi's temple, he replies:

> *O Deviri, they belong to one caste,*
> *And we belong to another caste.*
> *They eat buffaloes and sheep like they do in the palace*
> *I shouldn't go.*

Not only do the co-wives beg him to go, but they also give him their wedding ornaments to take to Chamundi. The story concludes with Nanjunda and Chamundi returning together to Nanjangudu, where Deviri blesses Chamundi and accepts her as her little sister.[64]

Where the Odda version of the story ends with quiet acceptance, the Kamsale version ends with a reversal of the dominant attitude toward caste-mixing and ritual-difference. The rituals associated with the "lower castes" are shown to be powerful and cunning, and the resistant "high castes" learn that caste discrimination is a sin that requires expiation. For all parties involved, the resolution of social change provides a happy ending to their tumultuous tale.

Conclusion

Within this engaging and comedic narrative, the Kamsale balladeers tackle the large social issue of caste- and ritual-mixing. While it is a story about gods and goddesses, the story reflects the society of southern Karnataka, embedding mundane concerns within the lives of the deities. Using the well-known narratives of the local deities, the singers are able to push the envelope by casting the beloved goddess Chamundi as the "low-caste" woman and Nanjunda as a "high-caste" Lingayat. The story highlights the complexities of religious practice and its relationship to caste identity, including Lingayatism, which often claims to be inclusivist and/or egalitarian. Throughout the entire narrative, anticaste discrimination sentiments are at the forefront, with the audience hoping that the lovers can overcome this difference in order to be together. Indeed, *Chamundi of the Hill* expertly and innovatively pushes its audience to rethink the differences between caste and the power of rituals that exist between "high" and "low" traditions, to which we turn in the next chapter.

Chapter Five

"I live on the top of the hill . . . you remain near its base"

"High" and "Low" in the Goddess Traditions of Southern Karnataka

For those who visit the temple of the goddess Chamundeshwari, or Queen Chamundi, atop Chamundi Hill outside the city of Mysore, the goddess bears little resemblance to images of emaciated and fierce Chamunda or Chamundi that worshippers encounter in various other parts of India. Instead, in her iconography, she is transformed into a regal goddess, taking a form more befitting a queen, like that of Durga, or—in the case of her processional image—she is a sweet-faced infant goddess. The fierce and ghoulish form that Chamundi takes in other contexts, however, is not forgotten from the collective religious memory of the city. At the bottom of the hill in a much smaller temple dwells Chamundi's younger sister Uttanahalli. Uttanahalli exhibits all of the characteristics and performs all the dirty deeds normally attributed to Chamundi in the more widely known Sanskritic narratives (see chapter 2). She drinks the blood of demons, she aids the mother goddess when her demon foes become too great and/or numerous, and in daily practice, she accepts offerings of meat sacrificed at her temple. Uttanahalli, however, doesn't have the same acclaim throughout India as her elder sister, and the narratives of Uttanahalli's deeds are absent from the broader Indic devotional traditions.[1] Following their iconography, the rituals that are publicly and regularly performed in and around the temples reflect their respective identities as benign royal goddess and bloodthirsty fierce goddess, respectively. In contemporary practice, Chamundi (/eshwari) is generally considered a vegetarian goddess; while daily rituals at Uttanahalli include offerings of chickens and goats that are openly walked to the temple entrance and then slaughtered at a nearby building that houses a kitchen for preparing and cooking the meat of the slaughtered animals.[2]

The iconography and ritual practices dedicated to these goddesses demonstrate two temples that, most likely, had similar foundations but have developed in different directions as a result of external influences, including the extensive royal patronage that the Chamundeshwari temple has received since the 17th century. It is easy to look at these two goddesses and their iconography, temples, and ritual practice and determine that they now exist as two distinct traditions at odds, which are often construed in various dichotomies: "Sanskritic/vernacular," "brahminic/folk," "vegetarian/bloodthirsty," "benevolent/malevolent."[3] The oral tradition of the Mysore region contained in songs like *Chamundi of the Hill* tells another story, one in which their ritual worlds are part of one large network of religious stories, practices, and devotion that is constructed and connected through their spatial relations. Therefore, when speaking of local traditions, especially local goddess traditions, the more meaningful, relational descriptors might be "high" and "low" traditions.

As we have seen throughout this book, the oral narratives of *Chamundi of the Hill* reflect local folk practices and values and envision a devotional world that is localized through mythological immanence, building networks of people and sacred sites through vivid and captivating storytelling. This concluding chapter seeks to extend this thesis, reflecting on the role of space and relationality within *Chamundi of the Hill* and as a means to reconsider how we understand folk religion in India, specifically goddess traditions of southern Karnataka. The terms "high" and "low" are reflective of both an implied and enacted relationality of religious practice and of the actual spatial arrangement of the goddesses of *Chamundi of the Hill*, their temples, their attendant rituals, and their deeds. That is to say, not only are the deities and their histories situated within the region, but they are embedded in the topography of the proximate area with Chamundi installed at the top of the hill and Uttanahalli remaining at its base. This concluding chapter seeks to demonstrate how the spatial arrangement of the goddesses atop and below Chamundi Hill is emphasized in the songs themselves. Highlighting the spatial relationships of the deities will allow us to see how local folk practitioners perceive the movement within and throughout various local traditions as they are negotiated up and down the hill, creating and reifying "high" and "low" traditions within the local religious community. In the end, using the songs' emphasis on space, this chapter suggests that there is an indigenous, local spatial understanding of deities and their attendant rituals that manifest into literal "high" and "low" traditions that can help us to understand how seemingly disparate ritual worlds fit into one cohesive religious landscape.

Highs and Lows: Space, Relationality, and Religion

Though many of us never stop to think about the implications, every day we order our worlds through the language of vertical space. In the morning we need our coffee "pick me *up*"; when we feel depressed, we are "feeling *down* in the dumps"; we look for struggling athletes to "*elevate*" their games; and we even ask friends and followers to "hit me *up* on DM." Verticality is also important in religious language: "god, on *high*," "*depths* of hell," "as *above*, so *below*." The vertical ordering of space in religion and everyday language is perfectly encapsulated in the term "hierarchy" from the ancient Greek *hierarkhēs* meaning "sacred ruler" or "rule of *high* priest." Slowly the term evolved into a system of ordering heavenly beings and religious clerics, and eventually to the common meaning today, a vertical system of ordering anything in which one can be high or low, above and below.

Building off of the common linguistic usage of spatial references, religious studies scholar Kim Knott has argued for a "spatial turn" in the academic study of religion.[4] Knott, following Michel Foucault, Madeleine Bourdieu, and Henri Lefebvre, understands the role of space as vital for understanding the dynamic relations of modernity and laments that spatiality has been undertheorized in scholarly works on religion.[5] She argues for an approach in which: "'space' is not seen as the passive container or backdrop in or against which religious activity takes place. Space cannot be separated from notions of embodiment and everyday practice, knowledge and discourse, and production and reproduction, and is an engaged and dynamic arena for religion no less than for other aspects of social and cultural life."[6]

The spatial turn in the study of religion helps us to better understand how space figures into sacrality and the creation of sacred spaces. It does so in five meaningful ways: (1) space is necessary for the process of setting things apart; (2) this process produces distinctions, demarcating "sacred" spaces, people, and so on; (3) religious or sacred space is, therefore, inherently a site of contestation, between things set apart and placed in contradistinction with one another; (4) these religious spaces are then reproduced through material culture and ideological positionality; and (5) in modernity space and its production are within a dynamic context and must be considered within a broad range of culture and social relations.[7] Space and its demarcation are the determinants that give birth and form to sacrality and also the means through which sacrality is replicated. What we learn from Knott's methodology is not only that space is a critical concept for the production of religion in the etic theoretical sense, but also that space is central within emic categories of sacrality as well, as bodies, persons, and spaces are regulated through the language of boundaries and borders.[8]

As a site through which sacrality is worked out in Knott's theoretical formations, space can be read primarily as a "site of contestation."[9] Knott's conceptualization of spatial contestation is developed from Michel Foucault's discussion of power and Émile Durkheim's formulation of religion: "a unified system of beliefs and practices relative to sacred things, that is to say, things set apart and forbidden."[10] Theorization of space through contestation was also prevalent in the work of religious studies scholar Jonathan Z. Smith. For Smith, religious space is produced through its position in the broader social hierarchy: "Place is not best conceived as a particular location with an idiosyncratic physiognomy or as a uniquely individualistic node of sentiment, but rather a social position within a hierarchical system."[11] While the Foucauldian emphasis on contestation certainly opens many avenues for thinking and rethinking religious space and identity, it also obfuscates other aspects of religious space and its function for religious practitioners. Space in religion is more than just the process of setting apart through the production and reification of boundaries. Sacred space and space in religion, more generally, is also about connection.[12] As discussed in chapter 3, the songs of *Chamundi of the Hill* reflect and build a regional network of pilgrimage and devotional sites, horizontally connecting temples and communities in Chamundi Hill, Uttanahalli, and Nanjangudu. This network, as we see below in the subsequent section, is also described through its vertical spatial relations—high, low, up, down—often turning *upside down* our assumptions about how these terms reflect assumed hierarchies.

Despite the spatial turn in the study of religion/s, "high" and "low" are no longer terms that are generally used in reference to religious traditions, and for good reason. For too long, the terms high and low were used to demarcate and separate cultures that were deemed to be elite from the cultures of the everyday, of the common folk. Selective works of art, music, and literature gained approval from elite circles of critics and identified as the elements that made one "cultured." This formulation granted those with access to these limited cultural resources "higher" than those that did not of those that did not recognize their inherent worth. As scholars like Lawrence Levine have shown, the selective elevation of certain aspects of culture as "high culture" is completely intertwined with class economics and colonial rhetoric that exalted European (and to a lesser degree American) culture over that of indigenous and colonized peoples. Levine has also noted that even the related terms for elite and popular/folk culture, "high brow" and "low brow," are related to phrenology, a pseudoscience popular in the 19th and 20th centuries that was built on racist and white supremist assumptions about teleological progressive evolution and the size and location of a person's eyebrow.[13]

The presentation of "high" and "low" culture has also been applied to the study of religion, privileging religious traditions that place greater emphasis in belief systems and abstract philosophy as compared to traditions that place importance in ritual that were deemed "superstitious" or "magical." As any survey of the readings of Durkheim, Tylor, Frazer, or Weber (etc.) will show, many of the "fathers of the study of religion" reify these boundaries, some more subtly than others.[14] Perhaps the clearest portrayal of the separation of "high religion" from the "low religion" of the folk can be seen in Walter Lippman's 1929 *A Preface to Morals*. Lippmann was a notable journalist and cultural critic who is often called the "father of modern journalism," coined the term "stereotype," and popularized the concept of the "Cold War." Early in his career, he was also a strong proponent of the natural separation of elite and popular culture, and in his 1922 book, *Public Opinion,* he argued that the educated elite should utilize popular media and create stereotypes to guide the "herd" into the correct way of seeing the world.[15] In *Preface to Morals,* Lippmann praised the values of philosophical, "disinterested" high religion while recognizing the mass appeal of popular religion, comparing both to Christianity and Philistines.[16] For Lippman, "adherents of a popular religion necessarily include an enormous number of people who are too young, or too feeble, too dull or too violent, too unstable or too incurious, to have any comprehension whatsoever of anything but the simplest scheme of rewards and punishments."[17] These religious traditions were defined by "supernatural rules, commands, punishments, and compensations."[18] "High Religion," however, is for the few: "High religion has in all ages seemed so unapproachably high that it is reserved for a voluntary aristocracy of the spirit."[19] The primary difference between high and low religion, for Lippmann, was that high religion was conceived of as the art and theory of the internal life of man, while the folk viewed religion only as cosmic government that exacted rules and regulations.[20]

In the 20th century, the separation between "high" and "low" culture started to disintegrate as artists and scholars began questioning the distinction between high and low/popular in their work. Kickstarted by Marcel Duchamp's *Fountain,* the critique of high and low art sparked a postmodernist cultural movement that generated an entirely new era of art production with figures such as Andy Warhol, Roy Lichtenstein, and in India, Jamini Roy, who incorporated popular and folk arts into the world of "high" art. As folk and popular culture become integrated with the "high" art world, more and more folk from all walks of life began to appreciate the sophisticated nature of popular art, music, and literature that had previously been considered "low." Evidenced in the acclaim of visual artists such as Jean-Michel Basquiat and Banksy and the critical recognition of popular musical genres, exemplified by Bob Dylan's 2016 Nobel Prize in Literature, Lin-Manuel Miranda's 2016 Pulitzer Prize for *Hamilton,* or Kendrick Lamar's 2018 Pulitzer Prize for *DAMN,* these formerly rigid boundaries are now eschewed by all but a few. Luckily, the outlook that separates elitist and popular culture regarding religion was also soundly critiqued, giving rise to new fields of study within the study of religion, including ritual studies, postcolonial studies, performance studies, and so on, that continue to demonstrate the complexity of popular religious practice and belief in order to break down arbitrary divisions between religious systems.[21]

The reconsideration of "high" and "low" culture and the attendant power structures surrounding these distinctions was both necessary and welcome, and provides especially in light of the spatial turn in the study of religion, scholars of religion with an opportunity to rethink how we employ the terms "high" and "low" when discussing religious traditions and their associated practices and beliefs. Particularly, we have the opportunity to include indigenous perspectives into our categories in order to develop more nuanced theoretical apparatuses. For the remainder of this chapter, I return to *Chamundi of the Hill* in order to demonstrate how the ballad engages with different religious traditions through the lens of "high" and "low" religions. In order to elucidate this emic perspective, the details provided within the songs are contextualized alongside the ritual practices in the region, particularly focusing on rituals to the goddesses Chamundi and Uttanahalli at the top of the hill and at its base. Through this analysis, we find that the ballad expresses anxieties about the indigenous systemic valuation of religious traditions that assesses greater worth to some religions at the cost of others; however, the songs of *Chamundi of the Hill* and the ritual practice to Chamundi and Uttanahalli in contemporary Mysore construct ritual worlds of "high" and "low" practice that are not in conflict with one another nor are assessed greater or lesser value but that provide parallel systems of expressing and performing religious devotion.

High and Low traditions: Removing Hierarchy from Devotion and Ritual Practice in Mysore

High and Low in *Chamundi of the Hill*

Even before one begins the narrative of *Chamundi of the Hill*, the title orients the reader to the centrality of space as the goddess is specifically connected to the hill. Moreover, the space of the hill by definition implies that it is a space that is raised or that is higher than the surrounding area.[22] Within the grammatical structure of this common epithet of the goddess "Chamundi of the Hill," the place is important as it is the hill that possesses the goddess and not the other way around.[23] As one moves into the ballad itself, after she defeats Mahisha and Aisu, the very first narrative song grounds Chamundi on top of the hill. It is also in this same moment that Uttanahalli is grounded at the base of the hill:

> "Oh, little sister, you shouldn't go far away.
> I live in the midst of this hill.
> I am the house god of Chamaraja Wodeyar.
> Once a year I take worship,
> but I live on top of the hill.
> You should remain near [its base]."
>
> "Tell me, Sister, where should I live?"
> asked Uttanahalli.
>
> Chamundi said,
> "Little Sister, if you remain near the base of this hill
> in the town of Uttanahalli,
> I will arrange an annual worship for you.
> I will ensure your homemade offerings.
> I will make *tambittu* and send it to you."
>
> Mother Chamundi of the hill
> blessed her like this.

Here within the conclusion of the foundational myth—and it is really Uttanahalli's foundational myth—the ballad configures the two powerful goddesses through space. It is clear, however, that the space is not separate space, but it is connected through ritual practice and through the strong bond between the goddesses. And, while Chamundi is the progenitrix of Uttanahalli and is her elder sister, the text does not imply that this is a subordinate position but is in fact a blessing to Uttanahalli and ensures her readiness to come to the aid of the elder sister.

The vertical positionality of the two goddesses is also emphasized when Uttanahalli is called into action in the fourth song "Go, Give My Love to Your Brother-in-Law Nanjunda, and Tell Him to Return." In the song, when Chamundi's perturbation about her absentee husband is ignited by an unsettling nightmare, the goddess arises from her bed and climbs the seven levels of her temple tower (*gopura*) to look for help. From her perch, she spots her sister down in her temple in Uttanahalli and promises the younger goddess a tongue of fire if she once again comes to her aid.[24] The text emphasizes Uttanahalli's trek from the foot of the hill up to its top, where the sisters are blissfully reunited with hugs. As discussed in chapter 3, Uttanahalli's journey up the hill recreates the pilgrimage that connects the two cities and that connects Chamundi Hill with the southern pilgrimage sites that are important for many in the region. Unlike the clear imbalance of power within the deity-devotee relationship that is inherent in the pilgrimage and its attendant rituals, *Chamundi of the Hill* casts Chamundi as in need of Uttanahalli's help. In order to aid her sister, Uttanahalli quickly descends the hill to take action and bring Nanjunda back to her lovesick sister.

In these scenes, for the first time we see some of the characteristics that distinguish the "high" and "low" goddesses become clearer. Being at the top of the hill or "high" allows the goddess to survey the realms. We see this at the beginning of the second song when Chamundi looks around her region for a place to bathe and in the fourth song as she looks for Uttanahalli. The same is true for Uttanahalli as she climbs the hill of Mulluru to look for Nanjunda and then climbs up a pepal tree to call out to him in "You Aren't Thinking about Your Wife." Being "high" provides broader perspective, but it also removes the deity from the action. It is a place that one can see and call to others, but one needs to come down to facilitate connections. After her original establishment on the hill (i.e., the slaying of Mahisha and Aisu), it is only when Chamundi comes down that she effectively engages in the narrative (i.e., marriage to Nanjunda and her role in his "resurrection"). The position of Chamundi on the hill makes sense given her role as the protector of the region and formerly of the kingdom of Mysore. She requires a higher perch to watch over her entire purview. It is also, perhaps, reflective of the ritual worlds of Chamundi, where she regularly receives visitors to whom she doles out blessings, but she only descends from her hill to give authority to the king and, in precolonial times, to reinvigorate him before his annual military expedition. Uttanahalli, however, is always *down* in the thick of things and always down to help those who ask. While being high comes with perspective, being low makes one agile and active.

High and Low Rituals to Uttanahalli and Chamundi

In many ways, the same structure is present within the ritual worlds of both goddesses. Like other places and goddess traditions throughout India, much of the negotiation of the identity of goddesses revolves around food, the types of food that the goddess accepts from her devotees, especially pertaining to rites of animal sacrifice.[25] Animal sacrifice in India is a touchy subject and has been the subject of critique for millennia. At least since the Buddhist and Jain critiques of the Vedic sacrifice in the 6th century BCE, there has been resistance to the ritual killing of animals. As Hinduism developed, rules regulating diet and the killing and consumption of meat become normalized in elite, brahminic religious regulations.[26] These religiosocial dietary conventions also prescribe the types of foods that can be consumed by different castes if they are to maintain their position of relative ritual purity: vegetarianism being considered purer and meat eating ritually polluting in many normative religious contexts.[27] This, of course, further reified caste inequality that took concrete manifestation through regulations of commensality (i.e., with whom one can and will eat) that is linked to rules of caste purity and social hierarchy in which people from "higher" castes cannot eat with or accept food from those who are "lower" on the scale of ritual purity. The subject of commensality, meat eating, and animal sacrifice is intimately tied into concepts of caste hierarchy and has been a topic of debate and discussion in Indian *bhakti* (devotional) traditions.[28] For some *bhakti* traditions, devotion outweighs one's caste background, which is demonstrated through narratives of deities either accepting meat offerings from people whose custom it is to eat such foods and who would normally be considered "lower" on the ritual purity hierarchy.[29] Other traditions, namely, those associated with devotion to the formless (*nirguna*) absolute or god in Vaishnava (relating to the god Vishnu) forms, such as Krishna or Rama, often deride traditions that engaged in animal or blood sacrifice, especially those related to goddess worship.[30] As Kathleen Erndl has shown, the narratives of goddess traditions "display a strong concern about issues of *high* and *low* caste, purity and pollution" and a "general anxiety about meat eating and blood sacrifice"; however, "it comes out overwhelmingly in favor of the view that the power (*śakti*) of the Goddess makes caste irrelevant, as there is no *high* or *low* in Devī's *darbār* [court]."[31] However, the ambivalence over these rituals often leads to great debates over the propriety of the rituals and the proper spaces in which they should be conducted.[32]

During my time conducting fieldwork in Mysore, I was always (and continue to be) struck by how the devotional and ritual complexes of Chamundi and Uttanahalli are worked out spatially. Chamundi's temple at the top of the hill is markedly vegetarian, in which she only accepts *pakka* (cooked/refined) offerings of sweets, money, and saris. At Uttanahalli's temple, on the other hand, one regularly sees devotees bringing goats and chickens to the temple gates to offer them to the goddess before taking them a few hundred meters down the road to slaughter them as blood offerings to the protective goddess. My first inclination was that while Uttanahalli has maintained her local *gramadevate* identity and ritual landscape, Chamundi has simply been sanitized, no longer accepting blood gifts, a marked contrast from sensationalist colonial British documents that provide a history of human and buffalo sacrifices on the hill.[33] One day while at the Chamundeshwari temple, I broached the topic of Chamundi and vegetarianism to the brahmin priests, including the head priest Shashishekhara Dikshita, asking them why a fierce and powerful goddess like Chamundi would be vegetarian. By this point in our relationship, we had become comfortable enough with one another that I felt like I could ask the question, and we had discussed other sensitive issues about the installation of Dikshita priests in the temple in the 19th century, the change to Shaiva *agamic* ritual in the temple at the same time, and the complex negotiation of caste amongst the temple priests and pujaris, and at each point everyone was very forthcoming with details. I, however, still expected a somewhat formulaic response about the polluting nature of meat eating and the purity upheld by Chamundi; these, after all, are vegetarian brahmin priests. Instead, I was shocked when they corrected me and explained that Chamundi accepts *all* offerings, even offerings of flesh. Confused, I asked for clarification, sure that they were either referring to historical Chamundi cults or, perhaps, small village Chamundi temples. Again, I was wrong, and they explained that Chamundi was *adishakti*, the primordial power, the goddess not only of priests but of kings and of the people, and as such, she accepted whatever offering she was given within any circumstance. Sensing my disbelief, they told me that if I wanted to see it, it was everywhere. I just had to go *down* from the temple.

Sure enough, with their help, I starting seeing the diversity of offerings that are given to Chamundi. On festival occasions, like Chamundi's birthday festival or her great festival, trucks deliver chickens for sacrifice to the top of the hill. Of course, these offerings aren't made inside the temple; instead, the sacrificial animals are taken a few hundred feet *down* from her temple, as small private blood offerings are made by the residents of Chamundi Hill in front of their homes. Similarly, one day during Dasara in 2013, while I was starting my trek up from the northern base of the hill, I noticed a family that was walking several goats to the first of the 1,000 steps lead up to the Chamundeshwari temple.[34] I watched as they stopped and briefly prayed and recited mantras and then poured water over the heads of the goats, which promptly shook off the excess water. I asked the devotees about this practice, and they explained that they were offering the goats to Chamundi, but that the goddess would only accept animals that freely offered themselves for the sacrifice. The goats had been asked for their consent when the water was being poured on them and had expressed their willingness by shaking. After the goats consented, the family led the animals and me over to an open spot where, they explained, devotees regularly ritually slaughter goats as a blood offering and then prepare, cook, and eat the goat meat. As the day went on, family after family followed the same pattern.

Animal sacrifice became a legal issue and was limited by laws like Section 295 of the Indian Penal Code of 1860 and subsequent decisions in the Calcutta (1882) and Allahabad (1887) High Courts. In 1948, shortly after Independence, Mysore passed the Mysore Prevention of Animal Sacrifices Act, which prohibited animal or bird sacrifices "in or within the precincts of Hindu Temples." This bill was extended to the state of Karnataka with the Karnataka Prevention of Animal Sacrifices Act, 1959, which was amended to include "any place of public religious worship or adoration and its precincts and to any congregation or precision connected with the religious worship in a public street."[35] Each time I asked if fear of legal repercussions was the reason that they were conducting the sacrifice at the base of the hill and not the top, the devotees similarly responded that the blood offering wasn't forbidden (even though it was technically illegal, but no one was trying to hide it, and several police officers even joined in); instead, they all concluded that it was *proper* to do these types of rituals *low* (*kelage*) on the mountain.

Conclusion

In both the narratives contained within the folk songs and in popular ritual action, the goddesses and their traditions are described spatially as "high" and "low." But in both cases, "high" and "low" aren't mapped onto similar "great" or "small" distinctions or part of a valuation system. Instead, these traditions and their attendant ritual apparatuses are expressed in three-dimensional space. The ritual offering of blood, which seems to be the most powerful offering to the goddess and the offering that is most efficient to bring about results, happens as part of a "low" ritual program that is conducted down the hill or at its base. The goddess at the peak of the hill, however, remains distinct from the intensity of this ritual life, accepting and speaking only about vegetarian offerings.[36]

When contemplating the goddesses' different roles in the narrative and ritual contexts, I couldn't help but think of discussions from my course Women, Goddesses, and Power in Hinduism, particularly when we talk about the Bhuktimuktipradayini, the common name for the Goddess in texts, mantras, and devotional songs. This topic is also one that I think is helpful for us to understand the relationship between high and low in the goddess traditions of southern Karnataka. Bhuktimuktipradayini is a Sanskrit compound that combines *bhukti* or "enjoyment," *mukti* "liberation," and *pradayini* "giver" (feminine); so, together *bhukti* + *mukti* + *pradayini* is translated as the "giver of both enjoyment and liberation." The discussion arises after reading the frame story of the Sanskritic *Devi Mahatmya*, as it details non*agamic* ritual phenomena that reflect the same concerns as *Chamundi of the Hill* and that pervades the goddess traditions of India. In this story, a king named Suratha and a merchant named Samadhi have lost their homes and their riches and while wandering through the wilderness happen upon Sumedhas, a sage's *ashrama* or hermitage. When they ask the sage about how they can overcome their grief that has arisen from their losses, the sage tells them the wonderous stories that proclaim the glorification of the Goddess (i.e., the *Devi Mahatmya*). After hearing the stories of the exploits of the Goddess in all her forms, the king and the merchant go to a riverbank to worship the Goddess. They cut themselves and make an earthen image of the Goddess; then they cut themselves daily, offering her their blood. They do this for three years; at which point the Goddess appears before them to grant them whatever they desire. The king asked for an imperishable kingdom. The merchant, however, asked not for riches but for knowledge that leads to liberation. The goddess grants both wishes and immediately disappears. The end.

Many of my students—as I did when I first encountered the text as an undergrad—are quick to criticize the king for choosing money and power over spiritual liberation. The text doesn't provide any commentary on the choices, nor does it explicitly or implicitly value one over the other. Indeed, one could actually argue the opposite, that the focus of the entire text was on the king because the entire narrative was predicated on the question about the king and the final verses focus on his subsequent birth as the universal ruler (*manu*).[37] The truth is that the interpretation that privileges liberation and the merchant tells us more about ourselves and our own religious value systems than it does about the king or the goddess traditions. The goddess traditions of India encourage the dual concerns of life, the material and the spiritual, and the Goddess and the many goddesses of India share in this, providing both physical and spiritual fulfillment. What is fascinating about the goddess traditions is that both can coexist without one necessarily being cast as more valuable or more meaningful than the other. This is perfectly encapsulated in the name Bhuktimuktipradayini. She gives both enjoyment and liberation.

In *Chamundi of the Hill* and the context from which it emerged and within which it continues to be a popular and meaningful story, we see a similar set of concerns that are manifested through a discourse of high and low. The goddess who remains high on the hill surveys her domain with a broad perspective. It is from these heights that she consumes only vegetarian food and, seemingly, concerns herself with the ritual purity that is required for the pursuit of liberation. As we move down the hill, however, the goddess becomes more concerned with action and engagement, helping those who seek her help with this-worldly problems. It is also within this tradition that the goddess accepts offerings of meat, perhaps needing the sustenance for the difficult tasks at hand. The goddess traditions of southern Karnataka not only accept both traditions, but in *Chamundi of the Hill*, we see that both are necessary parts of religious, ritual, and devotional life. Devotees and deities need the highs and the lows.

The ritual and devotional worlds of *Chamundi of the Hill* demonstrate that we need to continue to think about space in a three-dimensional sense when we consider how different ritual traditions work with, alongside, and parallel to one another. Indeed, in the tales of Chamundi and Uttanahalli, the goddesses and their attendant traditions are mapped within and *on top* of sacred landscapes. They construct traditions that are high and low that are mutually constituting and affirming. Simultaneously, however, there is a recognition of the normative social hierarchy. But these songs work to dispel the notion of superiority (or perhaps flip it upside down), demonstrating the value inherent in both the "high" and "low" goddess traditions.

Chapter Six

Chamundi of the Hill Translation

Note for Reading

*Lines in italics are sung,
and the lines in regular font are narrated.*

O Mother, Grant Me a Wish

of victory in combat, O Mother Chamundi
of a boon, O Goddess of Wealth[1]
of knowledge, O Goddess of Wisdom[2]
O Mother, grant me a wish

O Mother of Illusion,[3]
O Chamundi of the hill,
O Mother Chamundi,
you are the wife of Lord of Nanjangudu.[4]

Having taken the form of a woman,
you are the maker of illusion, O Chamundi.[5]
Having slaughtered Mahisha,
you are the house god of Chamaraja, O Chamundi.

You took the boon from Shiva,
O Chamundi of the hill

O mother, grant me a wish.
of nourishment and love
to your trusting devotees.

Sister, Stand on My Tongue and Fight![6]

A boon was given by Shiva
Mother Chamundi of the hill

With your ten shoulders and
with your twenty hands you did it.
You grabbed the sharpened sword and dagger.
You were granted a boon from Shiva
in the land of Mysore.

You won the battle
against Mahisha!

After the annihilation of Mahisha
Do you know what happens?
Aisu comes and grabs the forearm of Chamundi
but Chamundi grabs the sword with her hand.
She grabs the nape of Aisu's neck.
Wherever a little drop of his blood falls to the earth . . .

There, countless demons
are born.

The Maker of Illusion, Chamundi of the hill
has killed Mahisha.
She keeps fighting Aisu.
Aisu is a worthy opponent,
but Chamundi endures his trickery.
Inside the buffalo's belly,
he hides and schemes.
Countless demons are produced
from every little drop of his blood.
Then she leans on the buffalo's hoof and stands up.

She looks to the left and to the right
and thinks . . .

"I don't have the power
to destroy countless demons.
What should I do?"

Chamundi of the hill
looks to the left and right and thinks.

Sweat is pouring all over her body.
She sighs "Ughhh" and
wipes her sweat and slings it down.
She thinks, "Nobody can solve this problem alone.
I need to call someone."

Tears well in her eyes.
O Mother Chamundi, who belongs to the hill

O Chamundi of the hill!

Folks, tears are welling in her eyes.
But Shri Krishna, the supreme, realizes her predicament.

O Goddess of Wisdom![7]

He, husband to Rukmani,[8]
the one who plays on the seven seas,
He, the supreme soul, realizes,
"Ah, Rukmani, Chamundi of the hill
needs a boon from me
in order to kill Aisu.[9]
I've got to go!"
Shri Krishna, the supreme soul,
takes hold of Garuda[10]
and leaves Nanda's ranch.[11]

Shri Krishna, the supreme soul,
comes to the Mysore region.

Chamundi's in Mysore,
wiping her sweat and slinging it to the ground.

Shri Krishna, the supreme soul, watches
her sweat fall to the ground
and flow like a river.
He looks at the sweat, and
then, Uttanahalli Mari arises,
born from her sweat.

*Shri Krishna, the supreme soul,
gives the boon.*

After receiving the boon,
she is born.
Rising from the sweat,
she spreads her seven hoods
and sticks out her seven tongues.

*Look! The beautiful[12] Uttanahalli Mari
is already standing before you!*

Uttanahalli Mari grabs her by the hand and says,
"Sister, don't be afraid."

"Lady, who are you?"
Chamundi asks.

"Sister, don't you know who I am?
I took birth in your sweat."

Hearing this Chamundii is happy and says,
"Wow! Child of my sweat,
through your birth
you became closer
to me than all of my siblings.
You are now my sister."

Uttanahalli Maramma replies,
"Sister, those words are too great.
What is your trouble?"

"You asked, but
how do I reply, Sister?
I have killed Mahisha,
but if I strike Aisu
every small drop of his blood
that falls on the ground . . .

*Countless demons, Sister
will be born."*

Mother Uttanahalli feels
fire in her belly and says,
"Sister, when I am here, why should you fear?
His blood won't fall to the ground anymore!
Fight, Sister!"

"Sister, it isn't possible."

"Ugh! Why are you worrying?
At this moment, I am spreading
my seven tongues around the hill.

*Sister, Stand on my
seven tongues and fight!"*

"Sister, stand on my seven tongues
and fight," Uttanahalli says
as she spreads out her tongues.
Courage comes to Chamundi of the hill
Chamundi stands on her sister Uttanahalli,
the fire-starter's, tongue.

*She fights
with Aisu.*

Chamundi of the hill
Looks for the buffalo.
When she spots the buffalo,

he's going to die.
Chamundi of the hill looks around the hill.

She looks here.
She looks there.
But wherever she looks
there is no sign of Aisu.

Then she says,
"Sister, Sister, I've gone
and searched the mountains and hills,
and there is no sign of Aisu."

Uttanahalli replies,
"Sister Chamundi,
This buffalo is dead.
Now, thrust the trident
through his corpse-like body."

"Who are you, Uttanahalli Maramma?"[13]

Hearing the words of her little sister,
Chamundi of the hill
thrusts her trident, and
the buffalo is split in two.

The real Aisu
comes outside.

When the true form of Aisasura comes out,
he looks like a huge hill.
His teeth look like huge radishes.
He sticks his tongue out like a monkey.
His mouth is wide-open, like a metal pot.

He comes to grab
Mother Chamundi.

She exclaims, "Oh no! He's coming this way!
How can I kill him?"
Then she meditates on Shiva, and
Brahma becomes aware of her tears.

He says, "Uh-oh, Chamundi
is fighting the demon Aisu.
I gave him a wish,
and he asked,
'If a drop of my blood falls to the ground
countless like me
should be born.'
He has no fear
There is no one who can defeat him.
Agh, Chamundi!
Shiva, also gave him a blessing,
but now death must come to Aisu.
I must support Chamundi."

Brahma makes an oath
and sends the fiery lion.

Brahma Deva sends the fiery lion.
The fiery lion comes
to Parvati-Chamundri
and bows before her.

"Oh! A little lion!"
Chamundi of the hill says,
and then she sits on the lion-vehicle.

She fights
with Aisu.

With ten shoulders
and twenty hands she does it.
She stares at him with her burning eyes
and her lolling tongue.

Seated on her lion vehicle,
she grabs Aisu's long hair.
O Chamundi of the hill!
She fights him, and she kills him!

Uttanahalli Maramma worries and asks,
"Sister, I can't bear to see your trouble.
Produced from you, I took birth.
What should I do now, Sister?"

"Oh, little sister, you shouldn't go far away.
I live in the midst of this hill.
I am the house god of Chamaraja Wodeyar.
Once a year I take worship,
but I live on top of the hill.
You should remain near [its base]."

"Tell me, Sister, where should I live?"
asked Uttanahalli.

Chamundi says,
"Little sister, if you remain near the base of this hill[14]
in the town of Uttanahalli,
I will arrange an annual worship for you.
I will ensure you get homemade offerings.
I will make *tambittu*[15] and send it to you."

Mother Chamundi of the hill
blessed her like this.

She Bathes in the Kapini and Kaveri

Standing on the top of the hill
during the middle of the night
when stones and water melt into one,
she looks around her neighborhood and says,
"God, I need a bath.
Where should I go?"

She is looking
all around the seven regions.

Chamundi of the hill
looks all around the seven regions.
In the region of Nanjangudu,
which is equal to Kailasa,[16]
the Kapini River flows.
Thinking that she ought to bathe,
Chamundi goes to the river.
She says to the lion,
"Honorable lion, you stay here.
I am going to bathe and purify myself."
She gives her word and leaves
to come and bathe.

After killing countless demons
when she crosses through Mysore
the stain of their blood
remains on her right hand;
so the Mother comes to bathe
in the Kapini River.

She goes into the Kapini-Kaveri
and bathes.
She puts on a fancy white sari.
Chamundi of the hill
magically makes a golden comb
with a golden handle

and combs her long
knotted hair.

Mother Chamundi of the hill
combs her knotted hair.

Chamundi of the hill
combs her knotted hair.

Who Are You Wise Woman? You Are So Charming!

Hello, Nanjangudu!
The *jangama*'s city[17]
is equal to Kailasa.

Imagine this
they sleep peacefully
on a fiery bed.

The lord, Nanjunda,
who has the medicine for all internal issues,
thinks "I ought to go bathe."
So he gets off his fancy bed,
dressed in ochre
with his staff, shawl, and rosary[18]
and grabbed a copper pot in his right hand.

The god-king Nanjunda Swami
is coming to bathe too.

He comes to bathe too.
Nanjunda reaches the river and dunks himself
Then he puts on clean golden clothes,
a *linga* on his neck,[19]
a *linga* on his leg,
and his rosary around his neck.
In the hand of Lord Nanjunda,
there was another *linga*.
Holding that *linga* in his palm,
Nanjunda takes a *lakki* leaf, a *bilva* leaf, and a *tambe* leaf,[20]
places the sacred ash mark on the *linga*,
and performs Shiva worship to the *linga*.

Nanjunda Linga performs
Shiva worship to the linga.

Nanjunda turns and looks nearby.
Chamundi is there combing her long hair.

She looks as bright as the sun as she combs her hair.
Nanjunda just stares.

He fixes his sights
upon Chamundi.

Nanjunda comes galloping [toward her]
and says to himself,
"Who is this girl that I see,
who came in the middle of the night, and
stands here now? Oh wow!
If my two wives saw me now!
Somaji, the younger sister of Vishnu,
and Big Deviri, the daughter of Indra from the world of
    the gods,[21]
are already married to me,
[but] she is much better looking
than Deviri and Somaji, my housewives.
I have to talk to this girl!"
He makes up his mind
and comes and grabs her hand.[22]

"Madam, who are you?"

"Sir, release my hand,"
she says as she plucks her hand away
from Nanjunda's grasp.
"Sir, who speaks to me so forwardly,
who are you?"

"Madam, I killed Nandakasura.
I live in Nanjangudu, and
I am called Nanjunda.
Who are you, wise woman?
You are very charming."

"Sir, I am the house god of Chamaraja
I live in Mysore, and

I am the daughter of Uncle Lingayya,[23]
who resides in the Himalaya Mountains."

Nanjunda replies,
"Ah ha! You're the daughter of Uncle Lingayya,
who lives in the Himalaya Mountains?
Then, your father is my mother's brother.
You are my Salavali.[24]
Chamundi, marry me!"

"Sir, you say 'marry me,'
but aren't you already married?"

"Madam, I am married to two wives,
plump Deviri and
old Somaji," he answers.

"What is that proverb, Sir?
'Even a corpse will object
to a marriage with a co-wife.'
I don't want to live with *two* co-wives."
In this way, Chamundi refuses.

"Madam, I'll leave my wives.
I can't leave you,"
promises Nanjunda.

Touching the river
Nanjunda makes the promise.

"Sir, touching the river, you've promised.
Don't cheat me," she replies.

Then Chamundi and Nanjunda become one.

They go to Mysore Hill and
King Swami Nanjunda
lays his head
on Chamundi's arm
and falls asleep.

Nanjunda comes to Mysore Hill
and on Chamundi's round arm . . .

Swami Nanjundayya
has a good sleep.

For two weeks
Nanjunda rests well.
But the third week comes, and
the full moon festival is coming near.

"Woman, the festival has come
people from all corners of the land
will bow and pray for a boon.
After I look upon all their intentional and unintentional
    misdeeds,
I will return.
You wait here,"
Nanjunda says this to Chamundi,
giving her his word.

The god who dwells in Garalapura[25]
goes to Nanjangudu.

Go, Give My Love to Your Brother-in-Law Nanjunda, and Tell Him to Return

Chamundi of the hill,
the magic-maker stays there,
eating milk, rice, honey-sugar,
and blessed milk sweets.

She sleeps well
because of her husband's fortune.

I'll tell you how
Chamundi of the hill sleeps.

She puts large jasmine garlands
on her bed.
She puts sweet smelling rice
in her pillow.
She sleeps well
on this fancy bed.

Chamundi of the hill, the magic-maker
sleeps well.
That same night, however,
Nanjunda is sleeping
with Deviri on his left
and Somaji on his right.

You see Mr. Nanjunda Linga
is also sleeping very well.

With Deviri on his left
and Somaji on his right
between his two wives,
he is also sleeping well
enjoying the fortune of his wives.

Chamundi must remain
in her place in Mysore.

Since she was the house god of Chamaraja,
she gave him twelve lakh rupees.
So Chamaraja built a twelve-tiered temple
for her with his own hands.
On the temple, he carved an elaborate tower.

She is on the fancy bed.
It had been made spectacular.

When Chamundi of the hill
is on her fancy bed and
Nanjunda is on the bed in his house,

She sees a terrible vision.
She has a nightmare and
immediately opens her eyes and
looks to her right and left.
Mother Chamundi had dreamt that
she was wearing a fancy sari
and was engulfed in fire.
She was also wearing the jewelry of a married woman.[26]
Then all the ornaments shattered.
She immediately woke,
and looking to the left and right
she thinks,

"Oh God! I dreamt a terrible
nightmare while in this fancy bed.

Who should I tell
about my dream?

Oh God! Who should I tell
about my dream?
I want to tell someone
about this troubling thing, but
my father, mother, aunt, or uncle aren't here.
Neither are my elder or younger brothers or sisters."

If she looks back to the riverbank
her husband, Nanjunda, wouldn't be there.

If she looks back to the riverbank
her renowned husband, the poison-throated Nanjunda,
   wouldn't be there.
"Who should I tell about
this troubling dream that has come to me?"

The Mother climbs
the seven-leveled tower.

Chamundi climbs
the seven-leveled tower
and turns and looks nearby.
She sees Uttanahalli Maramma, the fire-starter.
"Ah! My little sister Uttanahalli, the fire-starter, lives here.

I don't know about
her happy times, O Shiva.
She doesn't know of
my troubles, O Shiva.

I should call my little sister, Uttanahalli Maramma, the
   fire-starter.
I should tell her my troubles,"
thinks Chamundi of the hill.

She shouts to her sister,
Uttanahalli Maramma.

How did she call her?

Chamundi of the hill
affectionately calls
Uttanahalli Maramma, the fire-starter.

"*Sister, who dwells in Uttanahalli,*
who has the tongue of fire,
little sister get up and come here.

While I was sleeping,
I had a nightmare.

Sister, I've called you because
if you come to me
I will not need any other comfort.
O Sister, Mysore is like a ship
that is sinking.[27]
What use is there in living, sister?
Madam, if you come
and answer my call, I promise
I will make you a tongue of fire."[28]
Chamundi of the hill
asks three times
and even a fourth time.

He left, and Mother
sleeps on the fancy bed.

But as Chamundi, the magic-maker
lies on her fancy bed,
Uttanahalli Maramma is
over there in Uttanahalli.

The little sister heard the sound
of her elder sister's call.

"Oh man! This day my sister
Chamundi of the hill is calling me.
She doesn't call about anything.
She has never called.
She doesn't call for festivals.
She doesn't call for the boat festival or the fair.
But now she is calling.

I don't know why the charming one
has called me."

She thinks,
"Why is she calling me?

She's calling with such urgency.
I should go
to my sister's temple quickly."

She quickly comes
to the bathing tank.

She comes to the bathing tank
and purifies herself.

She puts on an expensive sari.
She puts on a fancy blouse.
She parts her hair.
She puts it in a bun.
She puts a golden ornament
on the side of her bun.

Uttanahalli Maramma decorates
her whole head with
Mysore jasmine and white jasmine.

The exquisite Uttanahalli Mari
makes herself beautiful.

Uttanahalli Maramma
takes magical ash
and ties it in her sari.
Then, she grabs neem leaves in her left hand.[29]

The little sister opens her fiery eyes,
lolls her fiery tongue,
grabs a bamboo stalk,
and comes to her sister's temple.

Let me tell you how Uttanahalli Maramma, the fire-starter,
comes to her older sister's temple.
She went through Uttanahalli,
through the streets of Sakkalli,
through Nalatadripura,

through Barighatta,
across the edge of Doddakere tank.

The beautiful Uttanahalli Maramma
arrives at the foot of the hill.

Let me tell you how she comes
to her older sister's temple.
As she climbs the hill,
she wipes away the beads of sweat
and flips her beautiful hair.
Uttanahalli Maramma
climbs the hill, and then
she stands in front of her older sister's temple.

She knocks on the door
and calls to Chamundi.

She knocks on the door
and calls her sister,
"Sister, the cock has crowed
and sunlight has come to the world.
Open this heavy door.
Madam, the cock has crowed
and the eastern sky is red.
Open this heavy door."
Chamundi was sleeping
on her fancy bed.

She hears her little sister's call
and quickly gets up from the bed,
removing her ankleted foot from the bed
and placing it on the floor.
She opens the heavy door and
sees her sister's face.
She hugs her neck
and is happy.

"O sister Chamundi!
Why did you call me?"

"Little sister . . ."

Madam, I was sleeping in the bed
and had a nightmare.
Go, give my love to Nanjunda, your brother-in-law,
and tell him to return.

"Sister, you say call my brother-in-law
Nanjunda and give him your love."

Sister, I'm too modest
to call him brother-in-law.

"Little sister, how does modesty matter
in calling him brother-in-law?"

Sister, how has he become your husband?
How have you become his wife?
How am I his sister-in-law?
How is he my brother-in-law?
I haven't seen any coconut arrangements.
I haven't seen any wedding calculations.
I haven't seen the washerman Macayya come
and lay out any freshly washed wedding garments.
I haven't seen the 5 married women come[30]
and drop rice on the married couple.
I haven't seen the singers sing any folksongs
about Sita or Savitri.[31]
The family hasn't gathered.
I haven't seen any thali tied.[32]
I haven't seen any food being eaten.
I haven't seen any betel nut being taken.
Sister, I'm too modest
to call him brother-in-law.

Sister, I heard your call, and
I came and stood at the temple door.

But if I were to call out 'O brother-in-law Nanjunda,
O brother-in-law Nanjunda, my sister
is calling you,'
then Big Deviri would come and say,
'This lowly woman is calling my husband Nanjunda.'
Sister, they would come quickly,
grab my head,
and tie me to that pillar there!"

They would really take care of me.
They would grab me and make the evil spirit leave.

Listen, sister, magic-maker,
Chamundi of the hill,
They would really take care of me.
They would grab me and make the evil spirit leave.

Tell me clearly, Magic-Maker,
How has he become my brother-in-law?"

Listen, little sister, Uttanahalli Maramma, the fire-starter,
I killed a clan of countless demons
in Mysore,
and then I killed Mahisha.

I calmed myself
and crossed the hill into Mysore.
I killed all of them
and their blood became my forehead mark.
On that side was Nanjangudu
and on this side was the orchard of Hejjige.
In the middle of these two
flowed the Kapini Kaveri River.

Little sister, I bathed in the Kapini Kaveri
and put on clean clothes.

I was sitting and combing my knotted hair
and I joined him, but where is he now?[33]
That liar's mother ought to die.

I joined him, but where is he now?
His life breath ought to leave him.
He ran galloping towards me
and grabbed the end of my beautiful sari.
I thought the poison-throated one was worthy of my love.

Little sister, I bathed,
put on clean clothes,
and brushed my hair.
Sister, Nanjunda *is* your brother-in-law.
He grabbed my hand and asked,
"Whose daughter are you?"
I pulled my hand back and asked,
"Whose son are you?"
He responded,
"I killed Nandikasura,
and I live in Nanjangudu.
I am Nanjunda."
Then he said,
"Now, tell me whose daughter you are."
I said, "I am the daughter of Mavūru Lingayya
Chamundi of the hill."
Then he said, "Since you, Chamundi of the hill,
are the daughter of Mavūru Lingayya
you ought to be my wife."
That's how he became your brother-in-law, little sister.

Little sister, he touched the sword
and promised, and then he left.[34]

"Little sister, Maramma, the fire-starter,
he touched the sword and promised.
Your brother-in-law Nanjunda
said something else too."

"What did he say, sister?"

"Well, I said, 'Hey Nanjunda,
I see you already have two wives.

I won't be just another addition.'
And he told me 'Hey Chamundi,
I'll leave my two wives, but
I can't leave you.'
After he made that promise, he became your brother-in-law,
but who witnessed that promise?"

The sky witnessed that promise.
Mother Earth witnessed that promise.

"Little sister, for nine months he was here
Then he said, 'The full moon festival has come, and
I will go to Nanjangudu-Kailasa and
give boons to all the people
who have gathered from the four directions.

Afterwards, I will return.'
Little sister, your brother-in-law left
this young girl on this stone hill,
and longing for my co-wives
he went back to Nanjanguda.
Little sister, he forgot me.

"Listen, Little sister,
He brought me
from the mountains of the Himalayas.
He stopped me on this stone hill
of southern Kashi.[35]
But now he has longed for my old co-wives in Nanjangudu
whose hair has already turned gray.
Little sister, he forgot me.
For a month and a half
I hoped that
he would return the next day, Little sister.
He won't give me the pleasure
or the happiness of showing his face.
Little sister, that man, whom I trusted,
your brother-in-law, has cheated me.
Why hasn't an illness befallen him?

He ought to be bitten by a snake!
He ought to feel the deep discomfort of a stomach ache!
Because he has broken a promise
to his beloved, who trusted him,
a snake ought to bite Nanjunda!
He ought to be pierced by a scorpion!
He ought to feel the deep discomfort of a stomach ache!
Little sister, my king has gone!"

There hasn't been any romance.
We haven't bathed in turmeric water.
Flowers haven't been placed in my hair, Little sister.
Your brother-in-law hasn't come back for any romance.

Since my husband left
I haven't combed my hair
I haven't put Mysore jasmine in my hair
O sister, your brother-in-law ought to die!
He hasn't come back.

Little sister, every second
I remember
Nanjunda, your brother-in-law,
who left during Kalaratri.[36]

Since the day before yesterday,
I haven't been able to eat
because of my memories of him.
It seems like a lifetime
O Little sister, He ought to die!
He hasn't come back.

"Listen, little sister, this isn't all.
I will tell you more.
As I slept on the fancy bed,
I had a terrible nightmare.

I dreamt that Mysore
was like a sinking ship.

The Seven Durgas,
the children of Bijjalaraya
came from the region of Ujjain.
They tied a chariot on top of another chariot.
They became like the images on top of that chariot, sister.
They spread their seven tongues.
Their tongues covered the world.
They came to wage war on Mysore.

"Listen little sister, they came to wage war."

Who are the children of Bijjalaraya?
Let me tell you.
They are Akkamma, Cikkamma, Cikkadevi, Baddare, Balamane, Kali,
and the eldest of all these is Akkaji Doddamma.

"I dreamt that they were seated on top of that chariot
and came to Mysore
and were looting the region.
Those people are my co-wives,
the seven Marammas.
I'll tell you what I dreamt.

I dreamt the little ones
died on the little streets.
I dreamt the big ones
died in the big areas.
I dreamt that in Virangere[37]
they were putting the dying people outside the house.[38]
I dreamt that in Bandikeri
the seven Marammas
were binding the death carts.
I dreamt that in the clock tower street[39]
there were loud screams.
I dreamt that in Sunnakeri[40]
they were looting.
In Hallakeri
they scooped up men.

*I dreamt that in Bandikeri
they buried corpses.
I dreamt that on Mother Kali Road*[41]
*all the people on the road
were screaming and praying
to Mother Kali.*

Listen, little sister . . .

*I dreamt that the seven Marammas
were killing
all of the people of Mother Kali Road.
I dreamt that all the people on Mother Kali Road
were praying to Mother Kali.*

While their street was being looted, they cried out,
'Mother, you have to give us a boon!'

*They were cramming
all the newborns into anthills.*

They asked the goddess for a boon
but she didn't give them one.

[Then] I dreamt that in Kannanbadi[42]
Cannabasavanna[43] *was attracted
to a very beautiful tribal woman*[44]
*I dreamt that he was attracted
to the beautiful women.
I dreamt that he fell in love with her.
I dreamt that he chopped off a buffalo's head
in front of the beautiful women.
I dreamt that he waved a light
over the buffalo's head.*[45]

Little sister, I dreamt that he waved a light
over the buffalo's head
Listen, Uttanahalli Maramma, fire-starter,
I dreamt another horrible nightmare

about Nanjanguda Linga, your brother-in-law,
who lives in Nanjangudu.

I dreamt that a horrible thing will happen.
His affection for me will dry up and wilt.

I dreamt that a horrible thing will happen
to your brother-in-law Nanjunda.
His affection for me will dry up and wilt.

He was being carried by four people[46]
and brought to the Hejjige Kere.
A body-length grave was dug,
and he was put in the grave.
I dreamt this, sister.

Little sister, your brother-in-law Nanjunda
was carried by four people and taken to Hejjige Kere.
They put Nanjunda to rest in a grave.
Sister, they erected a tombstone
for Nanjunda.
His wife Big Deviri sat
on top of his tombstone.
She removed her golden bangles
and broke them over his grave.
I dreamt this, sister.
Nanjunda's youngest wife, Somaji,
ripped out her leaf-earrings
and threw them into a bush.
Little sister, go and come back, my dear one.
Go to Nanjangudu.
Madam, call your brother-in-law Nanjunda.
If you call upon him and return,
I will arrange a yearly festival for you.
Listen, Maramma, fire-starter.
If you call your brother-in-law Nanjunda
and come back
I will arrange a yearly festival.
I will also make a fiery tongue for you."

"If I tell you something, will you listen?
Listen, Chamundi of the hill . . .

He is from one caste.
We are from another caste.
He ties the linga.[47]
He dresses like a jangama.
He wears ochre.[48]
He uses the ascetic staff.[49]
We, like fierce demons,
eat chickens and goats.
We have nothing in common
with that place or the lord who resides there.

Sister . . .

Sister, if I shout and call
Nanjunda, will he come?

Have You Lost Interest in Your Wife?

She says, "Sister,
I will go and bring back Nanjunda."

*The little sister hears the words of her elder sister
and immediately mounts a horse and rides off
shouting loudly three times.*

She sits on the hill of Mullūru
as if she were Mullūru's village goddess

*She calls
to her brother-in-law Nanjunda the Great,*

How does Uttanahalli Maramma call
to her brother-in-law Nanjunda? I'll tell you.

*O Brother-in-law Shiva, please speak up.
I will be drawn by your voice.
Dear one, please speak up.
Get up and come to the street.
Show your beautiful face.
Will you speak sweetly?
Come, come out to this beautiful street.
Nanjunda whose crown is the moon,
have you lost interest in your wife?*

*O Bhasuvasa, healer of pox,
Nanjunda, supreme lord,
Please speak with Shri Chamundi.
Nanjunda whose crown is the moon,
have you lost interest in your wife?*

*Nanjunda, you love the feeling of devotion.
You love the smoke offering.*[50]
*You love when hands are uplifted to you.
But you've become the victim of the bow and arrow.*[51]
You've become the victim of the bow and arrow.

King Nanjunda, you've become the victim.
Please come to Mysore for your jasmine.
Nanjunda whose crown is the moon,
have you lost interest in us?

You are the greenery with which
I have adorned my hair.
O maker of confusion, get up and speak up.
Nanjunda guru, who is dwelling in the middle of the forest,
have you lost interest in your devotees?

Sir, you are the jasmine with which
I, the beloved, have adorned my hair.
Lover, please speak up.
Swami, Swamishekhara Nanjunda,
have you lost interest in your devotees?

Swami, what happened
while you were inside the Kapini, sir?
O poison king, don't you want her?[52]
O one, who has drank poison, please come.
Nanjunda whose crown is the moon,
have you lost interest in us?

Forget about Nanjangudu.
Forget about the cotton bed.[53]
Forget about your two wives.
Please speak about Chamundi of the hill, your beloved.
Nanjunda whose crown is the moon,
have you lost interest in your devotees?

Nanju, you are like 100,000 lamps.
In the hands of devotees coming in procession,
you are their torches, please speak up.
Nanjunda whose crown is the moon,
have you lost interest in your devotees?

Mount your elephant
and come to Karutu street.

*O lover, Enamored one, please speak.
Swamishekhara, Lord Nanjunda,
have you lost interest in your devotees?*

*There is a pepal tree.
In the new-moon night,
Uttanahalli Maramma of the hill, the fire-starter
climbs up the pepal tree
and lovingly calls out
to her brother-in-law, Nanjunda.*

*Sir, the regal Parvati,
whose man has gone from Nanjangudu,
that beautiful one has sent me.
The beautiful one sent me because
her man went on a quest beyond Nanjangudu
and hasn't returned.
Nanjunda whose crown is the moon,
have you lost interest in your wife?*

*Swami Nanjunda, who dwells in the middle of the forest
where palms grow and shake,
there, where palms are growing and shaking,
is a bird sanctuary, banyans, and
jasmine fields.*

*In Nanjangudu,
there are four or five doors,
five pillars and five banners.
There is one pillar, five banners,
and fifteen auspicious women with lamps, O Nanjunda Lingayya,
have you lost interest in your devotees?*

*In Nanjangudu, he celebrated with
the image of Shri Kaṇṭha that was mounted on
the dolled-up seven-axled chariots.
O Shiva, while celebrating
in Nanjangudu
all the people on the king's street saw him.*

*All the people on king's street who saw Shri Kanṭha
joined their hands and raised them up.
Swami King Nanjunda, who dwells in the middle of the forest,
have you lost interest in your devotees?*

*Mother Deviri, whom he calls "Big,"
where has your husband gone?
He went to the temple
in the middle of the river, which is beyond Narasipura.
He has come to the confluence of rivers
beyond Narasipura.
Nanjunda, whose crown is the moon,
have you lost interest in your devotees?*

They give him salt and jaggery.
They paint with fiery colors.
They tie torches to their legs
and grab torches with their hands.
They worship on their sides.
They worship by rolling.

*People with pox on their legs,
people with pain in their ankles,
people with headaches,
people with stomach pain and asthma
all grabbed Swami's feet.
They ask Swami for a boon.
They pray to Shrikara.
Nanjunda whose crown is the moon,
have you lost interest in your wives?*

*You are the blossom, which
I, the wise one, pluck and place in my hair.
O wise king, please speak up.
Nanjunda, whose crown is the moon,
have you lost interest in your devotees?*

*You put the sandalwood on your forehead
and plucked the fragrant leaf.*

You took the bow
and grabbed the arrow with your hand
and killed the demon.
Nanjappa, please speak up.
O Shankara, please speak up.
O king, please speak.
O Guru, please speak.
Lord Nanjunda whose crown is the moon,
have you lost interest in your devotees?

You are the palm leaf, which
I split and place in my hair.
O Nanjunda, the maker of rightness, please come.
Guru Nanjunda, whose crown is the moon,
have you lost interest in your devotees?

You've forgotten the temple of Okuli (Holi).
You've forgotten the Jangamma Matha.[54]
O One with the blessed throat
aren't you attracted to Chamundi of the hill?[55]
O Creator, please speak up.
Lord Nanjunda, whose crown is the moon,
have you lost interest in your devotees?

Who picks the fragrant maruga
from the field of weeds?
Only he who is drawn by its fragrance.
Shankara, aren't you drawn.[56]
Swami Nanjunda Linga, who live in the middle of the forest,
have you lost interest in your devotees?

Like a hornets' nest,
in tiny Nanjangudu
O Shankara, an ornately carved pillar was erected.
Sir, your stone pillar was carved and erected.
In Nanjangudu, a stone pillar was carved and placed.
Lord Nanjunda whose crown is the moon,
have you lost interest in your devotees?

"One with the blessed throat,
who has become my brother-in-law,
you haven't spoken with me.
I can't see anything that I've done wrong.
You should lovingly call back."
Uttanahalli Maramma said.

*Only you are the sandalwood paste, which
I take and rub on myself.
O Candrashekhara, please speak up.
O Hara, please speak up.
Lord Nanjunda whose crown is the moon,
have you lost interest in us?*

*Nanjangudu is beautiful.
The marriage hall is beautiful.
Our Swami, whom we worship, is very beautiful.
Hara is bliss.
Swami Nanjundappa, who dwells in the middle of the forest,
have you lost interest in your devotees?*

The women of Nanjangudu
wear dolled-up pleats
and golden bangles.
The women, who wear bangles, have come.
They've come to do **arati** to Nanjunda.
O Hara, they wave it.
O Shiva, they wave it.
O Nanjunda, they wave it.
Brother Nanjunda, whose crown is the moon,
have you lost interest in your devotees?

*O Shiva, who picks the fragrant leaves
from the burrows of the field?
Shri Kanthamūrthi aren't you drawn to the fragrance of the leaf.*[57]
*Who is the mother of that which is born of the earth?
Lord Nanjunda, whose crown is the moon,
have you lost interest in your devotees?*

Sir, there is a flock of 770 million peacocks
on Nanjayya's boat
and on your chariot.
A flock of 770 million peacocks sit there.
They take the ghee and gave it to Shankara.
They give it to Shiva.
They bow low and offer it.
They prostrate and offer it.
They stretch out and offer it.
Sai Sai, Lord Nanjunda whose crown is the moon,
have you lost interest in your devotees?

You are the jasmine and the maruga.
You are the champaka and the sunflower[58] *with which*
I adorn my head, please speak up.
O Hara, please speak up.
O Guru, please speak up.
Get up and come to the hill.
Hara, Hara, Hara, Hara, Nanjunda Linga,
have you lost interest in your wife?

She spreads her seven tongues,
opens her fiery eyes,
dishevels her long hair,
and approachs the one with blessed throat,
Nanjunda of Nanjangudu
in her ferocious form.
Then, she lovingly calls
to Nanjunda.

She says, "O brother-in-law, I am yours."
She says, "O Shankara, I am yours."
Who can be trusted in this life, Sir?
You aren't thinking about your wife.
O brother-in-law, remember your wife.
Brother Nanjunda whose crown is the moon,
have you lost interest in us?

O guru, the cock has crowed.
Light has come to the world.
O king, how long is this sweet sleep?
O Shankara guru,
How long is this sweet sleep?
Brother Nanjunda whose crown is the moon,
have you lost interest in your devotees?

O Shiva, many people have come
from the northern region.
They've come from the northern country, O guru.
They have fallen down and are begging for boons.
They fallen down and are asking you
for a boon, O King Nanjunda.
Sir, get up and give the boons.
Give it to them, Sir.
Nanjundesha, who dwells in the middle of the forest,
have you lost interest in your devotees?

About seventy clicks from here
in beautiful Nanjangudu
there is an ippe orchard alongside the river.[59]
O God, there is an ippe orchard
alongside the river in Nanjangudu.
O God, who has drunk the poison, please speak up.
O Nanjunda Linga, who dwells in the middle of the forest,
have you lost interest in your devotees?

O Nanjunda Linga,
why are you angry with your devotee?
There is a lamp pillar with a small peacock at the top.
O guru, there is a peacock lamp.
You saw the peacock, your elder wife's body,
and thought it was nice.
O Swami, Nanjundappa, who dwells in the middle of the forest,
have you lost interest in your wife?

Jallagombina Basava
of Mallana Mule

be tender and come to Mysore.
Lord Nanjunda, whose crown is the moon,
have you lost interest in your wife?

You are the champaka flower, with which
I adorn my hair.
Rajendra, please speak up.
O Shankara, please speak up.
Guru Nanjunda, whose crown is the moon,
have you lost interest in your devotees?

You are from the solar lineage.
O Sun, Nanjunda Linga,
you've enjoyed your hoes, now come back.[60]
O Hara, please come.
O Shankara, please come.
O guru, please come.
Get up and come to the mountain.
Hara Hara Hara Hara Nanjunda Linga,
have you lost interest in your wife?

Uttanahalli Maramma, the fire-starter,
calls to Nanjunda, who lives in the middle of the forest,
three times.
She calls to him three times.

Then she turns around
and returns to her sister's temple.

She says, "O sister, the maya-maker
Chamundi of the hill,
put your glorious feet on my head,"
to her older sister.
Then both the elder and younger sisters, depressed,
go to her fancy bed and sleep.

Tripping over Himself, He Runs to Chamundi of the Hill's House[61]

On this side of Nanjangudu,
Nanjunda
is cuddling between his two wives.
The fierce one
concentrates and listens to
the words spoken by Uttanahalli Maramma.
He wakes up quickly and
listens to the call of
his sister-in-law, Uttanahalli Maramma, the fire-starter.

*Lord Nanjunda, who dwells in the middle of the forest,
hears this with his own two ears, and
the memory saddens him.
Remembering her, he feels great pain.*

O Chamundi of the hill,
who is like my wife,
she made Uttanahalli call me.

*It'll be great
if I can go to my ho Chamundi's house
I'd have to be a horrible person
not to go.
But what sort of trick can I do to be able to go to Chamundi's house?
If I get up on the left side,
there is young Deviri. That'd be trouble.
If I get up on the right side,
there is little Somaji. That'd be trouble.
But if I stay here,
there will trouble from my ho on the hill.*

*There is trouble from all three wives.
"The night is always trouble for the day."[62]
Chicks are always trouble . . . a lot of trouble.[63]
O God, chicks are trouble . . . a lot of trouble . . . just like death.[64]
Leaving one alive, which of the three should be killed, God?*

Who amongst the three wives
should die?
Who should live?
My wives, who I married first,
they ought to die immediately.
And goodness and fulfillment should come
to Chamundi of the hill.
After such a short time I can't leave the
one who made love to me and cares for me.
She trusted me, and even if my breath leaves me,
I can't leave my life's breath.

If I get up and go
to Chamundi of the hill's house . . .

My housewives
are leaning against me, the Eagle Stone.[65]
They sleep cuddling up against me.
How can I go about
sneaking away like a thief in the night? O Lord!

Ah-ha![66]
In order to get an arm's length
between me and my wives, Big Deviri and little Somaji . . .

[I will pretend to be] bitten by mosquitoes during the day.
[I will pretend to be] bitten my bed bugs during the night.

Deviri, roll to that side.

Mosquitoes are buzzing.
Bed begs are biting.
Your house is ruined.
Wife, slide to the side.

Somaji sees
Nanjunda's antics.
It seems like mosquitoes are biting
her husband Nanjunda.
It seems like bed bugs are attacking him.

So, she leaves an arm's length of space.
She sleeps on the right side and rolls to the left,
and Deviri does the opposite.

Slowly Swami gets
an arm's length of space.

Nanjunda Linga thinks,
"Today is a good day.
Today, I will be happy."
Nanjunda thinks,
"My housewives
have left enough space,
but if I leave and go out,
at any time, they could realize that I have gone.
I should make a believable husband-dummy
to lie down, and then I should go."
He takes the pillow on which his head had laid
and laid it between his two wives.

Brother Nanjunda sits near
his two wives.
His two wives are mumbling "Husband, Husband."
Quarrelling in their sleep,
they hug the pillow tightly.
"Wives, hold this pillow
as if it were your dear and affectionate
husband Nanjunda Linga,
and don't let go
until I return from going
to my ho Chamundi's house.
Girls, hug this old pillow,
as if it were me, your husband."

He thinks,
"I've tricked my housewives.
But I don't have any money
to give to my ho Chamundi,
if I go to her house.

I don't have any money.
But, God, I can't think about abandoning her.
I have to go to the house of
Chamundi, the illusion-maker."

So, he comes to the temple
of the seven-hooded serpent Kalinga,
and he says,
"Hey Kalinga Serpent,
are you resting on your treasure chest
with your seven hoods open?
A great illness has come to
your elder sister, Big Deviri.
I can't give her any medicine because I don't have any money.
Sir, give me some money."

Brother Shesha says,
"Take some and go."

Nanjunda thinks, "Today is a good day,"
as he breaks open the large temple donation box[67]
and stuffs loads of money into his bag.

Then he runs away quickly
like a little lamb.

He leaves the chariot street, but
where does he go?

He comes to the market
and haggles.

Nanjunda thinks,
"If I have to go to the house of
my ho Chamundi of the hill,
I shouldn't take money.
I should buy her a golden ornament and then go."

He goes to a gold shop and haggles.
He buys a nice diamond earring
for his ho Chamundi.
He buys her a nose ring.
He buys her a colorful waist-chain.
He buys a toe ring.
He buys a chain anklet.[68]
He buys a locking waist chain.
He wraps them in a box and
puts them in his bag.
He buys a sari fit for a queen.
He wraps it in a box and
puts it in his bag.
He takes round jasmine and Mysore jasmine,
betel nut and betel leaves, which had been picked and cut,
and sweet limestone from Nagamangala, and
wraps them in a box.

O God, King Nanjunda is coming
to the house of Chamundi.

Nandi sees him as he was coming from [the market].[69]
"Brother-in-law, why are you coming [this way]?"

"Oh brother-in-law, Nandi, don't you know?
It seems like a tumor
has come to the girl in Mysore.
Sir, I'm going to give her medicine."

"Of course, Nanjunda.
Your name is known far and wide [as a healer],
but when I look at your bag it seems quite full.
What is that, Sir?"

"This is medicine."

"Ugh, you just take whatever you want.
And now you are going to that ho Chamundi's house.

Brother-in-law, shame on you.
Disgrace has come upon your name."

"O God, I thought no one would see;
so, I came.
But wouldn't you know you showed up: Nandi.
Nandi, if you allow me this one time,
I will give you a bell and tie it around your neck."

Basavanna replied, "O.k. Fine" and let him go.

The seven-hooded serpent, Kalinga,
saw this from his door and said,
"Brother-in-law, where are you going?"

"O brother-in-law, Kalinga, sir,[70]
do you know Kare Bilayya?
He has been holding court for six months,
and for three months all the people have been assembled.
He sent me a summons that said
'If Nanjunda doesn't come,
I will fine him.'

Therefore, I must go
O brother-in-law Kalinga."

"Brother-in-law, I can't allow you to go.
My sister is coming; so, you wait here."

Nanjunda becomes furious.
He picks up a stick and gives him three welts.
He watches the snake squirm as he curses him.
Then he says, "Let me go, and I will give you
an annual festival
called Subrahmanya Shrishti."[71]

He runs tripping over himself
to the house of Chamundi of the hill.

He can't see the stones,
He can't see the weeds.
He can't see the forest.
He can't see the houses.
He can't see the villages or cities.
He can't see the stream or the boats.
Tripping over himself, he climbs the hill.
He knocks on the door of Chamundi's house.
In the darkness of night,
he can't see on either side
from the front of the pearl's house.
He knocks on the diamond's door and
says "Chamundi, come and open the door."

Chamundi
immediately hears him,
gets up from the fancy bed, and
comes to meet her strong man.

She comes extremely quickly
and with her nose ring glimmering
opens the door.
Then she brings the water pot,
washes his feet,
touches her own eyes, and smiles.

First Chamundamma
followed by Nanjunda Linga
goes and sits down
on the golden bed, O Swami.

Nanjunda says,
"Girl, now that I've come, I can't leave.
Baby, my lil' parrot, come here.
Golden one, you are mine, come here.
Rambe,[72] *Chamundi, come here."*
Then he pulls her close.
He makes the young Chamundi love him,
and she is happy.

Batting Your Eyes, You called

At some point over there [in Nanjangudu],
Deviri had woken up and
Brother Nanjunda's wife Somaji woke up too.
They said we should wake Nanjunda,
so he can go bathe.

The pillow rolled
like it was a sack of lentils.

Deviri sees that
and says,
"O Somaji, that thief has tricked us.
His life ought to end.
His father ought to die.
His family tree ought to wither.
He really tricked us!
He went to Chamundi's house."

She comes to the hill,
peeps through the window of the temple,
and sees Nanjunda and Chamundi
sitting and talking about
all their dreams and disappointments.
After seeing this, anger sprouted,
and Deviri becomes furious.
Then Deviri scolds Chamundi.
"Batting your eyes, you called
my unwitting husband, Nanjunda.
Ugh! You, my co-widow, you've called my husband.
Now your eyeballs ought to burst!"

Chamundi becomes furious and screams.
Then Chamundi and Deviri start fighting with each other.
Nanjunda is watching and says,
"Uh-oh! This girl won't stop.

And that girl won't stop.
They are both Parvati."
Then he leaves from their fight.

Like Gandhari[73]
he left without a sound.

I Can Raise the Dead!

Nanjunda goes to Nanjangudu,
and then his wife Deviri arrives.
She grabs his hand,
"Oh no, Nanjunda . . .

*You went to the house
of that terrible buffalo and cat-eating demoness.
And now you come back here?
Stop! Just stop outside!"*

Having said that, she rips off his rosary.
And even if he wanted to clean his face,
she wouldn't even give him a handkerchief.

*She pushes him outside
as naked as the day he was born.*

Nanjunda spots
the flag cloth on a chariot that was being built.
He takes it and ties it around his waist.
Then, he goes to Brahma Loka.
He says, "Brahma, go and tell
my wife a false *shastra*."
Then, he goes to Chamundi's temple,
and says [to Chamundi], "You should dress like fortuneteller[74]
and come to Nanjangudu."
Then, he goes back to Nanjangudu
and lies down pretending to be dead.
Deviri and Somaji see him.

*"Nanjunda Linga
is dead,
making us widows
in our young age!"*

They say this, bursting into tears, and crying.
Then Brahma shows up and says,

"Woman, this is a bad day.
Your husband's breath has gone."
Then he gives them the false *shastra* and
goes back to his Brahma realm.
Chamundi sees all of this
and disguises herself as the fortuneteller.

"I can raise the dead!
I can kill the living!
I can recite any mantra or yantra
from every shastra I've ever seen."
She announces this prophecy
in the streets of Nanjangudu.

Deviramma sees her
and says,
"Little sister, I don't know who she is
but she says she can raise the dead.
She says she can kill the living.
Our husband Nanjunda's life-breath has gone.
Call her."

"Mother, Mother, Come here Mother." She called.
"Mother recite a *shastra*," she said.

Chamundi replied,
"Madam, which *shastra* should I recite?
Your own mouths have cursed
the goddess Chamundi.
'You put it in the belly of a Holiya
after taking it from the belly of a Madiga.'[75]
What you said [to her] was wrong.
You need to make a sin offering to Chamundi,[76]
and your husband will raise."

The two wives listened to her words.
"O Mother Chamundi,
my curse was absolutely wrong.
Let us all have the status of married women.
Let my husband live in your house for six months,

and let him live in our house for six months.
No make our husband rise."
Saying that, Deviramma makes a sin-offering.

Nanjunda Linga Swami
arises with a sigh.

Then Chamundi disappears.

Nanjunda seems like he didn't know what was going on,
"Deviri, why are you sitting near us?"

She answers,
"Oh, Swami your breath had left you!
We prayed to Chamundi.
You ought to go to Chamundi's temple."

Swami Nanjunda Linga says,
"O Deviri, they belong to one caste,
and we belong to another caste.
They eat buffaloes and sheep like they do in the palace.
I shouldn't go."

"Swami, please, sir,
You need to go to Chamundi's hill,
if you don't go, your breath will leave you!"
Saying that, Deviri pushes him out.

"Deviri, if you want me to go to Chamundi's hill,
Give me your diamond earring,
Give me your nose-ring,
Give me your head-ornament,
Give me your pearl necklace,
Give me your toe-ring,
Give me your golden bangle,
[Give me] the gold, which your father Devendra has given
    you.
Put your precious gold in my bag."
Saying this, he takes it all.

Then, he, who dwells in Goralapuri,
goes to Chamundi's hill.

While sleeping on the round arm of
Big Mother Chamundi of the hill,
he tells her,
"If my wives Big Deviri and little Somaji
were to see you, they'd be very happy.
But you always stay here on this stone hill.
He tells her to come to Nanjangudu and brings her there.
He tells Deviri,
"Please give her a plot of land
in Mullana Mule."

Deviri says,
"O little sister, Chamundi of the hill,
since you married our husband, you're our little sister.
Live in the Kapini-Kaveri
and be worshipped there."

Deviramma, who is called Big,
blesses her there.

Dharma Should Be with Us

O Mother, who wears the colorful sari,
who wears the colorful bangles,
who wears the round-eyed toe-ring,
O Mother Chamundi.

She looks nice and round
like a lemon.

She killed Mahisha
and dwells on the middle of the hill.

The seven sisters met and
came to the mortal world.
They stood in the middle of the kingdom.
They were worshipped
by the communities of the borderlands.

Mother look after your children.
Protect us, Mother.

Balannadu sulannadu[77]
Gracefully, O God!
Gracefully, she tied
the sari with flair.

O Shiva, who has tied his ox to the bhuja tree.
The beauty of the black-throated one,
who is like a pearl,
whose mouth is like a large water pot,
who wears the hair bun [drawn] on her cheek,[78]
the beauty, who looks in the mirror,
O Mother of the golden tank in Ukkuda.

Yadavale Banuvale
On the left side of Nanjangudu,
there is the big Dundalakere
very close to Chamalapura

O Mother Chamundi,
you're the one who protects this place.

O Mother, your innocent children have come.
They are asking for a boon from you.
They anointed your head,
O Mother, who protects us.

They make a kannadi on the small tiger.
O great Mother, they light the camphor to you.
They put the freshly bloomed flower on your head.
O Mother, who protects us.

O Mother, please give a boon.
Please give a boon.
They anoint your head with flowers.
Please give a boon.

They gave the incense and lamps to God.
They gave the incense to the Goddess.
Now, you give the flower,
which was kept on your head to us.[79]

O Mother, who wears beautiful colors,
who wears bangles,
who wears the golden round-eyed toe-ring,
O Chamundi, come, come.

Big Deviri, Little Somaji, and
Chamundi of the hill
dwell in Nanjangudu.
Shiva, you have married these three women, and
your devotees have come.
Now give a boon and
give them wealth.

Swami now dwells
in Nanjangudu.

*Merit comes to all
who have told the story of Chamundi and
to all who have heard her story.
Dharma should be with us.*

Appendix

"Wodeyar Origin Narrative" from Great Kings of Mysore

Yaduraya Comes from Dwaraka and the Details of his Dream

According to instructions received from Shri Krishna in a dream, Yaduraya left the borders of Dwaraka. He reached the goddess, who dwells in the Vindya mountains. While he performed austerities there, Vindhyavasini, was pleased and said, "I have lived on the Mahabala Mountain [another name for Chamundi Hill], which is between the Kaveri and Kapila, and there I'm called Chamundeshwari [Lady Chamundi]. If you go to Mahabala Mountain and worship me, you will marry the daughter of the king of the city named Mysore, which is next to the mountain, and this city will become yours." After the goddess's command, Yaduraya awoke happy, and he, along with his younger brother Krishnaraya, left for the Vindhya mountains. They came through Vijayanagara to Yadavagiri [Melukote]. They bathed in the temple tank and took *darshana* of many gods including Yoga Narasimha, Lord Narayana, and Lord Cheluva Narayana, who was the god of great king Yadu Shekhara's family. After crossing the Kaveri River and climbing the Mahabala Mountain, he worshipped the goddess Chamundi, who is *adishakti* [primordial power], the mother of the universe, and dwells on the mountain. He bowed with devotion to Shri Kantheshwara [Shiva], who is the lord of Bhukailasa [Nanjangud], which is 20 miles from the mountain. That night Yaduraya slept peacefully, meditating on the feet of the goddess.

At daybreak, the goddess came in the form of a woman and said, "Go to the southeastern portion of my mountain first thing tomorrow morning. Just as you have worshipped me, worship the goddess Jwalajjihwa [Uttanahalli], who killed Raktabija and resides there. Then, go to the Kodibhairava shrine beside the temple tank inside the Shiva temple worshipped by the Sage Trinabindu, which is on the east side of Mysore City and stay there. At that time, a man wearing the robes of a *jangama* and a *linga* will come. When he sees you, he will say a few words. If you do as he says, everything I promised you in the Vindya mountains will become yours." After she said this, Chamundeshwari vanished.

The Blessing of Shri Shri Kantheshwara

Yaduraya awoke and told his brother about the dream. Following the instructions of the goddess, he joyously worshipped Jwalamuhki [Uttanahalli]. Then after breakfast, they left and waited at the Kodibhairava shrine near the tank behind Mysore's Trineshwara temple. A great *jangama*, who was wearing a saffron robe and a *linga* came just as the goddess Chamundeshwari had told in the vision. When he saw the *jangama*, Yaduraya joyously arose and honored the ascetic by touching his lotus feet. He sat down and thought, "The words spoken by the Goddess in the dream are coming true." Then the great *jangama* asked in the words of the ordinary folk, "Prince, who are you? Where are you from? What are your intentions?" Then Yaduraya told him his own history and said, "I have been expecting the *darshana* of your feet as was prophesied by the goddess Chamundeshwari. I will follow your every command."

Upon hearing Yaduraya's words, the great *jangama* said, "Prince, I will tell you a secret. Previously, a valiant, brave, and wealthy king named Shuradevaraya was born in the lineage of Bhoja from the Gautama gotra in the city of Mathura. He, along with his family, left that city and came to Karnataka, gained wealth and the kingdom of Mysore, and lived happily because of the blessings of Shri Chamundeshwari. In the lineage of Shuradevaraya, a king named Chamaraya was born and ruled the kingdom. He had a jewel of a daughter, but he died without a son. The city was without a king. Now, an evil general named Maranayaka is threatening Devajammani, the wife of the deceased king. With my blessings, you will gain the power to kill that wicked man. Another great *jangama* will come and give you all the instructions in detail. If you follow this, not only will you marry the king's daughter, but you will obtain kingship and your lineage will prosper eternally (literally: "will become like the sun and the moon"). You will live happily. If you do whatever that great *jangama* requests, I will be very happy." After saying this, he vanished. When Yaduraya and Krishnaraya saw this, they were astonished and determined "Shri Kantheshwara, who lives in Nanjangudu, just came here to this hill in the form of this great *jangama*). If we fulfill these commands given by the goddess then just like the goddess Shri Chamundeshwari is our family goddess, Nanjunda Kantheshwara will become our family god." And they worshipped him.

The Dream of the Devajammanni, the Wife of the King of Mysore

At daybreak Parameshvara [Shiva] came to the suffering wife of Chamaraja in dream because she could not bear the troubles caused by Maranayaka. He said, "O Queen, don't worry. Calm your mind and listen to my words of comfort. Two princes, brothers born into the lineage of Yadu and the Atreya *gotra* have come to the Kodibhairava shrine of Mysore City. The eldest prince is a suitable match to marry your daughter. Send a wise and friendly man to them to tell them about all the things that have happened here. Have him bring them to the city. Give your daughter to the eldest prince. If you do this, you will have great peace. He will kill all of your enemies with his martial prowess. He will rule your kingdom with righteousness. He will have many descendants." After he said this, he vanished. The queen immediate arose and was happy. She woke up her daughter and told her the events of the dream. The two summoned a man, who, as had been described in the dream, had a peaceful countenance and wore a *linga*. They told him what was said in the dream and sent him to the princes. Excited, she called two more servants and said, "Servants, immediately go to the Bhairava temple, which is beside the tank of the city. Go so that no one knows and find out physical features, intellect, and qualities of the men who are there, and tell us with whom they speak and events about which they speak." Then she sent them away. As they had been commanded, the servants went immediately. They heard the words that the two princes spoke to the *jangama*. They observed their youthful form and beautiful qualities until they became tired. Then they quickly returned. The servants properly and secretively narrated all these observations to the queen, and she was immensely happy. Meanwhile, the great *jangama* enquired about the *gotra*, culture, and family of the princes. He asked about their health and wealth. The *jangama*, then, in a condensed manner, told them about the event that had transpired in the city, the queen's heartfelt desires, and the brave deeds that needed to be done, saying, "I will come again and take you inside the fort." Then he came to the palace, and as the *jangama* was narrating all the events that took place, Queen Dēvajammanni thought, "All the prophesies that were made by Parameshwara, are true." They were confirmed by the great *jangama*, and she was happy. In order to find out the next thing to do, she called the two scribes, named Timmarasayya and Naranayya, who had been very close to her for a long time. She thoroughly told them all these events. She told them, "I will make whatever arrangements are necessary in order for you, with your intelligence, to bring the princes here." Then she sent them away.

Yaduraya Enters the City

The two scribes received the command of the queen, and they convinced a few brave men to sign a treaty of peace and became enemies of the general Maranayaka. Secretly, these people, who were now close to them, were stationed with weapons near the gatekeepers at the palace gate. Then Timmarasayya and Naranayya, along with the one who wore the *linga* went to the Bhairava temple to talk with the princes. They conversed about all the events with the princes and told them, "Kill your enemies either by your strength or by deceit. If you do this, all of us will be happy." Having heard those words, the princes excitedly joined the three men from the palace. When they entered the city, the gatekeepers, who were allied with Maranayaka, attempted to stop them from entering the gates of the city; however, the gatekeepers were quickly killed, and the brothers entered the city and arrived in the courtyard of the palace per the queen's command.

The Assassination of Maranayaka

Maranayaka heard what happened and, along with this army, came and confronted the brothers. Maranayaka, holding a sword, shouted, "Who are you? Where are you from? Why have you killed my men? You've made a big mistake, and, now, I will kill you both." But Yaduraya and brave men who were installed in secret by the scribes engaged their enemy. The brothers' coalition quickly killed Maranayaka and his allies. They had obtained the goddess of wealth. Then they remembered Shri Chamundeshwari and Shri Kantheshwara and prayed. When they entered the city, as the two scribes proclaimed their victory in battle to their leader, Queen Devajammanni. They were then commanded to bring Yaduraya into the royal court of the palace with the honor worthy of a king.

The Marriage of Yaduraya

Yaduraya honored his army and then sent them away. He called the two scribes, the *linga*-wearing *jangama*, and his younger brother. He bowed to the queen, who was behind the curtain in her inner chamber, and sat down and crossed his arms. The queen looked at that prince and was pleased. She lovingly said, "Prince, you with the blessing of Shri Chamundeshwari were the answer to all my problems. You have obtained the goddess of kingship without obstacles; according to the scriptures, take the hand of my daugher Devajammanni. Be happy, and stay here protecting this kingdom." She gave him clothes and flower and leaf ornaments and ordered the scribes and other people to follow the orders of Yaduraya. She decorated the city, erected many canopies, prepared all the things which were necessary for marriage—clothes, ornaments, etc.—and invited everyone, including their relatives. At the time, which the astrologer had said was auspicious, according to the tradition of the palace, she worshipped Shri Kantheshwara and Shri Chamundeshwari, who were the family gods. The bride worshipped Indra's wife, Sacidevi, and Queen Devajammanni fulfilled her vow and, through her cousin Kenchalagudu Nanjarajayya, gave her daughter, who looked like Krishna's wife Rukmani, to Yaduraya. Yaduraya after completing a pilgrimage to Kashi (Benares), put on all the ornaments, looking like Shri Krishna, and they celebrated the marriage festival.

The Royal Coronation of Yaduraya

In the auspicious time on Monday the 5th day of the waxing moon in the month of Vaishakha in the year Pramathi, which happened in 1322 year of the Shalivahana shaka, Yaduraya was crowned king of Mysore. He having been offered the regions, the treasury, and the royal signet ring, Yaduraya doubled in brilliance. When he was ruling the kingdom, he appointed the work of the palace correspondence to the two scribes, who had done the highly secret work. Having made it their family tradition as requested by the *jangama*, who had been pleased by these actions, they commanded that all the rulers who had the royal coronation be called by the name Wodeyar and that saffron cloth, which is symbol of the *jangamas*, be included in their flag. Having come to know that his father-in-law's cousin, named Karagalli Shantarajayya, would oppose him, he curbed him. He married his younger brother Krishnaraya to Shantarajayya's daughter, and Krishnaraya became the ruler of the village of Karagalli.

Notes

Chapter One

1. P. K. Rajashekhara, *Bettada Chamundi* (Mysore: Ta. Vem. Smaraka Granthamale, 1972), 25, 51. The elements of the *Chamundi of the Hill* story highlighted by Rajashekhara align well with a Segalian model for the analysis of myth. Jon Mills, "Deconstructing Myth," in *Explaining, Interpreting, and Theorizing Religion and Myth: Contributions in Honor of Robert A. Segal*, eds. Nikolas P. Rouebekas and Thomas Ryba (Leiden: Brill, 2020), 233–47.

2. Roderick Main, "Myth, Synchronicity, and the Physical World," in *Explaining, Interpreting, and Theorizing Religion and Myth: Contributions in Honor of Robert A. Segal*, eds. Nikolas P. Rouebekas and Thomas Ryba (Leiden: Brill, 2020), 249.

3. Robert A. Segal, *Myth: A Very Short Introduction* (New York: Oxford University Press, 2015), 3–5; see also Laura Feldt, "Fictioning Myths and Mythic Fictions: The Standard-Babylonian Gilgameš Epic and Questions of Heroism, Myth, and Fiction," in *Explaining, Interpreting, and Theorizing Religion and Myth: Contributions in Honor of Robert A. Segal*, eds. Nikolas P. Rouebekas and Thomas Ryba (Leiden: Brill, 2020), 282–98. See also Roderick Main, "Myth, Synchronicity, and the Physical World," in *Explaining, Interpreting, and Theorizing Religion and Myth: Contributions in Honor of Robert A. Segal*, eds. Nikolas P. Rouebekas and Thomas Ryba (Leiden: Brill, 2020), 248–62.

4. This is typical of Puranic narratives. For example, see Travis L. Smith, "Renewing the Ancient: the *Kāśikhaṇḍa* and Śaiva Varanasi," *Acta Orientalia Vilnensia* 8.1 (2007), 83–108.

5. P. K. Rajashekhara, *Bettada Chamundi* (Mysore: Ta. Vem. Smaraka Granthamale, 1972), 53. Compare with A. K. Ramanujan, *Speaking of Shiva* (New York: Penguin, 1993) or H. S. Shivaprakash, *I Keep Vigil of Rudra: The Vachanas* (New Delhi: Penguin, 2010).

6. In his introduction, Rajashekara uses the first four lines of the opening hymn as an example. In that verse, the first two lines resemble the *raga* Anandabhairavi, and the second couplet is similar to Shankarabharana. P. K. Rajashekhara, *Bettada Chamundi* (Mysore: Ta. Vem. Smaraka Granthamale, 1972), 53.

7. Compare with A. K. Ramanujan, *Speaking of Shiva* (New York: Penguin, 1993); H. S. Shivaprakash, *I Keep Vigil of Rudra: The Vachanas* (New Delhi: Penguin, 2010); Indira Vishwanathan Peterson, *Poems to Śiva: The Hymns of the Tamil Saints* (Delhi: Motilal Banarsidass Publishers, 1991); Archana Venkatesan, trans. *A Hundred Measures of Time, Tiruviruttam* (New York: Penguin Books, 2014); or the Shakta poetry in Rachell Fell McDermott, *Singing to the Goddess: Poems to Kālī and Umā from Bengal* (New York: Oxford University Press, 2001). It is important to keep in mind that the Kamsale performers are devotees of Shiva, particularly in his form as Madeshwara, "lord of the seven hills," and not Chamundi. K. K. Presad, C. N. Ramachandran, and L. N. Bhat *Male Madeshwara: A Kannada Oral Epic as Sung by Hebbani Madayya and His Troupe.* Collected by. New Delhi: Sahitya Akademi.

8. Freda Matchett "The Purāṇas" *The Blackwell Companion to Hinduism,* ed. Gavin Flood (London: Blackwell Publishing, 2003), 138.

9. Quoted in Freda Matchett "The Purāṇas" *The Blackwell Companion to Hinduism* ed. Gavin Flood (London: Blackwell Publishing, 2003), 138.

10. Yi-Fu Tuan, *Topophilia: A Study of Environmental Perceptions, Attitudes, and Values* (New York: Columbia University Press, 1990), 4. See also Anne Feldhaus, *Connected Places: Region, Pilgrimage, and Geographical Imagination in India* (New York: Palgrave Macmillan, 2003), 5.

11. Space is another category of inquiry that is discussed in chapter 5. Space is more open-ended and is "an engaged and dynamic arena for religion." Kim Knott, "From Locality to Location and Back Again: A Spatial Journey in the Study of Religion," *Religion* 39, no. 2 (2009): 156.

12. My presentation of locality is inspired by both Knott and Appadurai. Kim Knott, "From Locality to Location and Back Again: A Spatial Journey in the Study of Religion," *Religion* 39, no. 2 (2009); Arjuna Appadurai, *Modernity at Large: Cultural Dimensions of Globalization* (Minneapolis, MN: University of Minnesota Press, 1996), 183–84.

13. As Appadurai explains, the process of locality production is "inherently colonizing, in the sense that it involves the assertion of socially (often ritually) organized power over places and setting that are views as potentially chaotic or rebellious." Arjuna Appadurai, *Modernity at Large: Cultural Dimensions of Globalization* (Minneapolis: University of Minnesota Press, 1996), 183–84.

14. Arjuna Appadurai, *Modernity at Large: Cultural Dimensions of Globalization* (Minneapolis: University of Minnesota Press, 1996), 180.

15. I use community here as an informal shorthand as the broader narrative of the Chamundi and Nanjunda transcend any one distinct community, religious tradition, and/or caste; however, when the songs are sung by people who identify with different castes or religions, the stories are told in different ways. See chapter 4, especially the notes, for examples of the songs from other castes and communities. I have never witnessed the inclusion of these songs within the temples, which operate according the Shaivagamas, brahminic ritual handbooks. Inside the temples, the story of the Goddess is told through recittions of the *Devi Mahatmya* (also called the *Durga Saptashati*).

16. Anne Feldhaus, *Connected Places: Region, Pilgrimage, and Geographical Imagination in India* (New York: Palgrave Macmillan, 2003), 5–6.

17. See Caleb Simmons, "History, Heritage, and Myth: Local Historical Imagination in the Fight to Preserve Chamundi Hill in Mysore City," *Worldviews* 22 (2018): 216–37.

18. In my final year of working on this book, I returned to Mysore to see that massive construction projects had begun on top of the hill.

19. In Promode Kumar Misra, *Cultural Profile of Mysore* (Mysore: Archaeological Survey of India, 1978), 62, Morab states that Wodeyar king Krishnaraja III gave land grants to Tamil (Smarta) brahmins in 1819, which was the official invitation of the brahmin priests. However, in a book-length study of the temple coauthored with B. B. Goswami, Morab says that it was in 1848 that the Shivarchaka priests were officially replaced by the Tamil Dikshita brahmins. B. B. Goswami, and S. G. Morab, *Chamundesvari Temple in Mysore* (Calcutta: Anthropological Survey of India, 1991), 2. Epigraphic evidence supports both claims. For more on Krishnaraja Wodeyar III's program of expanding the religious scope of his court, see Caleb Simmons, *Devotional Sovereignty: Kingship and Religion in India* (New York: Oxford University Press, 2020).

20. Shivarchakas still play an important role in the daily ritual life of the temple and in the important festivals that take place on the hill. There are also several other priestly castes that serve in the temple, including, in descending order of ritual hierarchy, Hoysala Karnataka brahmins, Smarta (Ayyar) brahmins, and Lingayatas. For more on the dynamics of caste in Mysore temples, see G. Saraswathi, *The Study of Socio-Economic Conditions of the Temple Priests of Southern Mysore* (Calcutta: Anthropological Survey of India, 2000).

21. Bihani Sarkar, *Heroic Shāktism: The Cult of Durgā in Ancient Indian Kingship* (Oxford: Oxford University Press, 2017), 61, 116, 254; Michael W. Meister, "Regional Variations in Mātṛkā Conventions," *Artibus Asiae* 46, nos. 3/4 (1986), 233–62.

22. These are similar to the small votive charms called *milagros* in the Mexican Catholic tradition.

23. Kyathanahalli Ramanna, *Subbakka Haadida Nanjundeshwara Kavya* (Bangalore: Dinakara Prakashana), 10.

24. Kyathanahalli Ramanna, *Subbakka Haadida Nanjundeshwara Kavya* (Bangalore: Dinakara Prakashana), 7.

25. Kyathanahalli Ramanna, *Subbakka Haadida Nanjundeshwara Kavya* (Bangalore: Dinakara Prakashana), 5–6. http://jssonline.org/sri-suttur-math/ accessed on Aug 22, 2020. This is the foundation story from the Sutturu Matha's website:

> The founding of the Math can be traced to a fascinating historical event. When Adi Jagadguru Sri Shivarathreeshwara Shivayogiji was doing penance on a rock in the middle of the Kapila River, King Rajaraja of the Chola dynasty, who was on his way to fight a war with King Rachamalla IV of the Gangas of Talakad, was passing nearby. At this point, King Rajaraja's horse changed direction and brought the King to the place where Adi Jagadguru Sri Shivayogiji was doing penance. Sri Shivarahtreeshwara Shivayogi made King Rajaraja realise the futility of war. The King heeded to the words of Sri Shivayogi and thus ended the hostility between Rachamalla IV of the Gangas of Talakad and Rajaraja of Cholas, which was about to break up into a large-scale war. The two kings became friends and later at the request of King Rajaraja, the seer graciously consented to establish a Math on the banks of the River Kapila at Suttur." http://sutturmath.org/sutturu-srikshetra/ accessed on Aug 22, 2020.

26. Kyathanahalli Ramanna, *Subbakka Haadida Nanjundeshwara Kavya* (Bangalore: Dinakara Prakashana), 5.

27. In this tradition, Shiva is characterized as "elderly, hemp-smoking, [and] poverty-stricken. Rachel Fell McDermott, *Mother of My Heart, Daughter of My Dreams: Kali and Uma in the Devotional Poetry of Bengal* (New York: Oxford University Press, 2001), 148. For examples of this, see the *Āgamanī* and *Vijayā* poems in Rachel Fell McDermott, *Singing to the Goddess: Poems to Kālī and Umā from Bengal* (New York: Oxford University Press, 2001), 123–51.

28. In all the different versions of this story that exist, Nanjunda has two wives, and Deviri is always the eldest. The younger goddess, however, is known by different names, including Parvati and Kaveri. P. K. Rajashekhara, *Bettada Chamundi* (Mysore: Ta. Vem. Smaraka Granthamale, 1972), 37. Masti Venkatesh Iyengar, *Karnataka Janapada Sahitya* (Bangalore: Jivana Karyalaya, 1937), 26–27.

29. In many ways, the situatedness of goddesses has been acknowledged even in the ways devotees speak about sacred sites associated with female

deities. Common nomenclature typically refers to sacred sites in general as *tirtha*s or "crossing places." Important pilgrimage sites relating to goddesses or the Goddess, however, are called *pitha*s, "seats" or "place." While this is not a hard and fast rule, the common use of these terms demonstrates the importance of goddesses in their locale and their relationship with the material landscape that they imbue with sacrality and power. The term *shakti pitha* is most commonly deployed in reference to the sites where the body parts of Sati are said to have fallen as Shiva, her distraught consort, carried her charred remains back to their mountain abode after she immolated herself on the sacrificial fire of her father, Daksha, sacrificial fire in the (in)famous Puranic tale. There are various accounts that relate the number and places of these *shakti pithas* that range from the most common 51 sites to larger groups of 108 and sometimes even more. See Dineschandra Sircar, *The Śākta Pīṭhas* (Delhi: Motilal Banarsidass, 1973), and Kathleen M. Erndl, *Victory to the Mother* (New York: Oxford University Press, 1993). Regardless of the number of shrines associated with this myth, the site and the surrounding landscape embody the sacred power that imbued the body of the goddess. In many cases, the landscape itself is the embodiment of the anatomy of the sacred: hills are the breasts of the goddess; cleft stones become her *yoni* (vulva), etc. Often these sites are very difficult to reach and prior to modern transportation would require a very arduous pilgrimage. This was also the case at Chamundi Hill until Dodda Devaraja Wodeyar installed the steps leading up to the temple in the 17th century. It is possible that the difficulty of the pilgrimage to these remote shrines associated with goddesses might have something to do with the epithet "Durga," which means "She who is hard to go to."

30. Kathleen M. Erndl, *Victory to the Mother: The Hindu Goddess of Northwest India in Myth, Ritual, and Symbol* (New York: Oxford University Press, 1993), 37–60. Similarly, there is a conception of the seven sisters in South India; however, they are not connected with the seven sisters of northwest India and are commonly identified as Poleramma, Ankamma, Muthyalamma, Dilli Polasi, Bangaramma, Mathamma/Matangi, and Renuka. Wilber T. Elmore, "Dravidian Gods in Modern Hinduism: A Study of the Local and Village Deities of Southern India" (PhD dissertation, University of Nebraska, 1915). The identity of Uttanahalli as Chamundi's sister conforms to popular worship of pairs of goddesses that can be found throughout India, including the temples of Chotila and Chamunda near Rajkot, Gujarat.

31. For more on similar practices, including those from Jwalamukhi in Himachal Pradesh, see Alejandro Jiménez Cid, "Blood for the Goddess: Self-Mutilation Rituals at Vajreśvarī Mandir, Kāngrā," *Indi@logs* 3 (2016): 37–55.

32. Sujatha Akki, *Chama Cheluve* dir. Mandya Ramesh (Mysore: Vismaya Prakashana, 2012). Original run scheduled July 12–17, 2012. It ran for 100 performances with a large celebration of the 100th performance taking place

on September 4, 2016, at Ravindra Kalashetra in Bangalore. The longer than intended run cause issues with the performers with Disha Ramesh eventually taking over the lead role as Chamundi.

33. Suhasini Hegade, "Chama Cheluve yashasvi nurne prayoga; nirdeshaka Mandya Ramesh manadaleda matu," *Siti Tude* (Bangalore), Sept. 3, 2016. Translation mine.

34. In the Kannada scholarly tradition, these songs have been recorded and studied in a variety of collections since the colonial period and have been adapted into other creative media, like plays and published poetry. K. R. Krishnaswami, *Janapada Kathana Geetagalu* (Mysore: Janapada Sahitya Academy, 1959 and 1962). *Naada Melella Haridave*; J. S. Paramashivayya, *Janapada Kavya kathegalu* (Mysore: Surachi Prakashana, 1970), *Helavaru and Their Kavyagalu* (n.p. 1972.), and *Kannada Vruttigayaka Kavyagalu* (n.p. n.d.); A. B. Rangaswamy. 1933. *Huttida Halli Halliya Haadugalu* and 1958. *Janapada Sahitya Chitragalu*; Goruru Ramaswamy Ayyangar, *Halliya Haadugalu* (Bangalore: Satyasodhana Pustaka Bhandara, 1938); J. S. Paramashivayya. and n.d. *Kannada Vruttigayaka Kavyagalu*; K. Maralusiddhappa. *Lavanigalu* (Bangalore: n.p., 1974); P. K. Rajashekara, *Chamundi Siri Chamundi* (Mysore: Honnaru Janapada Gayakaru, 1994); Mathighatta Krishnamurthy, *Kannada Janapada Sahitya Bhandara Geetegalu* (Bangalore: n.p., 1975); Kyathanahalli Ramanna, *Subbakka Haadida Nanjundeshwara Kavya* (Bangalore: Dinakara Prakashana); Ramegauda, *Chamayi* (1981); N. Chandrashekhar, *Bedagugara Nanjunda* (1998); H. Gangadaran, *Chamundeshwari Mahime* (2000).

35. P. K. Rajashekara, *Bettada Chamundi* (Mysore: Ta. Vem. Smaraka Granthamale, 1972).

36. P. K. Rajashekara, *Chamundi Siri Chamundi* (Mysore: Honnaru Janapada Gayakaru, 1994); and *Chamundi Siri Chamundi: Janapada Puranakavya Adharita Nataka* (Mysore: Chaitra Prakashana, 2012).

37. In *Bettada Chamundi*, Rajashekhara muses, "The same song is sung by the same artist several times, but it is sung in different ways. However, two different singers sing the same version in the same way. This is the challenge of the folk scholar." P. K. Rajashekhara, *Bettada Chamundi* (Mysore: Ta. Vem. Smaraka Granthamale, 1972), 48.

38. I am deeply grateful to P. K. Rajashekhara for allowing me permission to use his work in this book. I have relied on this text and personal communication to clarify terminology (including the titles of most songs), fill in gaps missing in the narrative, and for the overall structure of the ballad that in its oral form is dynamic and at times difficult to contain.

39. P. K. Rajashekhara, *Janapadada Virakavya Piriyapattanada Kalaga* (Mysore: Honnuru Janapada Gayakaru, 1990).

40. While they are multivalent in identity and composition, they are also extremely visible politically. For an overview of the Lingayat/Virashaiva

tradition, see Prithvi Datta Chandra Shobhi, "Pre-modern Communities and Modern Histories: Narrating Vīraśaiva and Lingayat Selves" (PhD dissertation. University of Chicago, 2005), 24–89.

41. The most well-known connection between the Sharana philosophy and Protestantism was made by Max Weber in Max Weber, *The Religion of India*, trans. and ed. Hans H. Gerth and Don Martindale (New York: The Free Press, 1958). For a discussion of this comparison, see R. Blake Michael, "Liṅgāyats," *Brill's Encyclopedia of Hinduism*, ed. Knut A. Jacobsen, Helene Basu, Angelika Malinar, and Vasudha Narayanan (Leiden, Boston: Brill), 378–92; Gil Ben-Herut, *Śiva's Saints: The Origins of Devotion in Kannada according to Harihara's Ragalegalu* (New York: Oxford University Press, 2018), 4–5; and Robert Zydenbos "Vīraśaivism, Caste, Revolution, Etc." *Journal of the American Oriental Society* 117, no. 3 (1997), 525–35.

42. In the program that was passed out on opening night of *Chama Cheluve*, Sujatha Akki states, "The message that 'love is not under the obligation of caste' is the inspiration for writing this work." This is also a broader message of the *katha* traditions of Karnataka; see Gayathri Rajapur Kassenbaum, "Communal Self and Cultural Imagery: The Katha Performance Tradition in South India," in *Self as Image in Asian Theory and Practice* ed. Roger T. Ames (Albany: SUNY Press, 1998), 260–79.

43. For a detailed history of the establishment of the study of folklore in India, see Frank J. Korom, *South Asian Folklore: A Handbook* (Westport, CT: Greenwood Press, 2006), 17–49.

44. In this way, this book is positioned with similar studies of songs from an ethnographic methodology. I am especially inspired by the work of Anne Gold, Kirin Narayan, and Anne Feldhaus. See Ann Gold and Bhoju Ram Gujar, *In the Time of Trees and Sorrows: Nature, Power, and Memory in Rajasthan* (Durham, NC: Duke University Press, 2002); Anne Gold and Gloria Goodwin Raheja, *Listen to the Heron's Words: Reimagining Gender and Kinship in North India* (Berkeley: University of California Press, 1994); Anne Grodzins Gold, *A Carnival of Parting: The Tales of King Bharthari and King Gopi Chand as Sung and Told by Madhu Natisar Nath of Ghatiyali, Rajasthan* (Berkeley: University of California Press, 2003); Kirin Narayan, *Everyday Creativity: Singing Goddesses in the Himalayan Foothills* (Chicago: University of Chicago Press, 2016); Anne Feldhaus, *Connected Places: Region, Pilgrimage, and Geographical Imagination in India* (New York: Palgrave Macmillan, 2003); and Anne Feldhaus et al., *Say to the Sun "Don't Rise," and to the Moon, "Don't Set": Two Oral Narratives from the Countryside of Maharashtra* (New York: Oxford University Press, 2014).

45. Cf. Alf Hiltebeitel, *Rethinking India's Oral and Classical Epics: Draupadi among Rajputs, Muslims, and Dalits* (Chicago: University of Chicago, 1999). While this book is a remarkable presentation of local and regional oral epics, the model implicitly assumes the priority of the classical tradition and "to

rethink the classical epic" and how it was "reworked" into regional and vernacular forms (1–3).

46. J. Edward Chamberlin and Daniel Frank Chamberlain, *Or Words to That Effect: Orality and the Writing of Literary History* (Amsterdam: J. Benjamins Publishing Co., 2016).

47. Frank J. Korom, *The Anthropology of Performance: A Reader* (New York: Wiley-Blackwell, 2014), 2–3; and "A Telling Place: Narrative and the Construction of Locality in a Bengali Village," in *Narrative Culture* 3, no. 1 (Spring 2016): 32–66; Kirin Narayan, *Everyday Creativity: Singing Goddesses in the Himalayan Foothills* (Chicago: University of Chicago Press, 2016).

48. As one small gesture, any royalties from this book will be donated to provide scholarships for underrepresented students to study in India. However, even if an author never earns royalties from a publication, the author still earns academic prestige and positions and promotions in institutions of higher education, something far more valuable than the few dollars of royalties that are earned from an academic monograph.

49. Kirin Narayan, *Everyday Creativity: Singing Goddesses in the Himalayan Foothills* (Chicago: University of Chicago Press, 2016), 29–33.

50. Primarily, I am referring to the introduction to *Bettada Chamundi*. Even at this early phase of his career, Rajashekhara identifies both as a scholar and a poet. P. K. Rajashekhara, *Bettada Chamundi* (Mysore: Ta. Vem. Smaraka Granthamale, 1972), 21–62.

51. P. K. Rajashekhara, *Bettada Chamundi* (Mysore: Ta. Vem. Smaraka Granthamale, 1972), 25.

52. P. K. Rajashekhara, *Bettada Chamundi* (Mysore: Ta. Vem. Smaraka Granthamale, 1972), 51.

53. P. K. Rajashekhara, *Bettada Chamundi* (Mysore: Ta. Vem. Smaraka Granthamale, 1972), 21.

54. P. K. Rajashekhara, *Bettada Chamundi* (Mysore: Ta. Vem. Smaraka Granthamale, 1972), 48.

55. P. K. Rajashekara, *Chamundi Siri Chamundi: Janapada Puranakavya Adharita Nataka* (Mysore: Chaitra Prakashana, 2012), xiii.

Chapter Two

1. E.g., P. G. D'Souza, *Annual Report of the Mysore Archaeological Department* (Bangalore: Government Press, 1925), 98; B. Lewis Rice, "Ch 102" *Epigraphia Carnatica Volume IV* (Mysore: Government Press, 1898); Promode Kumar Misra, *Cultural Profile of Mysore* (Mysore: Archaeological Survey of India, 1978), 9.

2. B. Lewis Rice, "My 16" *Epigraphia Carnatica Volume III.1* (Mysore: Government Press, 1894). While this inscription refers to the region as "buffalo

country," it calls what-is-now-known as "Chamundi Hill" by its older name "Mahabalachala" or "Hill of Shiva." This might indicate that the narrative of the buffalo demon and the goddess had yet to be associated with the hill or the local goddess who resides at its precipice.

3. The city was called Mayisuru in an inscription in which Timmaraja Wodeyar is granted two villages in 1551 CE, and the first record of the local goddess being associated with the slaying of the buffalo demon was in the Gajjiganahalli Copperplate Inscription of 1639, H. M. Nayak. "Nj 212" in *Epigraphia Carnatica Revision Volume III* (Mysore: Prasaranga, 1974).

4. The goddess Chamundi's local identity is evident in donative inscriptions that allude to her role as the guardian of a locale. A 10th-century hero stone from Chamarajanagara, south of Mysore City, describes a gift given to the town of Chamundapura or "City of Chamunda" in service of an unnamed deity. In a 12th-century inscription from the Hassan district, the Hoysala king Narasimha I bestowed a grant of land in the "land of Chaundeshwari" to a faithful minister. A badly damaged Tamil inscription from the 13th century records a list of eighteen towns that had been donated as a tax-generating land grant, including one whose inhabitants are called the "children of Chamundeshwari." Though none of these inscriptions explicitly connects the donation to the goddess Chamundi of Mysore, we must assume, given her relationship to the sites, that she was the goddess who presided over each locale, just like Pampadevi in Hampi, and served as the sites' gramadevate. Since none of these inscriptions directly connects Chamundi with Mysore, it remains unclear what relationship, if any, these goddesses had with the goddess who dwells on the top of Chamundi Hill. However, it seems unlikely that these inscriptions are in any way associated with the Mysore goddess since there was never any reference to Chamundi found in the area that is now Mysore city until the 17th century CE. The goddess of the hill was first called "Chamundi" in 17th-century inscriptions and literature from the Wodeyar court after they defeated the Vijayanagara viceroy in Shrirangapattana.

5. For how this has been incorpated as historical heritage within the region, see Caleb Simmons, "History, Heritage, and Myth: Local Historical Imagination in the Fight to Preserve Chamundi Hill in Mysore City," *Worldviews* 22 (2018): 216–37.

6. For those more familiar with the mythology of Mahisha and the goddess (see below), this narrative can prove quite confusing. In fact, through several performances of the song and readings of the transcription with Mysore Kannadigas, I was still unclear about the relationship between Mahisha and Aisa. I am deeply grateful to P. K. Rajashekara for meeting with me to help clarify the relationship between the two demons and the details of Chamundi's battle with Aisu. Personal communication June 28, 2017. The etymology of Aisu's name in *Chamundi of the Hill* is somewhat unclear. The

combination that was explained to me *aisu* ("that many") + *asura* ("demon") would result in his name being Aisasura with a short "a," but the name used is Aisāsura. One informant provided an alternate etymology of *aisayi* ("Christian") + *asura* ("demon") or the Christian demon. While this holds many possible intriguing avenues for hermeneutics, it does not seem likely nor was ever verified by a second source.

7. E.g., *Laws of Manu* 3.33.

8. This turn of events is foreshadowed in the demon's name, Aisasura, or the "demon that is *that* many."

9. The magnitude of the second greater demon is in some ways reminiscent of the Shakta *Adbhuta Ramayana*. See Thomas Coburn "Sītā Fights while Rāma Swoons: A Śākta Perspective on the *Rāmāyana*,"in *Breaking Boundaries with the Goddess: New Directions in the Study of Śāktism, Essays in Honor of Narendra Nath Bhattacharyya*, ed. Cynthia Ann Humes and Rachel Fell McDermott (New Delhi: Manohar), 35–59.

10. Indeed, for most of the Wodeyar history in Mysore, the kings have been great devotees and patrons of Chamundeshwari and her temple. It is even possible to trace the goddess's rise from a fierce goddess to a vegetarian Goddess using Wodeyar inscriptions and literature in which she goes from Chamundi of the hill in their earliest historical material (c. late 16th century) to Mahishasuramardini (17th century) to Mother of the Universe (*jagajjanani*; 19th century). See Caleb Simmons, "Goddess and the King: Cāmundēśvari and the Fashioning of the Wodeyar Court of Mysore" (PhD dissertation, University of Florida, 2014). Throughout their history, there is a steady Sanskritization of their ritual program and a vegetarianization of the goddess as portrayed in their official courtly texts. Uttanahalli, on the other hand, is absent from the courtly Mysore records until the 19th century when the *Shrimanmaharajara Vamshavaḷi* introduces her as Jwalamukhi, connecting this local fierce goddess to the *shakti pitha* of the fiery-tongue goddess in their foundation story. Caleb Simmons, *Devotional Sovereignty: Kingship and Religion in India* (New York: Oxford University Press, 2020), 107–32. Though it is clearly Uttanahalli given that she is said to reside at the base of the hill on its south side, the goddess is only referred to by a Sanskritic name with no additional details of her ritual or narrative background. This reference to Chamaraja provides no help in dating the songs because Chamaraja is the most common of all Wodeyar given names and appears throughout their history.

11. In my previous work, I have demonstrated that this narrative is a relatively late construction of the Wodeyar dynastic history that arises during the nineteenth century.

12. For the entire narrative, see chapter 3. For a discussion of the function of this royal history, see Caleb Simmons, *Devotional Sovereignty: Kingship and Religion in India* (New York: Oxford University Press, 2020), 107–32.

13. For more on Navaratri, see Caleb Simmons, Moumita Sen, and Hillary Rodrigues, eds., *Nine Nights of the Goddess: The Navarātri Festival in South Asia* (Albany: SUNY Press, 2018) and Bihani Sarkar, *Heroic Shāktism: The Cult of Durgā in Ancient Indian Kingship* (New York: Oxford University Press, 2017).

14. For more on contemporary Dasara in Mysore, see Caleb Simmons, "Dynastic Continuity and Election in Contemporary Karnataka Politics," in *The Conundrum of Worldly Power: Sovereignty in South Asian,* ed. Arild Ruud and Pamela Price (London: Routledge, 2019), 136–49 and "Domains of Dasara: Reflections on the Struggle for Significance in Contemporary Mysore," in *Nine Nights of Power* ed. Ute Hüsken, Vasudha Narayanan, and Astrid Zötter (Albany: SUNY Press, forthcoming).

15. There is an interesting manuscript in the Mackenzie collection in which a British military officer relates the traditional worship of Chamundeshwari on Chamundi Hill. He says that buffalo and goat sacrifices were a normal activity and that "not long ago" they were still offering her human sacrifice. *Traditionary Account of the worship of Chamoondee Sactee: or Chamoondee Betta the Hill of Mysore and of the Origin and Commutation of the Sacrifice of Men on that hill, compiled from information at Mysore in 1805,* Mackenzie General Collection Mss. 17.6: 17–19.

16. See note 21 in the introduction.

17. In the twelfth book of the Tamil epic poem the *Cilappatikaram,* the goddess Aiyai is clearly associated with the tribe and with their village as the ritual and song cannot commence until the "Eyiṉaṉs enclosed their village with a thorny fence." R. Parthasarathy, *Tale of an Anklet: An Epic of South India* (New York: Columbia University Press, 1993), 119. After the village is set apart from the rest of the forest, the oracle becomes possessed and demands that the Eyinans offer her sacrifices in fulfillment of their vow from which they received their martial prowess from the deity. Almost immediately, the great warriors begin to severe their own necks, offering their heads to the goddess. This imagery recalls the images of Dhyanu Bhagat offering his head to Jwalamalini, Chinnamasta severing her own head for her devotees, and the numerous images from medieval South India of a goddess standing on a buffalo head surrounded by devotees cutting off their heads and limbs. In the following hymn that predates the *DM* by about a century, the local goddess Aiyai is connected to other goddesses that fit Puranic descriptions. R. Parthasarathy, *Tale of an Anklet: An Epic of South India* (New York: Columbia University Press, 1993), 121–25; Also see R. Mahalakshmi, *The Making of the Goddess: Korravai-Durga in the Tamil Traditions* (New Delhi: Penguin Books, 2011). This leads to the situated goddess's simultaneous focus on locality and her association with transcendence.

18. See Sree Padma, *Inventing and Reinventing the Goddess: Contemporary Iterations of Hindu Deities on the Move* (Lanham, MD: Lexington Books, 2014)

and *Vicissitudes of the Goddess: Reconstructions of the Gramadevata in India's Religious Traditions* (New York: Oxford University Press, 2013).

19. Promode Kumar Misra, *Cultural Profile of Mysore* (Mysore: Archaeological Survey of India, 1978), 62. There is no consensus on this. In his essay in Misra's *Cultural Profile of Mysore* (1978), Morab states that Wodeyar king Krishnaraja III gave land grants to Tamil Smarta brahmins in 1819, which was the official invitation of the brahmin priests. However, in a book-length study of the temple coauthored with B. B. Goswami, Morab says that it was in 1848 that the Shivarchaka priests were officially replaced by the Tamil Dikshita brahmins. B. B. Goswami, and S. G. Morab, *Chamundesvari Temple in Mysore* (Calcutta: Anthropological Survey of India, 1991), 2. Epigraphic evidence supports both claims. My informants at the temple provided me with the caste names for the other priests (in descending order of ritual hierarchy): Hoysala Karnataka brahmins, Smarta (Ayyar) brahmins, and Lingayatas.

20. It should also be noted that many of the people who live atop the Chamundi Hill still practice these rituals, but they are often offered to the goddess Uttanahalli instead.

21. See Sree Padma, "From Village to City: Transforming Goddesses in Urban Andhra Pradesh," in *Seeking Mahadevi: Constructing the Identities of the Hindu Great Goddess*, ed. Tracy Pintchman (Albany: SUNY Press, 2001), 115–43, and *Vicissitudes of the Goddess: Reconstructions of the Gramadevata in India's Religious Traditions* (New York: Oxford University Press, 2013), 2. While, throughout the essay, she discusses these deities through the taxonomies of Sanskritization and Brahminization, it is quite clear that the processes are more complex and that there exists a great amount of slippage between the brahminic and village traditions to the point that the separation is perhaps more misleading than helpful, which indeed I believe is her point as she refers to the brahminic rituals as mere "window dressings" of the village traditions.

22. Thomas Coburn, *Devi Mahatmya: The Crystallization of the Goddess Tradition* (New Delhi: Motilal Banarsidass. 2002).

23. *Vicissitudes of the Goddess: Reconstructions of the Gramadevata in India's Religious Traditions* (New York: Oxford University Press, 2013), 2.

24. The subsequent details are a loose and abridged translation of the 7th chapter of the *Devi Mahatmya*.

25. This same myth is elaborated in *Padma Purana* 1.46.1–121; *Skanda Purana* 1.2.27–29; *Matsya Purana* 154–57.

26. DM 7.23- maya tavatropahritau candamundau mahapashu | yuddhayajñe svayam Shumbham niShumbham ca hanishyasi | | This scene conveys the importance of animal sacrifice within the tradition. Flesh offerings to fierce goddesses range from buffaloes to goats seemingly throughout India from the North to the South. See Alf Hiltebeital, *The Cult of Draupadi Volumes 1–2* (Chicago: University of Chicago Press, 1988, 1991) and William S. Sax, *Mountain Goddess: Gender and Politics in a Himalayan Pilgrimage* (New York:

Oxford University Press, 1991). During my first week of research in Mysore, I happened along a temple to Maramma, who is considered to be the sister of Chamundi. I arrived just after a goat had been offered to the goddess and was able to receive *mahaprasad*, at which time her devotees answered my questions about the deity. They told me that she was the sister of Chamundi and simultaneously the same Goddess. They went on to tell me that Chamundi used to receive similar offerings but that the brahmin priests would no longer allow it; so many people, who had not traditionally worshipped Maramma would now come to her when they desperately needed the aid of the Goddess. I have seen numerous goat and chicken sacrifices at the top and bottom of Chamundi Hill since.

27. *Devi Mahatmya* 7.25- *yasmaccandam ca mundam ca grihitva tvamupagata | camundeti hato loke khyata devi bhavishyasi | |* The text implies that the name of the goddess is derived from a combination of the names Chanda and Munda. While this etymology is quite clever, the imprecision in the construction of this epithet was taken up by Bhaskararaya, whose 18th-century commentary on the *Devi Mahatmya* the *Guptavati* offers another possible etymology. See Hari Krishna Sharma, *Durgasaptashati* (Delhi: Chaukamba Sanskrit Pratishthan, 2006), 10. Bhaskararaya suggests that the name is a combination of *camum* or "army" and *lati* or "eats;" so that Chamunda is "she who eats armies." Hari Krishna Sharma, *Durgasaptashati* (Delhi: Chaukamba Sanskrit Pratishthan, 2006), 10: *camum senam viyadadisamuharupam dati dalayoraikyallati | adatte svatmasatkarena nashayatiti vyutpatteḥ |*). In order to explain the shift from √la to √da, Bhaskararaya expounds that the *la* and *da* syllables have the same spiritual value and are therefore interchangeable in mantric algebra. Hari Krishna Sharma, *Durgasaptashati* (Delhi: Chaukamba Sanskrit Pratishthan, 2006), 11.

28. These references occur within chapter 8 verses 52 through 60. Raktabija is such a fierce opponent because every time that he is struck by one of the weapons of the Goddess each droplet of blood that falls on the ground manifested as another incarnation of the mighty demon making the Goddess's odds exponentially worse. This portion of the episode is particularly interesting with regards to the power of reproduction in the ancient world in which the queen/female was connected with the earth and the king/male with the seed (*bija*). In this scene, it is clear that the Goddess takes control of both the seed and the earth, and the all power of reproduction is controlled by her. For more analysis of this aspect of the narrative, see Kathleen M. Erndl, "Is *Shakti* Empowering for Women? Reflections on Feminism and the Hindu Goddess," in *Is the Goddess a Feminist: The Politics of South Asian Goddesses*, ed. Alf Hiltebeital and Kathleen M. Erndl (New York: New York University Press), 91–103.

29. These goddesses are the personification of the feminine energies (*shakti*) of Brahma, Maheshvara (Shiva), Guha (Skanda), Vishnu, Hari (Varaha), Narasimha, and Indra and in the later tradition become known as the "Seven

Little Mothers" (*saptamatrika*). It should also be noted that Chamunda is further incorporated into the Sanskritic fold in latter texts such as the *Shaktapramoda*, in which she replaces Narasimhi, the *shakti* of Vishnu's half man-half lion *avatara* Narasimha in the collection of *saptamatrikas*. See S. R. Devanandan, *Shaktapramoda* (Bombay: Khemraja Shrikrishnadasa Prakashan, 1973); and David Kinsley, *Tantric Visions of the Divine Feminine: The Ten Mahāvidyās* (Berkeley: University of California Press, 1997), 32. Historically, both in textual traditions (e.g., *Shaktapramoda*) and iconographical representations in temples from the 7th century until today, Chamunda is often depicted as one of the *saptamatrikas*, often replacing the lion-woman (*narasimha*). See Thomas Eugene Donaldson, "The Shava-Vahana as Purusha in Orissan Images: Chamunda to Kali/Tara," *Artibus Asiae* 51, no. 1/2 (1991): 107–41.

30. This is also taking place in the beginning of the third episode when the assortment of goddesses were being grouped together based on their personalities and appearance as epithets of Ambika. For example, Parvati is called *krishna* and *kalika*, which can be taken as descriptions of her color (dark and black) or as proper names, Krishna and Kalika, who are individual goddesses with their own mythology, iconography, rituals. Another example is given in that same scene in which Ambika is called *shiva, kaushaki,* and *durga*.

31. Thomas Eugene Donaldson, "The Shava-Vahana as Purusha in Orissan Images: Chamunda to Kali/Tara," *Artibus Asiae* 51, no. 1/2 (1991): 107–41.

32. Charlotte Schmid, "Du Rite au Mythe: Le Tueuses de Buffle de l'Inde ancienne" *Artibus Asiae* 71, no. 1 (2011): 115–61.

33. The emanation motif can also be found in the *Laws of Manu* 7.1–11. This chapter relates the duty of the king, and it begins with the origin of the first king, whose duty was to restore order and to protect the people of the world.

34. Coburn, *Encountering the Goddess* (Albany: SUNY Press, 1991) and *Devi Mahatmya: The Crystallization of the Goddess Tradition* (New Delhi: Motilal Banarsidass Publishers, 1988).

35. M. N. Srinivas, *Religion and Society among the Coorgs of South India* (Oxford: Claredon Press, 1952), 207–22.

36. J. Fritz Staal, "Sanskrit and Sanskritization," *The Journal of Asian Studies* 22, no. 3 (May 1963): 261–75. Despite the problems with the term, Sanskritization has been one of the most commonly employed theories to explain the Shakta tradition; however, within this context, the process is often described as the appropriation of goddesses from indigenous non-Sanskritic traditions into the Sanskritic pantheon because of their immense popularity and perceived power. This has been at the core of most studies that have looked at the goddess traditions since the time of Sir John Woodroffe and has continued through Mircea Eliade, *Yoga: Immortality and Freedom* (Princeton, NJ: Princeton University Press, 1973) and contemporary scholarship on the

Shakta tradition. See also Tracy Pintchman, *Seeking Mahadevi: Constructing the Identities of the Hindu Great Goddess* (Albany: SUNY Press, 2001); David Kinsley, *Tantric Visions of the Divine Feminine: The Ten Mahāvidyās* (Berkeley: University of California Press, 1997); Coburn, *Encountering the Goddess* (Albany: SUNY Press, 1991); and Alf Hiltebeital, *The Cult of Draupadi Volumes 1–2* (Chicago: University of Chicago Press, 1988, 1991).

37. A. L. Basham, *The Wonder that Was India* (New York: Grove Press, 1959) and Thomas Coburn, *Devi Mahatmya: The Crystallization of the Goddess Tradition* (New Delhi: Motilal Banarsidass Publishers, 1988), give the later date, but M. R. Kale argues that Bhavabhuti was active in the 7th century. M. R. Kale, *Bhavabhuti's Malatimadhava with Commentary of Jagaddhara* (Delhi: Motilal Banarsidass, 1967), 7–8.

38. H. H. Wilson, *Malati and Madhava or the Stolen Marriage: A Drama* (Calcutta: Society for the Resuscitation of Indian Literature Elysium Press, 1901), 5.

39. In this drama she is also called Karala (she whose mouth is gaping). It should also be noted that one of the *asuras* that is slain by the Goddess in the second episode of the *Devi Mahatmya* is named Karala (3.16). While this may be mere coincidence and simply references the description of the goddess in the hymn, I think it is more likely that the fierceness of Chamunda is being equated to demonic forces in this drama, and this reference concretizes her terrifying qualities

40. *Malatimadhava* 5.22; M. R. Kale, *Bhavabhuti's Malatimadhava with Commentary of Jagaddhara* (Delhi: Motilal Banarsidass, 1967), 102. Translation mine.

> devi camunde namaste namaste
> savashṭambhanizumbhasambhramanamadbhugikanishpidana
> nyañcatkarparakurmakampavigalahbrahmandakhandasthiti
> patalapratimallagallavivaraprakshiptasaptarnavam
> vande nanditanilakanṭhaparishahvyaktrddhi vaḥ kriditam

41. Their hymn to the goddess makes it clear that by the last part of the 7th century or the first part of the 8th Chamunda was associated with Shiva where there had been little or no connection between the goddess and Shiva in the *Devi Mahatmya*.

42. The same apprehension/admiration over Chamunda was present within the medieval Jain community as well. In the *Upakeshagaccha Pattavali*, an Osian text that is retold in a 16th century inscription, explains that the Jaina *acarya* Ratnaprabha pleaded with the Jain community to discontinue their worship of the fierce goddess Saccika, who is often associated with Chamunda and images of Chamunda had been depicted within Saccika Jain temples as far back as the 12th century CE. The text explains that the *acarya* warned

the Jain laity that the blood sacrifices required by the goddess caused them to break their Jaina *dharma*; however, because of the efficacy of the practice the people refused to forsake their worship of the Goddess and his attempt failed miserably. According to the text and the inscription, in order to protect the Jaina laity, Ratnaprabha converted Saccika to the Jaina path. John Cort "Medieval Jaina Goddess Traditions," *Numen* 34 Fasc. 2 (Dec. 1987): 243–44; and F. R. Hoernle "The Pattavali or List of Pontiffs of the Upakesa-Gachchha," *Indian Antiquary* 19 (1890): 237–38.

43. R. Parthasarathy, *The Tale of an Anklet: An Epic of South India* (New York: Columbia University Press, 1993), 120–25; *Traditionary Account of the worship of Chamoondee Sactee: or Chamoondee Betta the Hill of Mysore and of the Origin and Commutation of the Sacrifice of Men on that hill, compiled from information at Mysore in 1805*, Mackenzie General Collection Mss. 17.6: 17–19.

44. C. Mackenzie Brown, *The Triumph of the Goddess: The Canonical Models and Theological Visions of the* Devi-Bhagavata Purana (Albany: SUNY Press, 1990).

45. C. Mackenzie Brown, *The Triumph of the Goddess: The Canonical Models and Theological Visions of the* Devi-Bhagavata Purana (Albany: SUNY Press, 1990), 11.

46. C. Mackenzie Brown, *The Triumph of the Goddess: The Canonical Models and Theological Visions of the* Devi-Bhagavata Purana (Albany: SUNY Press, 1990), 11.

47. C. Mackenzie Brown, *The Triumph of the Goddess: The Canonical Models and Theological Visions of the* Devi-Bhagavata Purana (Albany: SUNY Press, 1990), 14.

48. Kathleen M. Erndl, *Victory to the Mother* (New York: Oxford University Press, 1993), 153–58; Lynn Foulston, *At the Feet of the Goddess: The Divine Feminine in Local Hindu Religion* (Sussex: Sussex Academic Press, 2003), 173–80; Ehud Halperin, "Is the Goddess Haḍimbā Tantric? Negotiating Power in a Western Himalayan Sacrificial Arena," in *International Journal of Hindu Studies* 23, no. 2 (2019): 195–212 and *The Many Faces of a Himalayan Goddess: Hadimba, Her Devotees, and Religion in Rapid Change* (New York: Oxford University Press, 2019).

49. See Caleb Simmons, "Family, God, and King: Vaṃśāvaḷi as Royalist Literature," in *Clio and Her Descendants: Essays in Honor of Keshavan Veluthat* ed. Manu Devadevan (New Delhi: Primus Books, 2018), 598–622.

50. For example, see Cynthia Humes, "Is the *Devi Mahatmya* a Feminist Scripture?," in *Is the Goddess a Feminist?: The Politics of South Asian Goddesses.* ed. Alf Hiltebeital and Kathleen M. Erndl (New York: New York University Press), 123–50. Cf. Sarah Caldwell "Waves of Beauty, Rivers of Blood: Constructing the Goddess in Kerala," in *Seeking Mahādevī: Constructing the Identities of the Hindu Great Goddess*, ed. Tracy Pintchman (Albany: SUNY Press, 2001), especially pp. 94–95.

51. See Stephanie Jameson, *Sacrificed Wife/Sacrificer's Wife: Women, Ritual, and Hospitality in Ancient India* (New York: Oxford University Press, 1996), 65–88.

52. The nearness (and sometimes farness) of mythic cycles is something I hope to develop more thoroughly in the future.

53. This, interestingly, places the mythic deeds within very recent human history or is a prophetic ancient account concerning the future devotion that she will be accorded . . . very Puranic.

54. Because of the vagueness of this ritual reference, the song does not shed any light on the date. It could be interpreted as either portraying the prenational integration Dasara rituals in the palace or her contemporary ride in the golden *hoda* on the elephant's back.

55. In later songs we find descriptions of other local festivals (*jatre*) like the chariot festival (*rathotsava*) in Nanjangudu.

Chapter Three

1. Dolores Hayden, "Placemaking, Preservation and Urban History" *Journal of Architectural Education* 41, no. 3 (Spring 1988): 45–51. Kumkum Chatterjee, "History as Self-Representation: The Recasting of a Political Tradition in Late Eighteenth-Century Eastern India" *Modern Asian Studies* 32, no. 4 (1998): 913–48.

2. Partha Chatterjee "Introduction: History in the Vernacular," in *History in the Vernacular*, ed. Raziuddin Aquil and Partha Chatterjee (Delhi: Permanent Black, 2008), 1–25.

3. See Berin F. Gür, "Local Performance in the Construction of National Identity: Plaka District of Athens during the Nineteenth Century," *Journal of Urban History* 38, no. 1 (2012): 39–70.

4. Anna Lise Seastrand, "Praise, Politics, and Language: South India Murals, 1500–1800 (PhD dissertation, Columbia University, 2013).

5. Diana L. Eck, *India: A Sacred Geography*, 1st ed. (New York: Harmony Books, 2012) and Anne Feldhaus, *Connected Places: Region, Pilgrimage, and Geographical Imagination in India*, 1st ed., Religion/Culture/Critique (New York: Palgrave Macmillan, 2003); Martha Ann Selby and Indira Viswanathan Peterson, *Tamil Geographies: Cultural Constructions of Space and Place in South India*, SUNY Series in Hindu Studies (Albany: State University of New York Press, 2008).

6. Ranjeeta Dutta, "Pilgrimage as Religious Process: Some Reflections on the Identities of the Srivaisnavas of South India," *Indian Historical Review* 37, no. 1 (2010): 17–38.

7. Emma Stein, "All Streets Lead to Temples: Mapping Monumental Histories in Kanchipuram, c. 8th–12th centuries CE" (PhD dissertation, Yale University, 2017).

8. For much more on this history, see Caleb Simmons, *Devotional Sovereignty: Kingship and Religion in India* (New York: Oxford University Press, 2020).

9. Aya Ikegame, *Princely India Re-imagined: A Historical Anthropology of Mysore from 1799 to the Present* (London: Routledge, 2013), 10. For example, in 1905, the Mysore first kingdom was the first kingdom in Asia to have electric street lamps in one of its cities (Bangalore).

10. J. F. Fleet "Mahishamandala and Mahishmati," *The Journal of the Royal Asiatic Society* (1910): 446–47. Some of these historians sought the history of the city in the Sanskrit "canon" examining references that were often said to be allusions to the region and its buffalo-demon past, especially in the *Mahabharata*.

11. See Mark Wilks, *Historical Sketches of the South of India in an Attempt to Trace the History of Mysoor from the Hindoo Government of that State to the Extinction of the Mohammedan Dynasty in 1799 Volumes 1 & 2* (Mysore: Government Branch Press, 1930) and G. R. Joyser, *The History of Mysore and the Yadava Dynasty* (Mysore: Coronation Press, 1939). These dynastic histories often speculated that the Wodeyar rulers might have arisen from local chieftains, but they, for the most part, were contented merely to raise the issue before turning to the lineage as it was presented in the courtly documents. As Nair points out, many British administrators worked from the assumption that the Wodeyar were indeed local agriculturalists, even referring to them as *shudra*s in some of their correspondence. Janaki Nair, *Mysore Modern: Rethinking the Region under Princely Rule* (New Delhi: Orient Blackswan Private Limited, 2010), 19.

12. For a full description and analysis of the different versions of the Wodeyar history of Mysore and their kingdom, see Simmons 2014.

13. The full title of the text is *Mysuru Samsthananda Prabhugalu Shriman Maharajavara Vamshavali or The Lineage History of the Glorious and Great Kings of Mysore. Mummadi Krishnaraja Wodeyar, Maisūru Samsthānada Prabhugaḷu Śrīmanmahārājaravara Vaṃśāvaḷi Volumes 1–2*, ed. B. Ramakrishna Row (Mysore: Government Branch Press, 1916 and 1922).

14. As I have shown elsewhere, this text adds many new details to the overall narrative, but it also retains the older elements mentioned above, See Simmons 2014, 2020.

15. For example, when printing presses made the publication of inexpensive periodicals possible, *The Great Kings of Mysore* was published as a serial in the journal *Hithibodhini* in 1881.

16. I have translated the following passage from Wodeyar, Mummadi Krishnaraja Wodeyar, *Maisūru Samsthānada Prabhugaḷu Śrīmanmahārājaravara Vaṃśāvaḷi Volumes 1–2*, ed. B. Ramakrishna Row (Mysore: Government Branch Press, 1916) 4–12. I previously translated and discussed this foundational story in the context of colonial politics in my work. See Caleb Simmons, *Devotional Sovereignty: Kingship and Religion in India* (New York: Oxford University Press, 2020), 121–27.

17. See "Family, God, and King: Vaṃśāvaḷi as Royalist Literature," in *Clio and Her Descendants: Essays in Honor of Keshavan Veluthat*, ed. Manu Devadevan (New Delhi: Primus Books, 2018), 598–622.

18. This is made particularly clear at the end of the ballad when Chamundi's co-wife Deviri grants Chamundi a large plot of land.

19. Interview with the maharaja September 2013. Furthermore, he directed me to the writings of James Tod from whom he said I could learn the most about Indian kingship. For more, see Caleb Simmons, *Devotional Sovereignty: Kingship and Religion in India* (New York: Oxford University Press, 2020), 1–5.

20. This is almost certainly a reference to the *mahotsava* at the Chamundi temple on Chamundi Hill that immediately follows Dasara. The other possibility is the *gramadevate* festival on Chamundi Hill that takes place in the spring. It is clear, however, that this is not a reference to the royal Dasara festival.

21. The song describes the seven Durgas as the "children of Bijjalaraya," a Kaladuri vassal who broke away from the Chalukyas of Kalyani. The song also states that they came from the region of Ujjain. I'm not sure what to make of these interesting details.

22. The area surrounding St. Philomena's cathedral.

23. This is a common practice in southern Karnataka. When people are near death, they are placed outside the home, so any evil spirits that come at the time of death will not enter the home.

24. This is Ashoka Road. The clock tower was built during the British Raj.

25. Near Sitappa Square.

26. This reference is unclear, but I have been told that it might refer to what is now Irving Road.

27. Krishnaraja Wodeyar IV was coronated as the maharaja of Mysore upon the death of his father in 1894; however, he was at the time a minor and did not take control of the administration of the kingdom until 1902.

28. Personal communication with CS Purnima 2013.

29. Given more time/space this would be fruit to analyze. That is, the establishment of the kingdom vis-à-vis the "imperial" goddess Chamundi / Mahishasuramardini and the seven sister goddesses of the "borderlands."

30. This refers to a beauty mark that is placed on the face of a beautiful woman, which is intended to draw in the gaze of others, averting the evil eye.

Chapter Four

1. Sandalwood is the equivalent nickname for Kannada cinema, which is largely based out of Bangalore. The name "Sandalwood" is both a play on "Hollywood" and "Bollywood" and was so named because of the production of sandalwood for which southern Karnataka is famous.

2. For more on the distinctions between purity, cleanliness, pollution, and dirtiness, see Kelley Alley, *On the Banks of the Gangā: When Wastewater Meets a Sacred River* (Ann Arbor: University of Michigan Press, 2002).

3. See *Jaimini Brahmana* 1.3.5–7. P.V. Kane, *History of Dharmasastra: Ancient and Mediaeval Religious and Civil Law in India Volume I Part I* (Pune: Bhandarkar Oriental Research Institute, 1953), 841–42.

4. The closest river for bathing from Chamundi Hill is the Kabini River in Nanjangudu (22kms); T. Narasipura is 11 kms farther (33kms).

5. For more on Kumbha Mela, see Kama McLean, "Making the Colonial State Work for You: The Modern Beginnings of the Ancient Kumbh Mela in Allahabad," *The Journal of Asian Studies* 62, no. 3 (2003): 877–79 and James Lochtefeld, *God's Gateway: Identity and Meaning in a Hindu Pilgrimage Place* (New York: Oxford University Press, 2010).

6. Compare this with the ethnographic work by Humes in which she describes a similar myth of the blood-seed demon Raktabija and the disconnect between the Goddess and women. Cynthia Humes, "Is the *Devi Mahatmya* a Feminist Scripture?" in *Is the Goddess a Feminist: The Politics of South Asian Goddesses*, ed. Alf Hiltebeitel and Kathleen M. Erndl (New York: New York University Press), 123–50.

7. Lingas are aniconic representations of Shiva that often serve as the primary image (*murti*) in Shaiva temples. Lingayats, which will be discussed at greater length later in this chapter, derive their name from the small personal (*ishta-*) lingas that they wear.

8. Nandikasura might be a local derivation (*tadbhava*) of Sanskritic deity Andhakasura, who is killed by Shiva in puranic narratives. P. K. Rajashekhara, *Bettada Chamundi* (Mysore: Ta. Vem. Smaraka Granthamale, 1972), 37. However, in his introduction to Kyatanahalli Ramanna's *Nanjundeshwara Kavya*, Rajashekhara explains that this is another local myth in which Nanjunda slays a demon giant in Nanjungudu. See Kyathanahalli Ramanna, *Subbakka Haadida Nanjundeshwara Kavya* (Bangalore: Dinakara Prakashana), 8.

9. Mavura is the genitive of *mava* (*māva*) a *tadbhava* of *mama*.

10. Maternal cross-cousin marriage is the traditional marriage in the Kuruba community from which the performers of *Bettada Chamundi* the Kamsales come. K. H. Basavarajappa, "Backward caste and class movement in Karnataka with special reference to Kurubas" (PhD thesis, Karnatak University, 1983), 131. https://shodhganga.inflibnet.ac.in/handle/10603/94009.

11. In various versions of this tale, Nanjunda's two wives have different names. Deviri appears in all versions of the story, though the Kamsale version often refers to her as Dundu or "Round" Deviri. The Kamsale version seems to be the only version that includes the name Somaji (or Somajamma). Others' iterations call her either Parvati, the name of Shiva's wife in Pan-Indic myth, or Kaveri, the local river goddess. See P. K. Rajashek-

hara, *Bettada Chamundi* (Mysore: Ta. Vem. Smaraka Granthamale, 1972), 37 and Masti Venkatesh Iyengar, *Karnataka Janapada Sahitya* (Bangalore: Jivana Karyalaya, 1937), 26–27.

12. The theme of Shiva marrying multiple wives and the rivalries that ensue is common in Shaiva literature. See David Shulman *Tamil Temple Myths: Sacrifice and Divine Marriage in the South Indian Śaiva Tradition* (Princeton: Princeton University Press, 1980), 267–94.

13. Special thanks to Gil Ben Herut for his many helpful comments and suggestions for this section.

14. See Gil Ben Herut, *Śiva's Saints: The Origins of Devotion in Kannada according to Harihara's Ragalegalu* (New York: Oxford University Press, 2018). For complications with this oversimplification, see Robert Zydenbos "Vīraśaivism, Caste, Revolution, Etc.," *Journal of the American Oriental Society* 117, no. 3 (1997), 525–35.

15. K. H. Basavarajappa, "Backward caste and class movement in Karnataka with special reference to Kurubas" (PhD thesis, Karnatak University, 1983), 112–18; R. C. Dhere, *Rise of a Folk God: Vitthal of Pandarpur* (New York: Oxford University Press, 2011), 240–41.

16. R. C. Dhere, *Rise of a Folk God: Vitthal of Pandarpur* (New York: Oxford University Press, 2011), 243–45. K. N. Sreenivasan, "Occupational mobility among Kurubas in Karnataka" (PhD thesis: Bangalore University, 2014), 90. https://shodhganga.inflibnet.ac.in/handle/10603/127361.

17. For a compilation of foundation myths, see K. N. Sreenivasan, "Occupational mobility among Kurubas in Karnataka" (PhD thesis: Bangalore University, 2014), 94–96, 100–104. https://shodhganga.inflibnet.ac.in/handle/10603/127361.

18. K. H. Basavarajappa, "Backward caste and class movement in Karnataka with special reference to Kurubas" (PhD thesis, Karnatak University, 1983), 109–10. https://shodhganga.inflibnet.ac.in/handle/10603/94009; Aya Ikegame, "Why Do Backward Castes Need Their Own Gurus? The Social and Political Significance of New Caste-Based Monasteries in Karnataka. *Contemporary South Asia* 18, no. 1 (March 2010): 57–70. K. N. Sreenivasan, "Occupational Mobility among Kurubas in Karnataka" (PhD thesis: Bangalore University, 2014), 107. https://shodhganga.inflibnet.ac.in/handle/10603/127361. For more on the Shaivization of the Kuruba deities, RC Dhere, *Rise of a Folk God: Vitthal of Pandarpur* (New York: Oxford University Press, 2011), 74–77.

19. There is also a movement to have the Kuruba classified as a "Scheduled Tribe." The Scheduled Tribe designation is a more limited classification that was created at the creation of the Indian Constitution, and members of these groups have greater protections from the national government. OBC is a more recent classification that was created in 1978 with the adoption of Article 304 of the Indian Constitution and is a broader category.

20. K. N. Sreenivasan, "Occupational Mobility among Kurubas in Karnataka." (PhD thesis: Bangalore University, 2014), 106. https://shodhganga.inflibnet.ac.in/handle/10603/127361.

21. Recently, debates over the identity of Lingayats and their relationship with Virashaivism have been part of the public and political discourse in India, especially in Karnataka. Gauri Lankesh provided a helpful, though contested and not scholarly rigorous, review of her interpretation of the distinction that was published on *TheWire.in* (August 8, 2017) that was republished after her murder for speaking out on issues related to religion in India, including her argument that Lingayats were not Hindus. Gauri Lankesh, "Making Sense of the Lingayat vs Veershaiva Debate," *TheWire.in*, September 5, 2017, https://thewire.in/history/karnataka-lingayat-veerashaive-debate/ .

22. For a discussion of the theological (i.e., not social) implications of Lingayat rejection of caste, see Dunkin Jalki, "Lingayat Tradition, Adhyatma and Caste: How Bhakti Traditions Understand Caste," *in Journal of Contemporary Thought* no. 41 (Summer 2015): 165–90.

23. See the beginning of the song "Who are you, wise woman? You are so charming!" for a description of the *ishtalinga* Shiva *puja* performed by Nanjunda.

24. The Lingayat acceptance of converts from all caste backgrounds makes Lingayatism an extremely caste-diverse tradition. This perplexed colonial administrators during the British period. Therefore, the colonial government classified all Lingayats as *shudras*, which has led to over a century of mischaracterization of Lingayat group identity. See Ramesh Bairy, *Being Brahmin, Being Modern: Exploring the Lives of Caste Today* (New Delhi: Routledge, 2010), 143–49.

25. Aya Ikegame, "Karnataka: Caste, Dominance, and Social Change in an Indian Village," *The Modern Anthropology of Indai: Ethnography, Themes, and Theory*, ed. Peters Berger, Frank Heidemann, Subrata Ghatak, and Paul Levine (London: Routledge, 2013), 128.

26. A. K. Ramanujan, *Speaking of Shiva* (New York: Penguin, 1993), 5–9.

27. Najunda is also said to be both the brother of Madeshwara and his classmate at the Kunturu Matha. Kyathanahalli Ramanna, *Subbakka Haadida Nanjundeshwara Kavya* (Bangalore: Dinakara Prakashana), 3–4.

28. To compare the details of this song with the details of Kuruba marriage and wedding rituals, see K. H. Basavarajappa, "Backward Caste and Class Movement in Karnataka with special reference to Kurubas" (PhD thesis, Karnatak University, 1983), 128–31. https://shodhganga.inflibnet.ac.in/handle/10603/94009 ; Edgar Thurston, *Castes and Tribes of Southern India Vol. IV* (Madras: Government Press, 1909), 144–47.

29. Rajashekhara 1972, 35.

30. H. H. Wilson, *The Vishnu Purana, A System of Hindu Mythology and Tradition* (London: John Murray, 1840), 189; B. Lewis Rice, *Mysore Inscriptions* (Bangalore: Mysore Government Press, 1879); B. Lewis Rice, *Mysore: A Gazet-*

teer Compiled for Government (New Delhi: Asian Educational Service [London: Archibald Constable and Company], 2001 [1897]); *MAR* (1925), 98. Fleet definitively disapproved the connection between Mahishamati and Mysore in 1910, but it has remained a popular connection ever since. J. F. Fleet, "Mahishamandala and Mahishamati," *Journal of the Royal Asiatic Society* (1910): 446.

31. P. K Rajashekhara, *Bettada Chamundi* (Mysore: Ta. Vem. Smaraka Granthamale, 1972), 35.

32. P. K Rajashekhara, *Bettada Chamundi* (Mysore: Ta. Vem. Smaraka Granthamale, 1972), 335.

33. P. K Rajashekhara, *Bettada Chamundi* (Mysore: Ta. Vem. Smaraka Granthamale, 1972), 335.

34. For more, see Sree Padma, *Inventing and Reinventing the Goddess: Contemporary Iterations of Hindu Deities on the Move* (Lanham, MD: Lexington Books, 2014) and *Vicissitudes of the Goddess: Reconstructions of the Gramadevata in India's Religious Traditions* (New York: Oxford University Press, 2013).

35. All of this information was taken from observations made 18–19 February 2014.

36. The scene is quite Carnivalesque with a great deal of merry-making. In 2014, the central display for the show was an effigy (*bombe*) of a man whose fuse led to streams of fire shooting from a cigarette he held in one hand and from his penis in the other before exploding to cheers from the crowd. When I asked my temple-worker friends about the effigy, they told me that it was simply supposed to be funny and had no greater meaning and did not represent anyone: mythological, political, or otherwise.

37. The shrine of the village goddess is easy to miss and is nestled just outside the south wall of the Chamundeshwari temple

38. My informants told me that these priests were Lingayats, who normally work in the large brahminic Chamundeshwari temple. However, as you can see in the photo, they were not wearing an *ishtalinga*. This and the firework procession are the only two functions given to priests from the Chamundeshwari temple.

39. A *harike* is a promise made to a deity that if X is done/given by the deity, then the devotee will do Y. In this way it is different from a *vrata* in which Y is done by the devotee first in expectation of X from the deity.

40. Information for this festival comes from my own limited observations and conversation in September 2013 and from B. B. Goswami, and S. G. Morab, *Chamundesvari Temple in Mysore* (Calcutta: Anthropological Survey of India, 1991). Additionally, the brahmin castes of Chamundi Hill celebrate the Chamundi *mahōtsava* (the great festival), which includes the *rathōtsava* (chariot festival) and *tepōtsava* (boat festival) immediately after Dasara.

41. The Raja Parivara ("family of the kings") or Palegar Nayaka ("Chieftain-Ruler") *jati* claims to be the descendants of the clan of former rulers and warriors of the region, and they, like the Bedas in the Shimoga district, claim

the sage Valmiki among their ancestors. During this festival period, all people from the region make offerings to their ancestors.

42. The following details about the *kannu kannadi* procession are taken from B. B. Goswami and S. G. Morab, *Chamundesvari Temple in Mysore* (Calcutta: Anthropological Survey of India, 1991).

43. Though I did not observe these rituals, I asked several of the non-brahmin temple workers about them. When I asked about the identity of these goddesses, I was told that they are the same as the seven little mothers (*saptamatrikas*), who are prominent in brahminic traditions. These seven goddesses, however, are often described by their Sanskritic names: Chamunda, Brahmi, Maheshwari, Indrani, Varahi, Vaishnavi, and Kumari. While this list is similar to the tradition list of the *saptamatrikas*, it varies from those described in the *DM* with Chamunda replacing Narassimhi. This is not particular to Mysore, though. This list can be seen as far back as the *Shaktapramoda*, a Shakta tantric text.

44. Goswami and Morab state that the traditional day for the celebration is the first Tuesday after the full moon day of Bhadrapada, but that in actuality it occurs "according to the peoples' convenience" (B. B. Goswami, and S. G. Morab, *Chamundesvari Temple in Mysore* (Calcutta: Anthropological Survey of India, 1991), 20.

45. The practice is quite similar to the festival of Mariyamman in Tamil Nadu and the festival to Pydamma in Andhra Pradesh. In fact, several people referred to the *gramadevata* as Maramma over the course of the day. Mariyamman is an agricultural goddess, who is associated with infectious diseases such as smallpox and cholera. See Elaine Craddock "Reconstructing the Split Goddess as Śakti in a Tamil Village," in *Seeking Mahadevi: Constructing the Identities of the Hindu Great Goddess*, ed. Tracy Pintchman (Albany: SUNY Press, 2001), 146–47. The festival in honor of Mariyamman which usually takes place in the Tamil month of Adi (Sanskrit: Shravana; July/August), though Younger observed the same festival in the town of Samayapuram during the second week of April. Paul Younger, "A Temple Festival of Mariyamman," *Journal of the American Academy of Religion* 48, no. 4 (Dec. 1980): 495. During this festival or at the onset of an outbreak of a disease, the devotees of the goddess, both male and female, place earthen pots on the top of their heads and walk in procession to the temple of Mariyamman. This procession is typically referred to as dancing because of the elaborate brisk walk or shuffle in which the devotees engage. The pot represents the seat of the goddess into which she is invited to "cool off." The connection between rituals to Mariyamman and Chamundi is even stronger when you consider that the Chamundi Hill *gramadevata* is also associated with infectious disease, such as smallpox and cholera, and is propitiated and "cooled off" in the earthen vessels carried by the Raja Parivara caste. Promode Kumar Misra, *Cultural Profile of Mysore*

(Mysore: Archaeological Survey of India, 1978), 68. This practice can also be seen in the Tamil diaspora in the Guyanese festival Kalimai Puja. However, in Guyana the earthen pot is replaced with a brass pot that is considered to be the womb of the goddess Kali, and the *marlo pujaris*, who carry the consecrated pots to the Kali temple inaugurating the festival, are only prepubescent boys. The carrying of earthen pots is also used in the annual festival of the Andhran village deity Pydamma of Visakhapatnam. However, in this case, they are not carried by virgin or prepubescent children but married women, who undertake this as fulfillment of a vow for the well-being of their children and husbands. Tracy Pintchman, *Seeking Mahadevi: Constructing the Identities of the Hindu Great Goddess* (Albany: SUNY Press, 2001), 125. Also in this case, the goddess is seen as an incarnation of Durgā, but she still accepts animal sacrifices (until recently including buffalo) and holds a cup for drinking blood offered to her by her devotees. In addition to the pot rituals, Richard L. Brubaker has pointed out that often buffaloes would be sacrificed at the onset of an epidemic. Richard L. Brubaker, "The Ambivalent Mistress: A Study of South Indian Village Goddesses and their Religious Meaning" (PhD diss., University of Chicago, 1978), 4, 332–43. The connection between the festivals of Mariyamman of Tamil Nadu, Pydamma of Visakhapatnam, and Chamundi Hill in Mysore is striking, and the former might demonstrate some aspects of south Indian local goddess ritual, which were part of the worship/veneration of the goddess of Chamundi hill prior to Wodeyar intervention.

46. Personal communication with Kannada language instructor C. S. Purnima.

47. For a detailed study of *jogatis*, see Lucinda Ramburg, *Given to the Goddess: South Indian Devadasis and the Sexuality of Religion* (Durham, NC: Duke University Press, 2014).

48. The ritual slaughter of buffaloes to goddesses during Navaratri is still practiced in various parts of India and Nepal. For a detailed study of the practice in Nepal, see Astrid Zotter, "Which Durgā? What Navarātra? Remarks on Reconfigurations of Royal Rituals in the Kathmandu Valley," in *Nine Nights of the Goddess: The Navarātri Festival in South Asia*, ed. Caleb Simmons, Moumita Sen, and Hillary Rodrigues (Albany: SUNY Press, 2018), 39–62.

49. In the traditions that are linked to the teachings of the Sharanas (Lingayatism and Virashaivism), participants do not cremate their dead as is the custom for most Hindu traditions. Instead, they bury their dead.

50. A reference to the Shiva *linga* worn by Lingayats.

51. A small brass bell worn by *jangamas*.

52. Reference to renunciation.

53. Another reference to asceticism, the *kamunda* is a short staff that is used to stabilize the arm while performing austerities.

54. See next chapter for a detailed discussion of this song.

55. In the Tambure version of the story, Najunda goes to the forest and creates an effigy that he places between his wives. P. K Rajashekhara, *Bettada Chamundi* (Mysore: Ta. Vem. Smaraka Granthamale, 1972), 46.

56. In other versions of the story, there is no confrontation. In the story told by a storyteller named Raghav, Chamundi calls Deviri as Nanjunda pretends to be sick and in need of her services as a fortune teller (Koravanji woman). P. K Rajashekhara, *Bettada Chamundi* (Mysore: Ta. Vem. Smaraka Granthamale, 1972), 49.

57. In the Tambure version, it is Parvati who scolds Nanjunda, but the confrontation is quickly dissolved by Deviri, who says that Nanjunda is free to take as many wives as he desires.

58. The association between "low-" caste identity, meat eating, and goddesses is a common triangulation. For an excellent discussion of this phenomenon in the context of *bhakti* devotional traditions, see Heidi Pauwels, "Who Are the Enemies of the Bhaktas?: Testimony about 'Saktas' and 'Others' from Kabir, the Ramanandis, Tulsidas, and Hariram Vyas," in *Journal of the American Oriental Society* 130, no. 4 (Oct.–Dec. 2010), 509–539. See also the section titled "Sacrifice and Pollution," in Kathleen M. Erndl, *Victory to the Mother: The Hindu Goddess of Northwest India in Myth, Ritual, and Symbol* (New York: Oxford University Press, 1993), 96–110.

59. K. R. Krishnaswami, *Janapada Kathana Geetagalu* (Mysore: Janapada Sahitya Academy, 1959). G. S. Paramashivayya, *Janapada Kavya Kathegalu* (Mysore: Surachi Prakashana, 1970).

60. The infighting of co-wives is another frequent theme in South Indian Shaiva literature. Often, these verbal altercations include accusations of caste inferiority that is linked to meat eating. See Shulman *Tamil Temple Myths: Sacrifice and Divine Marriage in the South Indian Śaiva Tradition* (Princeton: Princeton University Press, 1980), 284.

61. Gajanan Khergamker, "Keepers of the Craft," *Deccan Herald* (Mysore), May 5, 2019. https://www.deccanherald.com/sunday-herald/sh-top-stories/keepers-of-craft-731967.html.

62. Gajanan Khergamker, "Keepers of the Craft," *Deccan Herald* (Mysore), May 5, 2019. https://www.deccanherald.com/sunday-herald/sh-top-stories/keepers-of-craft-731967.html.

63. Holeyas and Madigas are also the two communities associated with the Tambure traditional performers, who also perform ballads that tell of the romance between Chamundi and Nanjunda. Gayathri Rajapur Kassenbaum, "Communal Self and Cultural Imagery: The Katha Performance Tradition in South India," in *Self as Image in Asian Theory and Practice*, ed. Roger T. Ames (Albany: SUNY Press, 1998), 260–79.

64. *Chamundi of the Hill's* narrative arch in which the goddess from a "lowly" background is accepted by or even exalted above other goddesses

after her performance of miracles is similar to the narrative of Santoshi Ma. Veena Das, "The Mythological Film and Its Framework of Meaning: An Analysis of 'Jai Santoshi Ma" in *India International Centre Quarterly* 8, no. 1 (March 1981), 43–56.

Chapter Five

1. In elite records since the 19th century and even through allusion in *Chamundi of the Hill*, Uttanahalli is sometimes connected with the lesser-known goddess Jwalamalini or Jwalamukhi. The connection with Jwalamalini, who is also well known in Jain Digambara traditions as the attendant to the eighth Tirthankara Chandraprabhu, has caused some scholars to speculate if both goddesses were originally Jain *yakshi*. See P. V. Nanjaraja Urs, *Maisūru: Nūrinnūru Varshagalu Hinde* (Mysore: Abhurrichi Prakashana, 2011).

2. Blood sacrifices are technically illegal in Karnataka, but while conducting research in Uttanahalli for this book, I frequent saw police observe and even take part in these blood sacrifices.

3. For example, see A. K. Ramanujan, *Speaking of Shiva* (New York: Penguin, 1993), 4–5.

4. Kim Knott, "Religion, Space, and Place: The Spatial Turn in Research on Religion," *Religion and Society: Advances in Research I* (2010): 29–43; "From Locality to Location and Back Again: A Spatial Journey in the Study of Religion," *Religion* 39, no. 2 (2009): 154–60; *The Location of Religion: A Spatial Analysis* (London: Routledge, 2005); "Spatial Theory and the Study of Religion" *Religion Compass* 2/6 (2008): 1102–16; "Inside, Outside and the Space in-between: Territories and Boundaries in the Study of Religion," in *Temenos* 44, no. 1 (2008): 41–66.

5. Kim Knott, *The Location of Religion: A Spatial Analysis* (London: Routledge, 2005), 94–123.

6. Kim Knott, "From Locality to Location and Back Again: A Spatial Journey in the Study of Religion," *Religion* 39, no. 2 (2009): 156.

7. Kim Knott, *The Location of Religion: A Spatial Analysis* (London: Routledge, 2005), 1–8, 122.

8. "Spatial Theory and the Study of Religion" *Religion Compass* 2/6 (2008). For an enlightening discussion of the language of borders as it pertains to religious identity, see Daniel Boyarin, *Border Lines: The Partition of Judaeo-Christianity* (Philadelphia: University of Pennsylvania Press, 2004).

9. E.g., Kim Knott, "Religion, Space, and Place: The Spatial Turn in Research on Religion," *Religion and Society: Advances in Research I* (2010); *The Location of Religion: A Spatial Analysis* (London: Routledge, 2005), 6.

10. Emile Durkheim, *Elementary Forms of Religious Life*, trans. Karen E. Fields (New York: Free Press, 1995), 36–37.

11. Jonathan Z. Smith, *To Take Place: Toward Theory in Ritual* (Chicago: University of Chicago Press, 1992), 45.

12. While Knott's theoretical apparatus tends to mask the connectivity of space, her methodology often highlights the networks—what she calls extensions—of religious practitioners across different geographical spaces, especially in her work on Hindu diaspora communities. See "Spatial Theory and the Study of Religion" *Religion Compass* 2, no. 6 (2008): 1109–10, for a succinct discussion of "extension."

13. Lawrence W. Levine, *Highbrow/Lowbrow: The Emergence of Cultural Hierarchy in America* (Cambridge, MA: Harvard University Press, 1988), 221–23.

14. For an overview of theories of the ways that many of these scholars portrayed "high" and "low" religion through the language of religion and magic, see Murray Wax and Rosalie Wax, "The Notion of Magic," *Current Anthropology* 4, no. 5 (December 1963), 495–518.

15. Walter Lippmann, *Public Opinion* (New York: Harcourt, Brace and Co., 1922).

16. Walter Lippman, *A Preface to Morals* (New York: Macmillan Company, 1929), 204–5.

17. Walter Lippman, *A Preface to Morals* (New York: Macmillan Company, 1929), 201.

18. Walter Lippman, *A Preface to Morals* (New York: Macmillan Company, 1929), 203.

19. Walter Lippman, *A Preface to Morals* (New York: Macmillan Company, 1929), 203.

20. Walter Lippman, *A Preface to Morals* (New York: Macmillan Company, 1929), 195.

21. There are many examples of this; however, one of my favorites is David Chidester, *Authentic Fakes: Religion and American Popular Culture* (Berkeley: University of California Press, 2005). In this book, Chidester eviscerates the assumption that popular culture is inferior, but shows that it functions in similar ways to religious traditions.

22. The Kannada term that is translated here as "hill" is *betta*, which denotes a "large hill or mountain." F. Kittle, *Kannada-English Dictionary* (New Delhi: Asian Educational Services, 2012 [1894]), 1136.

23. Again, this is quite clear in the Kannada *Bettada Chamundi* in which *betta* is declined in the genitive case as the possessor of *Chamundi*.

24. This is a reference to the goddess's Sanskritic identity as Jwalamukhi or Jwalajihva, which was part of her elite traditions (see chapter 2).

25. For an overview of sources that examine goddess binaries particularly through the lens of meat eating and vegetarianism, see Sree Padma, *Vicissitudes of the Goddess: Reconstructions of the Gramadevata in India's Religious Traditions* (New York: Oxford University Press, 2013), 35–38. For examples of

meat-eating local goddesses, see Sree Padma (ed.), *Inventing and Reinventing the Goddess: Contemporary Iterations of Hindu Deities on the Move* (Lanham, MD: Lexington Books, 2014).

26. For a helpful overview of meat eating and vegetarianism, see Ludwig Alsdorf, *The History of Vegetarianism and Cow-Veneration in India*, trans. Bal Patil and Nichola Hayton and ed. Willem Bollée (Routledge: New York, 2010).

27. For an overview of food theory and commensality in the Hindu traditions, see R. S. Khare, "Anna," *The Hindu World*, ed. Sushil Mittal and Gene Thursby (Routledge: New York, 2004), 407–28.

28. For more on the concept of commensality in *bhakti* (devotional) traditions, see Jon Keune, *Shared Devotion, Shared Food: Equality and the Bhakti-Caste Question in Western India* (New York: Oxford University Press, 2021).

29. For an excellent discussion of this phenomenon in the Virashaiva/Lingayat tradition, see the section titled "Animal Killing and Meat Consumption," in Gil Ben-Herut, *Śiva's Saints: The Origins of Devotion in Kannada according to Harihara's Ragalegalu* (New York: Oxford University Press, 2018), 145–51.

30. Heidi Pauwels, "Who Are the Enemies of the Bhaktas?: Testimony about 'Saktas' and 'Others' from Kabir, the Ramanandis, Tulsidas, and Hariram Vyas," in *Journal of the American Oriental Society* 130, no. 4 (Oct.–Dec. 2010), 509–39.

31. Kathleen M. Erndl, *Victory to the Mother: The Hindu Goddess of Northwest India in Myth, Ritual, and Symbol* (New York: Oxford University Press, 1993), 99–100. Emphasis added.

32. William S. Sax, *Mountain Goddess: Gender and Politics in a Himalayan Pilgrimage* (New York: Oxford University Press, 1991), 147–59. Goddess devotion takes on many forms. This is one source of the ambiguity over propriety. For a concise summary of different forms of goddess devotion, see June McDaniel, *Offering Flowers, Feeding Skulls: Popular Goddess Worship in West Bengal* (New York: Oxford University Press, 2004), 145–208.

33. Traditionary Account of the worship of Chamoondee Sactee: or Chamoondee Betta the Hill of Mysore and of the Origin and Commutation of the Sacrifice of Men on that hill, compiled from information at Mysore in 1805, Mackenzie General Collection Mss. 17.6. For more on this process, see Sree Padma, *Vicissitudes of the Goddess: Reconstructions of the Gramadevata in India's Religious Traditions* (New York: Oxford University Press, 2013).

34. The rituals described were observed in 2013.

35. In recent years the Indian Supreme Court has ruled in favor of allowing animal sacrifices on grounds of religious freedom, most notably the 2017 decision regarding Kullu Dussehra in Himachal Pradesh.

36. This might be related to the unique Goddess philosophy that stresses the simultaneous immanence and transcendence of the goddess, that is, the

goddess at the bottom of the hill acting as *bhuktipradayini*, while the goddess at the top of the hill is *muktipradayini*.

37. For a monograph focused on this connection, see Raj Balkaran, *The Goddess and the King in Indian Myth: Ring Composition, Royal Power and the Dharmic Double Helix* (London: Routledge, 2018).

Chapter Six

1. Lakshmidevi.
2. Sharada or Saraswati.
3. Mayakati.
4. The song says "Nanjalagudi" here. For sake of clarity, however, I have systematized each reference to this site to read "Nanjangudu."
5. Here the song says "Chamundeshwari." For sake of clarity, however, I have systematized each derivation of this epithet for the goddess to read "Chamundi."
6. Most of these songs are actually given in the present tense in Kannada because they are narrated by the performer as if they were unfolding in front of the audience. I have tried to replicate this where possible, although in written media, the present translation comes across awkwardly at times.
7. Sharada.
8. Rukmani is one of the wives of Krishna in Pan-Indic myth.
9. Literally having taken a boon from us, which could refer to either the group of gods or to Vishnu himself since he commonly refers to himself in the honorary plural.
10. Garuda is Krishna's eagle vehicle.
11. A reference to Krishna's childhood home.
12. The term translated as beautiful here is *rambe*. It could also be a reference to Indra's *apsara* of the same name.
13. The editor of the Kannada texts interprets it *"yaru? utnalli maramma!"*
14. The Kannada term *kibbi* is used here. It means the beginning or lower slope of the hill/mountain. It is also used to describe the lower part of the belly where it starts to rise (*kibboṭṭe*). It is etymologically linked to the term *kelagu* which means "bottom" or "low."
15. *Tambittu* is a rice dish that is formed by combining rice and jaggery and forming it into a ball or mound that is often offered to the goddess.
16. Kailasa is Shiva's divine abode in the Himalayan mountains.
17. *Jangama* refers to the wandering mendicants in the Lingayat tradition.
18. The term translated as rosary here is *rudraksha*. *Rudrakshas* are seeds from the *elaeocarpus ganitrus* tree that is used within Shaiva traditions, particularly for making garlands.

19. A *linga* is an aniconic representation of Shiva worn specifically by members of the Lingayat traditions.

20. Leaves used for Shiva worship.

21. She is literally called *dunda* Deviri or Big Deviri.

22. In traditional Kannada culture, if a man grabbed a woman by the hand, it meant they were married.

23. The term translated as "uncle" is *mavūra* or "maternal uncle."

24. Salavali is the female in a traditional Kannadiga marriage alliance in which the daughter of an eldest brother was betrothed to the son of the eldest sister.

25. Garalapura is a small village near Ramanagara outside of Bangalore. The reference here is unclear.

26. The text simply says nose-ring, etc., but the implication is the *accoutrements* of a married woman.

27. Literally "like a ship gone to ruin."

28. This is a reference to the Uttanahalli *murti* and its incredibly large tongue. Another name for Uttanahalli Maramma is Jwalatripurasundari, a combination of the goddess Jwalamukhi (the one with a face/tongue of fire) and the Shri Vidya goddess Tripurasundari (the beauty of the three cities).

29. These are the implements necessary for the exorcism of malevolent spirits (*bhuta*). The ash would be thrown on the victim, who is then beaten with the neem leaves until it leaves the victim's body. Moreover, neem leaves (along with tender coconut water and curd rice) are a typical offering to *marammas* that are taken as prasad and used to treat a variety of illnesses.

30. Five married women are part of the marriage ceremony. They come to the bride's home and offer plates with kumkum and flowers prior to the wedding. As part of this ceremony, they also throw rice on the couple.

31. Sita and Savitri are both females from Indian mythology and are frequently included in women's folksongs, particularly about married life, and often about its hardships.

32. This is the south Indian equivalent of a wedding ring or the north Indian custom of placing kum-kum in the part of the hair to denote a woman is married.

33. The verb used here is *doraku*, which literally means to come by, obtain, acquire, get, find, but given how incensed she is, I read it as a reference to their union on the river bank.

34. In the previous song, the lyrics cite Nanjunda touching the river. The cause for this discrepancy is unclear.

35. This usually refers to Nanjanguda, but here it is a clear reference to Mysore.

36. Kalaratri, here could be a reference to the new moon festival or the seventh night of *navaratri*.

37. The area surrounding St. Philomena's cathedral.

38. This is a common practice in southern Karnataka. When people are near death, they are placed outside the home, so any evil spirits that come at the time of death will not enter the home.

39. This is Ashoka Road. The clock tower was built during the British Raj.

40. Near Sitappa Square.

41. This reference to Kalamma Road here is unclear, but I have been told that it might refer to what is now Irving Road.

42. The area around KRS dam.

43. Cannabasava was a Virashaiva poet, who spoke out against ritual and animal sacrifice.

44. The meaning of *gangakati* is somewhat unclear. Some take it as simply a flirtatious woman, but others as a tribal woman, especially one who carries the image of the deity on her head during folk processions. This is probably an allusion to two people, who are from different *jatis* and different parts of society. Cannabasavanna was an antiritualistic *jangama* poet. He was a brahmin and vegetarian. The *gangakati* would have been from a low-caste village background and would have represented the animal sacrifice tradition associated with Chamundi and Uttanahalli worship. This is foreshadowing a response to Uttanahalli's complaint against Chamundi and Nanjunda's marriage.

45. This is an illusion to waving *arti* during puja in front of an animal sacrifice.

46. A reference to a funeral procession.

47. A reference to the Shiva *linga* worn by Virashaivas.

48. A reference to renunciation.

49. The *kamunda* is a short staff that is used to stabilize the arm while performing austerities.

50. The smoke which arises from frankincense that is thrown into a small flame outside of his temple.

51. This and the following line is an allusion to Kama's attack on Shiva.

52. Literally, "you are hungry."

53. *Mantapa* here is a reference to a village marriage platform.

54. Matha is a religious institution. This is likely a reference to the Suttur Matha in Nanjangudu.

55. This is actually given as a statement, but it seems to carry the sense of the interrogative.

56. Also given as a statement but with the sense of interrogative.

57. Give as statement but with the sense of an interrogative.

58. *Surugi*.

59. *Ippe* is a plant, the seeds of which were traditionally harvested to produce lamp oil. The term also means a wish or desire and is most likely

a double *entendre*, indicating that the Nanjunda temple on the bank of the river in Nanjalagudi is a wish-giving orchard.

60. I have chosen to translate the term *suli*, which literally means "prostitute" or "whore" as "ho" since it is used throughout the remaining songs both as an insult (as in this case) and a term of playful teasing by Nanjunda when referring to Chamundi. Though now a little dated, the closest equivalent in American English would be the term "ho" that is derived from "whore" and commonly used in popular media to represent a female sexual partner (often not the primary sexual partner) and can be used in both a flirtarious (albeit demeaningly) and pejorative sense. Another option would be the way that female friends in the United States sometimes refer to one another as "whores" or even perhaps "sluts."' Another possible translation would be "bitch," but it does not carry the same sexual connotation.

61. The name used in the song here is Chamayi, a common colloquial name for Chamundi.

62. This is a Kannada idiomatic proverb.

63. The term I have chosen to translate as "chicks" is *habbakki*, which literally means "birds."

64. Death here is Yama or the god who rules over the netherworld.

65. This is a reference to the Haddugallu mountain range near Nagamangala.

66. Literally, "Let it be."

67. The *hundi* is a box or chest in the main platform or *mantapa* of a temple in which offerings are placed by devotees.

68. Here the English word "chain" is used.

69. Nandi, here, is called Basavanna, a common name for the deity in southern Karnataka.

70. Here Kalinga is actually called Brother Shesha (Sheshanna), a connection between the serpent deity and the serpent Shesha on whom cosmic Vishnu rests.

71. This is an annual *naga* festival, which takes place in the Subrahmanya temple located on the road between Mysore and Shrirangapaṭṭana.

72. This is the name of the Apsara, who was the consort of Brahma.

73. This is a reference to Dhritarashṭra's wife, who blindfolded herself in solitude with her blind husband. The reference, however, is to her role as the mother of the Kauravas and therefore, the silent cause of the Mahabharata War.

74. The term here is *koravanji* or a fortuneteller. It is also the name of a lake in Mysore.

75. Holiya and Madigas are two of the lowest *jatis* in southern Karnataka. This idiom means that someone has scolded in the harshest way. It is similar to the English idiom "You treated her like a red-headed step-child."

76. Typically, when a devotee would commit an act that was seen as displeasing to the goddess, they would tie coins in a cloth and offer it to the goddess.

77. The meaning of this is absolutely unknown to everyone that I have consulted. It could be something that is very old and has been slowly changed over time to something unrecognizable.

78. This refers to a beauty mark that is placed on the face of a beautiful woman, which is intended to drawn in the gaze of others averting the evil eye.

79. When a devotee comes to the temple for a boon, they will offer flowers over the deity's head. If the flower falls to the right side of the image, the request will be granted. If the flower falls to the left side the request will not be granted.

Bibliography

Kannada and Sanskrit Sources

Akki, Sujatha. *Chama Cheluve*. Directed by Mandya Ramesh. Mysore: Vismaya Prakashana, 2012.
Ayyangar, Goruru Ramaswamy. *Halliya Haadugalu*. Bangalore: Satyasodhana Pustaka Bhandara, 1938.
Chandrashekhar, N. *Bedagugara Nanjunda*. N.p.: n.p., 1998.
Devanandan, S. R. *Shaktapramoda*. Bombay: Khemraja Shrikrishnadasa Prakashan, 1973.
Iyengar, Masti Venkatesh. *Karnataka Janapada Sahitya*. Bangalore: Jivana Karyalaya, 1937.
Hegade, Suhasini. "Chama Cheluve yashasvi nurne prayoga; nirdeshaka Mandya Ramesh manadaleda matu." *Siti Tude* (Bangalore), September 3, 2016.
Kale, M. R. *Bhavabhuti's Malatimadhava with Commentary of Jagaddhara*. Delhi: Motilal Banarsidass, 1967.
Mathighatta Krishnamurthy. *Kannada Janapada Sahitya Bhandara Geetegalu*. Bangalore: n.p., 1975.
Krishnaswami, K. R. *Janapada Kathana Geetagalu*. Mysore: Janapada Sahitya Academy, 1959.
———. *Naada Melella Haridave*. N.p.: n.p., 1962.
Maralusiddhappa, K. *Lavanigalu*. Bangalore: n.p., 1974.
Paramashivayya, J. S. *Helavaru and Their Kavyagalu*. Mysore: Institute of Kannada Studies, 1972.
———. *Janapada Kavya kathegalu*. Mysore: Surachi Prakashana, 1970.
———. *Kannada Vruttigayaka Kavyagalu*. N.p.: n.p., n.d.
Rajashekhara, P. K. *Bettada Chamundi*. Mysore: Ta. Vem. Smaraka Granthamale, 1972.
———. *Chamundi Siri Chamundi*. Mysore: Honnaru Janapada Gayakaru, 1994.
———. *Chamundi Siri Chamundi: Janapada Puranakavya Adharita Nataka*. Mysore: Chaitra Prakashana, 2012.

———. *Janapadada Virakavya Piriyapattanada Kalaga*. Mysore: Honnuru Janapada Gayakaru, 1990.
Ramanna, Kyathanahalli. *Subbakka Haadida Nanjundeshwara Kavya*. Bangalore: Dinakara Prakashana, 1980.
Ramegauda. *Chamayi*. N.p: n.p., 1981.
Rangaswamy, A. B. *Huttida Halli Halliya Haadugalu*. N.p.: n.p., 1933.
———. *Janapada Sahitya Chitragalu*. N.p.: n.p., 1958.
Urs, P. V. Nanjaraja. *Maisūru: Nūrinnūru Varshagalu Hinde*. Mysore: Abhurrichi Prakashana, 2011.
Wodeyar, Mummadi Krishnaraja, *Maisūru Saṃsthānada Prabhugaḷu Śrīmanmahārājaravara Vaṃśāvali Volumes 1–2*. Edited by B. Ramakrishna Row. Mysore: Government Branch Press, 1916 and 1922.

English Sources

Alley, Kelley. *On the Banks of the Gaṅgā: When Wastewater Meets a Sacred River*. Ann Arbor, MI: University of Michigan Press, 2002.
Alsdorf, Ludwig. *The History of Vegetarianism and Cow-Veneration in India*, trans. Bal Patil and Nichola Hayton and ed. Willem Bollée. Routledge: New York, 2010.
Appadurai, Arjun. *Modernity at Large: Cultural Dimensions of Globalization*. Minneapolis, MN: University of Minnesota Press, 1996.
Bairy, Ramesh. *Being Brahmin, Being Modern: Exploring the Lives of Caste Today*. New Delhi: Routledge, 2010.
Balkaran, Raj. *The Goddess and the King in Indian Myth: Ring Composition, Royal Power and the Dharmic Double Helix*. London: Routledge, 2018.
Basavarajappa, K. H. "Backward Caste and Class Movement in Karnataka with Special Reference to Kurubas." PhD thesis, Karnatak University, 1983. https://shodhganga.inflibnet.ac.in/handle/10603/94009.
Basham, A. L. *The Wonder That Was India*. New York: Grove Press, 1959.
Boyarin, Daniel. *Border Lines: The Partition of Judaeo-Christianity*. Philadelphia: University of Pennsylvania Press, 2004.
Brubaker, Richard L. "The Ambivalent Mistress: A Study of South Indian Village Goddesses and Their Religious Meaning." PhD dissertation, University of Chicago, 1978.
Caldwell, Sarah. "Waves of Beauty, Rivers of Blood: Constructing the Goddess in Kerala" *Seeking Mahādevī: Constructing the Identities of the Hindu Great Goddess*, edited by Tracy Pintchman, 93–114. Albany, NY: SUNY Press, 2001.
Cid, Alejandro Jiménez. "Blood for the Goddess: Self-Mutilation Rituals at Vajreśvarī Mandir, Kāṅgrā." *Indi@logs* 3 (2016): 37–55.

Chamberlin J. Edward and Daniel Frank Chamberlain. *Or Words to That Effect: Orality and the Writing of Literary History.* Amsterdam: J. Benjamins Publishing Co., 2016.

Chandra Shobhi, Prithvi Datta. "Pre-modern Communities and Modern Histories: Narrating Vīraśaiva and Lingayat Selves." PhD dissertation, University of Chicago, 2005.

Chatterjee, Kumkum. "History as Self-Representation: The Recasting of a Political Tradition in Late Eighteenth-Century Eastern India." *Modern Asian Studies* 32, no. 4 (1998): 913–948.

Chatterjee, Partha. "Introduction: History in the Vernacular." In *History in the Vernacular*, edited by Raziuddin Aquil and Partha Chatterjee, 1–25. Delhi: Permanent Black, 2008.

Chidester, David. *Authentic Fakes: Religion and American Popular Culture.* Berkeley: University of California Press, 2005.

Coburn, Thomas. *Devi Mahatmya: The Crystallization of the Goddess Tradition.* New Delhi: Motilal Banarsidass, 2002.

———. *Encountering the Goddess.* Albany, NY: SUNY Press, 1991.

———. "Sītā Fights while Rāma Swoons: A Śākta Perspective on the *Rāmāyana.*" In *Breaking Boundaries with the Goddess: New Directions in the Study of Śāktism, Essays in Honor of Narendra Nath Bhattacharyya*, edited by Cynthia Ann Humes and Rachel Fell McDermott, 35–59. New Delhi: Manohar, 2009.

Cort, John. "Medieval Jaina Goddess Traditions." *Numen* 34, Fasc. 2 (Dec. 1987): 237–255.

Craddock, Elaine. "Reconstructing the Split Goddess as Śakti in a Tamil Village." In *Seeking Mahadevi: Constructing the Identities of the Hindu Great Goddess*, edited by Tracy Pintchman, 145–170. Albany, NY: SUNY Press, 2001.

D'Souza, P. G. *Annual Report of the Mysore Archaeological Department.* Bangalore: Government Press, 1925.

Das, Veena. "The Mythological Film and Its Framework of Meaning: An Analysis of 'Jai Santoshi Ma." *India International Centre Quarterly* 8, no. 1 (March 1981): 43–56.

Dhere, R. C. *Rise of a Folk God: Vitthal of Pandarpur.* New York: Oxford University Press, 2011.

Donaldson, Thomas Eugene. "The Shava-Vahana as Purusha in Orissan Images: Chamunda to Kali/Tara." *Artibus Asiae* 51, no. 1/2 (1991): 107–141.

Durkheim, Emile *Elementary Forms of Religious Life.* Translated by Karen E. Fields. New York: Free Press, 1995.

Dutta, Ranjeeta. "Pilgrimage as Religious Process: Some Reflections on the Identities of the Srivaisnavas of South India." *Indian Historical Review* 37, no. 1 (2010): 17–38.

Eck, Diana L. *India: A Sacred Geography.* New York: Harmony Books, 2012.

Eliade, Mircea. *Yoga: Immortality and Freedom*. Princeton, NJ: Princeton University Press, 1973.
Elmore, Wilber T. "Dravidian Gods in Modern Hinduism: A Study of the Local and Village Deities of Southern India." PhD dissertation, University of Nebraska, 1915.
Erndl, Kathleen M. "Is *Shakti* Empowering for Women? Reflections on Feminism and the Hindu Goddess." In *Is the Goddess a Feminist: The Politics of South Asian Goddesses*, edited by Alf Hiltebeital and Kathleen M. Erndl, 91–103. New York: New York University Press, 2000.
———. *Victory to the Mother*. New York: Oxford University Press, 1993.
Feldhaus, Anne. *Connected Places: Region, Pilgrimage, and Geographical Imagination in India*. New York: Palgrave Macmillan, 2003.
Feldhaus, Anne, Ramdas Atkar, Rajaram Zagade. *Say to the Sun "Don't Rise," and to the Moon, "Don't Set": Two Oral Narratives from the Countryside of Maharashtra*. New York: Oxford University Press, 2014.
Feldt, Laura. "Fictioning Myths and Mythic Fictions: The Standard-Babylonian Gilgameš Epic and Questions of Heroism, Myth, and Fiction." In *Explaining, Interpreting, and Theorizing Religion and Myth: Contributions in Honor of Robert A. Segal*, edited by Nikolas P. Rouebekas and Thomas Ryba, 282–298. Leiden: Brill, 2020.
Fleet, J. F. "Mahishamandala and Mahishmati." *The Journal of the Royal Asiatic Society* 42, no. 2 (April 1910): 425–447.
Gold, Anne Grodzins. *A Carnival of Parting: The Tales of King Bharthari and King Gopi Chand as Sung and Told by Madhu Natisar Nath of Ghatiyali, Rajasthan*. Berkeley: University of California Press, 1993.
Gold, Ann, and Bhoju Ram Gujar. *In the Time of Trees and Sorrows: Nature, Power, and Memory in Rajasthan*. Durham, NC: Duke University Press, 2002.
Gold, Anne, and Gloria Goodwin Raheja. *Listen to the Heron's Words: Reimagining Gender and Kinship in North India*. Berkeley: University of California Press, 1994.
Goswami, B. B., and S. G. Morab. *Chamundesvari Temple in Mysore*. Calcutta: Anthropological Survey of India, 1991.
Gür, Berin F. "Local Performance in the Construction of National Identity: Plaka District of Athens during the Nineteenth Century." *Journal of Urban History* 38, no. 1 (2012): 39–70.
Hayden, Dolores. "Placemaking, Preservation and Urban History." *Journal of Architectural Education* 41, no. 3 (Spring 1988): 45–51.
Hiltebeitel, Alf. *Rethinking India's Oral and Classical Epics: Draupadi among Rajputs, Muslims, and Dalits*. Chicago: University of Chicago Press, 1999.
———. *The Cult of Draupadi Volumes 1–2*. Chicago: University of Chicago Press, 1988 and 1991.

Hoernle F. R. "The Pattavali or List of Pontiffs of the Upakesa-Gachchha," *Indian Antiquary* 19 (1890): 237–238.

Humes, Cynthia "Is the *Devi Mahatmya* a Feminist Scripture?" In *Is the Goddess a Feminist: The Politics of South Asian Goddesses*, edited by Alf Hiltebeitel and Kathleen M. Erndl, 123–150. New York: New York University Press.

Ikegame, Aya. *Princely India Re-imagined: A Historical Anthropology of Mysore from 1799 to the Present.* London: Routledge, 2013.

———. "Karnataka: Caste, Dominance, and Social Change in an Indian Village." In *The Modern Anthropology of Indai: Ethnography, Themes, and Theory*, edited by Peters Berger, Frank Heidemann, Subrata Ghatak, and Paul Levine. 121–135. London: Routledge, 2013.

———. "Why Do Backward Castes Need Their Own Gurus? The Social and Political Significance of New Caste-Based Monasteries in Karnataka." *Contemporary South Asia* 18, no. 1 (March 2010): 57–70.

Jalki, Dunkin. "Lingayat Tradition, Adhyatma and Caste: How Bhakti Traditions Understand Caste." *Journal of Contemporary Thought* 41 (Summer 2015): 165–190.

Jameson, Stephanie. *Sacrificed Wife/Sacrificer's Wife: Women, Ritual, and Hospitality in Ancient India.* New York: Oxford University Press, 1996.

Joyser, G. R. *The History of Mysore and the Yadava Dynasty.* Mysore: Coronation Press, 1939.

Kane, P. V. *History of Dharmasastra: Ancient and Mediaeval Religious and Civil Law in India Volume I Part I.* Pune: Bhandarkar Oriental Research Institute, 1953.

Kassenbaum, Gayathri Rajapur. "Communal Self and Cultural Imagery: The Katha Performance Tradition in South India." In *Self as Image in Asian Theory and Practice*, edited by Roger T. Ames, 260–279. Albany, NY: SUNY Press, 1998.

Keune, Jon. *Shared Devotion, Shared Food: Equality and the Bhakti-caste Question in Western India.* New York: Oxford University Press, 2021.

Khare, R.S. "Anna." In *The Hindu World*, edited by Sushil Mittal and Gene Thursby. 407–428. Routledge: New York, 2004.

Khergamker, Gajanan. "Keepers of the Craft." *Deccan Herald* (Mysore), May 5, 2019. https://www.deccanherald.com/sunday-herald/sh-top-stories/keepers-of-craft-731967.html.

Kinsley, David. *Tantric Visions of the Divine Feminine: The Ten Mahāvidyās.* Berkeley, CA: University of California Press, 1997.

Knott, Kim. "From Locality to Location and Back Again: A Spatial Journey in the Study of Religion." *Religion* 39, no. 2 (2009): 156.

———. "Inside, Outside and the Space in-between: Territories and Boundaries in the Study of Religion" *Temenos* 44, no. 1 (2008): 41–66.

———. *The Location of Religion: A Spatial Analysis*. London: Routledge, 2005.

———. "Religion, Space, and Place: The Spatial Turn in Research on Religion." *Religion and Society: Advances in Research I* (2010): 29–43.

———. "Spatial Theory and the Study of Religion." *Religion Compass* 2, no. 6 (2008): 1102–1116.

Kittle, F. *Kannada-English Dictionary*. New Delhi: Asian Educational Services, 2012 [1894].

Korom, Frank J. "A Telling Place: Narrative and the Construction of Locality in a Bengali Village." *Narrative Culture* 3, no. 1 (Spring 2016): 32–66.

———. *The Anthropology of Performance: A Reader*. New York: Wiley-Blackwell, 2014.

———. *South Asian Folklore: A Handbook*. Westport, CT: Greenwood Press, 2006.

Lankesh, Gauri. "Making Sense of the Lingayat vs Veershaiva Debate." *TheWire.in*. September 5, 2017. https://thewire.in/history/karnataka-lingayat-veerashaive-debate/.

Levine, Lawrence W. *Highbrow/Lowbrow: The Emergence of Cultural Hierarchy in America*. Cambridge, MA: Harvard University Press, 1988.

Lippmann, Walter. *Public Opinion*. New York: Harcourt, Brace and Co., 1922.

———. *A Preface to Morals*. New York: Macmillan Company, 1929.

Lochtefeld, James, *God's Gateway: Identity and Meaning in a Hindu Pilgrimage Place*. New York: Oxford University Press, 2010.

Mahalakshmi, R. *The Making of the Goddess: Korravai-Durga in the Tamil Traditions*. New Delhi: Penguin Books, 2011.

Main, Roderick. "Myth, Synchronicity, and the Physical World." In *Explaining, Interpreting, and Theorizing Religion and Myth: Contributions in Honor of Robert A. Segal*, edited by Nikolas P. Rouebekas and Thomas Ryba, 248–262. Leiden: Brill, 2020.

Matchett, Freda. "The Purānas." In *The Blackwell Companion to Hinduism*, edited by Gavin Flood, 129–143. London: Blackwell Publishing, 2003.

McDaniel, June. *Offering Flowers, Feeding Skulls: Popular Goddess Worship in West Bengal*. New York: Oxford University Press, 2004.

McDermott, Rachell Fell. *Mother of My Heart, Daughter of My Dreams: Kali and Uma in the Devotional Poetry of Bengal*. New York: Oxford University Press, 2001.

———. *Singing to the Goddess: Poems to Kālī and Umā from Bengal*. New York: Oxford University Press, 2001.

McLean Kama. "Making the Colonial State Work for You: The Modern Beginnings of the Ancient Kumbh Mela in Allahabad." *The Journal of Asian Studies* 62, no. 3 (2003): 877–879.

Meister, Michael W. "Regional Variations in Mātṛkā Conventions." *Artibus Asiae* 46, nos. 3/4 (1986): 233–262.

Michael, R. Blake. "Liṅgāyats." In *Brill's Encyclopedia of Hinduism*, edited by Knut A. Jacobsen, Helene Basu, Angelika Malinar, and Vasudha Narayanan, 378–392. Leiden, Boston: Brill, 2011.

Mills, Jon. "Deconstructing Myth." In *Explaining, Interpreting, and Theorizing Religion and Myth: Contributions in Honor of Robert A. Segal*, edited by Nikolas P. Rouebekas and Thomas Ryba, 233–247. Leiden: Brill, 2020.

Misra, Promode Kumar. *Cultural Profile of Mysore*. Mysore: Archaeological Survey of India, 1978.

Nair, Janaki, *Mysore Modern: Rethinking the Region under Princely Rule*. New Delhi: Orient Blackswan Private Limited, 2010.

Narayan, Kirin. *Everyday Creativity: Singing Goddesses in the Himalayan Foothills*. Chicago: University of Chicago Press, 2016.

Nayak, H. M. "Nj 212." In *Epigraphia Carnatica Revision Volume III*. Mysore: Prasaranga, 1974.

Padma, Sree. "From Village to City: Transforming Goddesses in Urban Andhra Pradesh." In *Seeking Mahadevi: Constructing the Identities of the Hindu Great Goddess*, edited by Tracy Pintchman, 115–143. Albany, NY: SUNY Press, 2001.

———. *Inventing and Reinventing the Goddess: Contemporary Iterations of Hindu Deities on the Move*. Lanham, MD: Lexington Books, 2014.

———. *Vicissitudes of the Goddess: Reconstructions of the Gramadevata in India's Religious Traditions*. New York: Oxford University Press, 2013.

Parthasarathy, R. *Tale of an Anklet: An Epic of South India*. New York: Columbia University Press, 1993.

Pauwels, Heidi. "Who Are the Enemies of the Bhaktas?: Testimony about 'Saktas' and 'Others' from Kabir, the Ramanandis, Tulsidas, and Hariram Vyas." *Journal of the American Oriental Society* 130, no. 4 (Oct.–Dec. 2010): 509–539.

Peterson, Indira Vishwanathan. *Poems to Śiva: The Hymns of the Tamil Saints*. Delhi: Motilal Banarsidass Publishers, 1991.

Pintchman, Tracy. *Seeking Mahadevi: Constructing the Identities of the Hindu Great Goddess*. Albany, NY: SUNY Press, 2001.

Ramachandran, C. N. and L. N. Bhat. *Male Madeshwara: A Kannada Oral Epic as Sung by Hebbani Madayya and His Troupe*. Collected by K. K. Presad. New Delhi: Sahitya Akademi.

Ramanujan, A. K. *Speaking of Shiva*. New York: Penguin, 1993.

Ramburg, Lucinda, *Given to the Goddess: South Indian Devadasis and the Sexuality of Religion*. Durham, NC: Duke University Press, 2014.

Rice, B. Lewis. "Ch 102" *Epigraphia Carnatica Volume IV*. Mysore: Government Press, 1898.

———. "My 16" *Epigraphia Carnatica Volume III.1*. Mysore: Government Press, 1894.

———. *Mysore: A Gazetteer Compiled for Government* (New Delhi: Asian Educational Service [London: Archibald Constable and Company], 2001 [1897]).

Saraswathi, G. *The Study of Socio-Economic Conditions of the Temple Priests of South Mysore*. Calcutta: Anthropological Survey of India, 2000.

Sarkar, Bihani. *Heroic Shāktism: The Cult of Durgā in Ancient Indian Kingship*. New York: Oxford University Press, 2017.

Sax, William S. *Mountain Goddess: Gender and Politics in a Himalayan Pilgrimage*. New York: Oxford University Press, 1991.

Schmid, Charlotte. "Du Rite au Mythe: Le Tueuses de Buffle de l'Inde ancienne." *Artibus Asiae* 71, no. 1 (2011): 115–161.

Seastrand, Anna Lise. "Praise, Politics, and Language: South India Murals, 1500–1800. PhD dissertation, Columbia University, 2013.

Segal, Robert A. *Myth: A Very Short Introduction*. New York: Oxford University Press, 2015.

Selby, Martha Ann, and Indira Viswanathan Peterson. *Tamil Geographies: Cultural Constructions of Space and Place in South India*. Albany: SUNY Press, 2008.

Sircar, Dineschandra. *The Śākta Pīṭhas*. Delhi: Motilal Banarsidass, 1973.

Sharma, Hari Krishna. *Durgasaptashati*. Delhi: Chaukamba Sanskrit Pratishthan, 2006.

Shivaprakash, H. S. *I Keep Vigil of Rudra: The Vachanas*. New Delhi: Penguin, 2010.

Shulman, David. *Tamil Temple Myths: Sacrifice and Divine Marriage in the South Indian Śaiva Tradition*. Princeton: Princeton University Press, 1980.

Simmons, Caleb. *Devotional Sovereignty: Kingship and Religion in India*. New York: Oxford University Press, 2020.

———. "Domains of Dasara: Reflections on the Struggle for Significance in Contemporary Mysore." In *Nine Nights of Power*, edited by Ute Hüsken, Vasudha Narayanan, and Astrid Zötter. Albany, NY: SUNY Press, forthcoming.

———. "Dynastic Continuity and Election in Contemporary Karnataka Politics." In *The Conundrum of Worldly Power: Sovereignty in South Asian*, edited by Arild Ruud and Pamela Price, 136–149. London: Routledge, 2019.

———. "Family, God, and King: Vaṃśāvaḷi as Royalist Literature." In *Clio and her Descendants: Essays in Honor of Keshavan Veluthat*. edited by Manu Devadevan, 598–622. New Delhi: Primus Books, 2018.

———. "Goddess and the King: Cāmundēśvari and the Fashioning of the Wodeyar Court of Mysore." PhD dissertation, University of Florida, 2014.

———. "History, Heritage, and Myth: Local Historical Imagination in the Fight to Preserve Chamundi Hill in Mysore City." *Worldviews* 22 (2018): 216–237.

Simmons, Caleb, Moumita Sen, and Hillary Rodrigues. *Nine Nights of the Goddess: The Navarātri Festival in South Asia*. Albany, NY: SUNY Press, 2018.

Smith, Jonathan Z. *To Take Place: Toward Theory in Ritual*. Chicago: University of Chicago Press, 1992.
Smith, Travis L. "Renewing the Ancient: The *Kāśikhanda* and Śaiva Varanasi." *Acta Orientalia Vilnensia* 8 no. 1 (2007): 83–108.
Srinivas, M. N. *Religion and Society among the Coorgs of South India*. Oxford: Clarendon Press, 1952.
Staal, J. Fritz. "Sanskrit and Sanskritization." *The Journal of Asian Studies* 22, no. 3 (May 1963): 261–275.
Stein, Emma. "All Streets Lead to Temples: Mapping Monumental Histories in Kanchipuram, ca. 8th–12th centuries CE." PhD dissertation, Yale University, 2017.
Thurston, Edgar. *Castes and Tribes of Southern India Vol. IV*. Madras: Government Press, 1909.
Traditionary Account of the worship of Chamoondee Sactee: or Chamoondee Betta the Hill of Mysore and of the Origin and Commutation of the Sacrifice of Men on that hill, compiled from information at Mysore in 1805, Mackenzie General Collection Mss. 17.6.
Tuan, Yi-Fu. *Topophilia: A Study of Environmental Perceptions, Attitudes, and Values*. New York: Columbia University Press, 1990.
Venkatesan, Archana (trans). *A Hundred Measures of Time, Tiruviruttam*. New York: Penguin Books, 2014.
Wax, Murray, and Rosalie Wax. "The Notion of Magic." *Current Anthropology* 4, no. 5 (December 1963): 495–518.
Weber, Max. *The Religion of India*, trans. and ed. by Hans H. Gerth and Don Martindale. New York: The Free Press, 1958.
Wilks, Mark. *Historical Sketches of the South of India in an Attempt to Trace the History of Mysoor from the Hindoo Government of That State to the Extinction of the Mohammedan Dynasty in 1799 Volumes 1 & 2*. Mysore: Government Branch Press, 1930.
Wilson, H. H. *Malati and Madhava or the Stolen Marriage: A Drama*. Calcutta: Society for the Resuscitation of Indian Literature Elysium Press, 1901.
———. *The Vishnu Purana, A System of Hindu Mythology and Tradition*. London: John Murray, 1840.
Younger, Paul. "A Temple Festival of Mariyamman." *Journal of the American Academy of Religion* 48, no. 4 (Dec. 1980): 493–513.
Zotter, Astrid. "Which Durgā? What Navarātra? Remarks on Reconfigurations of Royal Rituals in the Kathmandu Valley." In *Nine Nights of the Goddess: The Navarātri Festival in South Asia*, edited by Caleb Simmons, Moumita Sen, and Hillary Rodrigues, 39–62. Albany, NY: SUNY Press, 2018.
Zydenbos, Robert. "Vīraśaivism, Caste, Revolution, Etc." *Journal of the American Oriental Society* 117, no. 3 (1997), 525–535.

Index

Basava, 13, 91, 101, 192n25
Bhagavad Gita, 50
Buddhism, 59, 118

caste
　and agriculturalists, 1, 10, 42, 91
　and brahminic regulations, 118
　of bramins, 42, 92, 191n20, 200n19, 211n40
　and caste hierarchy, 18, 41, 42, 47, 86, 90, 92, 93, 102–103, 104, 106, 107, 191n20
　and *Chama Cheluve*, 195n42
　and Coorgs castes, 47
　and deities of different castes, 60, 93, 101–105, 154, 175
　and devotion (*bhakti*), 118
　discrimination based on, 24, 83, 86, 90, 92, 93, 106, 107
　and goddess traditions, 118, 119, 200n19
　and Kuruba caste, 1, 17, 91, 100
　and landowning castes, 92
　and Lingayatas, 191n20, 200n19, 210n22
　and Lingayat identity, 42, 92, 104, 210n24
　and "low castes," 18, 41, 47, 91, 93, 96, 100, 101, 102, 104–105, 107, 118, 214n58, 220n44
　and marriage, 85–86, 90, 91, 93, 101, 102, 103
　and meat eating, 214n60
　in Mysore temples, 191n20
　and nonbrahmin castes, 48, 72, 99–100
　and "Other Backward Castes" (OBC), 18, 91, 209n19
　and "outcastes," 106
　and performance-based castes, 16
　and Raja Parivara, 100, 212n45
　and religious practice, 91, 92–93, 106
　and rituals, 8, 48, 100, 103, 104, 106–107, 118
　and the Sharanas, 101
　and Shiva *puja*, 92
　and Shivarchakas, 99, 100, 191n20
　and song "I Can Raise the Dead!," 175
　and subcaste Devaragudda, 1, 17, 18, 91, 92
　and Tammadi (also Tomadi) caste, 10, 42
　and the Vijayanagara Empire, 91
　See also Kamsales
Chama Cheluve, 16–17, 21, 22, 81, 81 fig. 3.1
Chamundeshwari temple
　and animal sacrifice, 120

Chamundeshwari temple *(continued)*
   and Chamundi Hill, 9–10, 17, 32 *fig.* 2.2, 38, 42, 54, 109
   and Dikshita priests, 10, 119, 191n19, 200n19
   and festival image, 96
   and goddess traditions, 54–55
   and Kamsale bards, 17
   and Lingayat priests, 211n38
   and ritual practice, 100, 109–10, 191n20
   royal patronage of, 110, 198n10
   and Shivarchakas, 200n19
   and shrines to goddesses, 211n37
   site of, 9, 10, 109
   and universal Goddess, 7, 37 *fig.* 2.3
   workers from, 98 *fig.* 4.2
   See also Chamundi

Chamundi
   and Aisu ("Many"), 31–33, 51–52, 69, 70, 71, 86, 116, 117, 127, 128, 130–33, 197–98n6
   and animal sacrifice, 120, 199n15, 201n26, 220n44
   and bathing, 86–88, 117, 134–35, 147, 148
   and caste, 105, 107, 154
   in *Chama Cheluve*, 193–94n32
   as Chamaraja's house deity, 34
   and Chamundeshwari, 218n5
   and Chamundi Hill, 6, 7–8, 11, 37–38, 53–54, 71, 72, 73, 77, 81, 96, 109, 115–16, 119, 125, 127, 128, 140, 177, 181, 199n15, 207n20
   and community, 7
   and consort Nanjunda, 1, 2, 3, 4–5, 6, 11, 13, 14, 16, 24, 31, 42, 54, 58, 69, 70–71, 72, 74, 77–79, 80, 85, 87, 88–90, 100, 103–104, 105, 116–17, 125, 138–39, 140, 141, 146, 147–50, 153, 170, 176
   as a co-wife, 5–6, 93, 94, 95, 103, 106, 151, 174–76, 207n18
   and cult of the seven little mothers, 10–11
   as deity of Mysore, 2, 4, 8, 9–11, 34, 35, 37–38, 52–54, 63–64, 72, 95, 117, 137–38, 197n4
   and devotion *(bhakti)*, 54, 119, 126
   festivals of, 37, 38, 39 *fig.* 2.4 a&b, 72, 96–100, 120, 211n36, 211n40
   and goddess traditions, 36–37, 123
   and human sacrifice, 199n15
   identity of, 42, 72, 88–90, 109–10, 119, 125, 197n4, 198n10
   images of, 8, 9 *fig.* 1.1, 33, 37, 38, 88, 100, 109
   and Kamsales, 190n7
   lion as vehicle of, 132–33
   as a local deity, 7, 9, 10, 27, 35–36, 41–42, 48, 53–54, 72, 77, 79, 93, 95, 99–100, 133, 141, 197n4
   and Maramma, 201n26
   and marriage, 220n44
   as a mother goddess, 8–9, 72, 125–26, 127, 128, 131, 133, 134, 135, 141, 143, 176, 177–78, 181, 198n10
   and myth, 29, 43–47, 52–54, 70–72, 95, 101, 208n6
   and name Chamunda, 8, 11, 43, 44, 45, 49, 109
   and name Chamundeshwari, or Queen Chamundi, 109
   and name Chamundeshwari [Lady Chamundi], 48, 63, 64, 80, 181
   nightmare of, 141–43, 146, 150–52
   offerings to, 119–20
   portrayals of, 7, 33
   power of, 63, 119, 181
   as protector of city, 80, 89–90
   as protector of region, 117, 177–78
   and relationship with Nanjunda, 214n56, 221n60

religious context of, 27, 35, 36–40, 81, 125
and ritual practice, 115, 117, 118–19
and romance between deities, 214n63
as ruler of Mysore, 52
in the Sanskritic/brahminic Mysore tradition, 8, 9
second nightmare of, 152–53
and slaying of buffalo demon Mahisha, 4, 8, 23, 27, 29, 30, 31, 33, 42, 52–54, 69, 70, 71, 86, 88, 89, 116, 117, 125, 127, 130, 131, 147, 177, 197–98n6
and song "O Mother, Grant Me a Wish," 125–26
songs about, 16–17, 18, 53–54, 58, 69, 70–71, 74, 77, 86, 125–54, 155–57, 161–70, 171–76, 177–79
temple of, 4, 5, 7, 9–10, 11, 37, 54–55, 81, 96, 106, 109–10, 117, 119, 120, 141, 144, 145, 146, 163, 173, 175, 198n10, 207n20
and Uncle Lingayya, 89, 90, 138, 148
as a vegetarian goddess, 110, 119, 122, 198n10
virility of, 52, 54
as a warrior goddess, 8–9, 90
worship of, 34, 97, 116, 133, 178, 181–82, 201n26
See also Chamundeshwari temple; goddesses
Chamundi of the Hill
and Aisu ("Many"), 197–98n6, 198n8
and *Bettada Chamundi*, 1, 190n6, 194n35
and Chamaraja's house god, 137
and Chamundi, 96, 115–16, 117, 125–35, 191n15
and Chamundi Hill, 113, 117

and community, 7, 58, 83, 113, 191n15
and copywrite issues, 22–23
dates of versions of, 1, 76–77
and deities' identities, 2, 13, 74
and devotion *(bhakti)*, 110, 112–13, 178
and devotional songs or poetry, 3–4, 77–81
and dharma, 1, 80, 177, 179
and folk history, 24, 70–71, 85
and folk locality, 7–8, 24
and folk traditions, 8–9, 19–20, 22–23, 24, 25, 28, 110–11, 121, 146, 194n37
form and style of, 2–4
as a group of songs, 1, 27
and helper goddesses, 51
and hierarchy, 24–25, 113, 123
high and low in, 19, 115–17, 122–23
and Kalinga, 81, 167, 169
Kamsale version of, 105–107
and Lingayatism, 94, 97, 107
and local deities, 6–7, 14, 29, 40–41, 71, 72, 77, 79, 80, 83, 92, 107
and local history, 28–29
and locality, 6, 23, 52, 73
as a *mahatmya* (glorification text), 4
and marriage, 85–86, 88, 90, 93–94, 105, 117, 138, 146, 174–75, 178
and meat-eating, 42, 175
and modern media, 16, 17
and Mysore, India, 6, 7, 57–58
and myth, 2–3, 4, 23–24, 27–28, 29, 42–45, 51–54, 57–58, 60, 70, 72–73, 82, 85, 86, 90, 110, 116, 189n1, 189n4
narrative of, 4–6, 13, 14, 21–24, 25, 27–28, 29, 44, 48, 52–54, 57–58,

Chamundi of the Hill (continued)
    69, 70–73, 77–81, 82, 85, 86, 88, 90, 91, 92, 104, 107, 110, 115–16, 117, 121, 125, 191n15, 194n38, 214–15n64
  Odda version of, 104, 105, 106
  and oral folk traditions, 20, 22–23, 110, 194n38, 195–96n45
  and Pan-Indian myths, 27, 28
  pilgrimage networks in, 73–74, 77, 79, 82–83, 112–13, 117
  and place, 20, 82
  and Puranas, 4, 189n4
  ragas (melodies) of, 3, 190n6
  and regional deities, 8, 24
  and religious practice, 107, 110
  and reproduction, 52, 53–54
  and ritual, 48, 74, 87–88, 95–96, 99, 110, 115, 116, 117, 121, 122–23
  and romance between deities, 3, 14, 24, 70–73, 74, 80, 85, 88–89, 90, 93–94, 102–103, 107, 150, 170
  and royal and Sanskrit traditions, 24
  and royal devotion and patronage, 34–36
  and sacred history, 4, 60
  and Segalian myth analysis, 189n1
  and "She Bathes in the Kapini and Kaveri," 86–90
  and "Sister, Stand on My Tongue and Fight," 27, 29, 30, 33–35, 38, 51
  and slaying of buffalo demon Mahisha, 28, 70, 71, 177
  and social change, 18, 24
  and song "Batting Your Eyes, You called," 171–72
  and song "Dharma Should Be with Us," 177–79
  and song "Go, Give My Love to Your Brother-in-Law Nanjunda . . . ," 116–17, 140–54
  and song "Have You Lost Interest in Your Wife?," 77–80, 155–63
  and song "I Can Raise the Dead!," 173–76
  and song "O Mother, Grant Me a Wish," 125–26
  and song "She Bathes in the Kapini and Kaveri," 134–35
  and song "Sister, Stand on My Tongue and Fight!," 127–33
  and song "Tripping over Himself, He Runs to Chamundi of the Hill's House," 164–70
  and song "Who Are You Wise Woman? You Are So Charming!," 136–39
  and song "You Aren't Thinking about Your Wife," 117
  and spaciality, 122–23
  translation of, 16–17, 21, 23, 25, 28, 125–79
  and the two-brother trope, 51
  and urban histories, 62, 77, 82–83
  Uttanahalli's role in, 40–41, 52, 73–74, 77
  and visions of Mysore's destruction, 74–76
  and worship of goddesses, 96
Chamundi Siri Chamundi (Akki), 22
Channabasava, 100, 101
Christianity, 114, 198n6

Dasara, 21, 38, 45, 54, 72, 99, 199n14
  See also Mysore; rituals
Devi Bhagavata Purana, 50, 71
Devi Mahatmya
  Chamunda in, 43, 44–45, 49, 201n27, 203n40

and goddess Durga, 42
and goddesses in brahminic
  pantheon, 47
and Goddess glorification, 121,
  191n15
goddess production in, 51
and nonagamic rituals, 121
plot of, 121–22
and slaying of buffalo demon,
  45–47, 71
and slaying of the demon Raktabija,
  41, 44–45
terrifying goddesses in, 50
Dylan, Bob, 114

Foucault, Michel, 111, 112

goddesses
  and Aiyai, 50, 199n17
  and Ambika, 45 fig. 2.5, 46
  and aniconic image of Chamunda
    Maramma, 96, 97 fig. 4.1
  and animal sacrifice, 213n45, 213n48
  and battles of the Goddess, 27,
    43–46, 45 fig. 2.5, 86, 127, 147,
    201n28
  blood sacrifices to, 15, 40–41,
    72, 118, 119, 121–22, 199n15,
    200n26, 204n42
  and brahminic tradition, 47,
    48–49, 96, 200n21, 212n43
  and Chamunda, 50, 94–95, 109,
    193n30, 197n4, 201n27, 202n29,
    203–204n42, 203n39, 203n40,
    212n43
  and Chamundeshwari, 109–10,
    181–82, 183, 185, 186, 197n4,
    199n15
  and Chamundi, 63, 95, 96, 97,
    109, 181–82, 193–94n32, 193n30,
    207n29

and Chamundi Hill, 110–11, 181,
  197n4, 199n15
and *Chamundi of the Hill*, 7, 8, 29,
  42, 71–72, 75, 94, 107
and demons (*asuras*), 44, 46, 51
devotion (*bhakti*) to, 13, 40, 54, 55,
  72, 94–95, 121, 199n17, 217n32
and Durga, 8, 42, 48, 88, 94, 109,
  151, 193n29, 207n21, 213n45
and festivals, 143, 212–13n45
and fire-walking, 97, 99 fig. 4.4
food preparation for, 98 fig. 4.3
and Goddess as creator, 46
and Goddesses *Mahadevi* and
  adishakti, 36–37
and goddess traditions, 42,
  47, 118, 122, 201n26, 202n30,
  217–18n36
and *gramadevates* (goddesses of
  villages), 13, 40–42, 95–97, 99,
  197n4, 207n20, 212n45
and Great Goddess tradition, 42,
  47, 122, 182
and Hidimba, 51
and "high" and "low" traditions,
  110–15, 118–19
and human sacrifice, 49, 199n15,
  199n17
identities of, 50–51, 95, 109–10,
  118, 119
and Jwalamukhi, 15, 41, 48, 182,
  193n31, 215n1, 216n24
and Kali, 15, 41, 42, 44, 45, 47, 48,
  51, 151, 152, 213n45
and Kali / Chamunda, 44, 47
and liberation, 25, 46, 50, 121, 122
and local deities, 1, 2, 5, 29,
  40–41, 42, 43, 72, 75, 80, 81, 90,
  94, 95–97, 110–11, 155, 197n2,
  199n17, 200n21
and local history, 54

goddesses *(continued)*
 and Mahadevi, 47
 and Mahakali, 94
 and Marammas *(gramadevatas)*, 95–96, 151, 152, 201n26, 219n29
 and Mariyamman's festival, 212–13n45
 and meat eating, 214n58, 216–17n25
 and Mysore tradition, 29, 37–38, 40–41, 73
 and myth, 3, 24, 29, 38, 41, 42, 45–46, 50, 51–53, 54, 96, 193n29
 and name of Bhuktimuktipradayini, 121, 122
 and Navaratri, 213n48
 and Pan-Indian goddesses, 41, 42, 88
 and pilgrimage sites, 193n29
 and ritual, 101, 118–20, 121
 and "Royal and Local Goddesses," 28
 and sacred sites, 192–93n29
 and the *saptamatrikas* (or "seven little mothers"), 10–11, 201–202n29, 212n43
 and Sati, 15, 48
 and seven sister goddesses, 15, 79, 95, 100, 177, 193n30, 207n29
 and *shakti pitha*, 193n29
 and Shiva, 42, 48, 193n29
 and Shri Kantheshwara, 65
 shrines for, 12, 95, 96, 97, 100, 193n29
 and slaying of buffalo demon Mahisha, 23, 24, 38, 45–46, 52, 53–54, 71, 85, 197n2, 197n3
 and songs of Bengal, 13
 and universal Goddess, 7, 36
 and Uttanahalli, 63–64, 182, 215n1, 219n28
 varied traditions of, 24–25, 42, 94, 95
 and Vindhyavasini, 35, 36
 and war against Mysore, 151–52
 of wealth, 185
 and wives Deviri and Somaji, 178
 worship of, 15, 96, 118, 121, 178, 181, 183, 204n42
 and wrath of Durgas, 75–76, 94
 and Yellamma, 105
 See also Chamundi; Dasara; *Devi Mahatmya*; Navaratri ("Nine Nights") festival; Uttanahalli
gods
 and Brahma, 33, 49, 52, 62, 105, 106, 132, 173–74, 221n72
 and *Chamundi of the Hill*, 8, 107, 132
 and demons *(asuras)*, 43
 and devotion *(bhakti)*, 55
 and Kalinga, 13, 72–73
 and Krishna, 32–33, 34, 35, 52, 62, 71, 73, 118, 128–29, 181, 186, 218n8, 218n10, 218n11
 and local deities, 1, 2, 69–70, 72–73, 186
 and Lord Cheluva Naranyana, 63, 181
 and Lord Naranyana, 63, 181
 and myth, 3, 30, 72–73
 and Nandi (or Basavanna), 13, 73
 and offering of war implements, 46
 offerings to, 118
 and Rama, 118
 and right-handed practices, 87
 and Shiva, 10, 11, 12, 13, 18, 30, 33, 36, 49, 63, 64, 65, 69, 70, 71, 73, 77, 78, 80, 88, 91–92, 93, 100, 125, 127, 132, 136, 142, 155, 157, 160, 161, 162, 177, 178, 181, 182, 183, 190n7, 192n27, 193n29, 197n2, 203n40, 208–209n11, 208n7, 208n8, 209n12, 210n23,

213n50, 218n16, 219n19, 219n20, 220n47, 220n51
and Vishnu, 10, 50, 62, 118, 137, 218n9, 221n70
worship of, 136, 178, 183
and Yadava line, 62
and Yama of the netherworld, 221n64
and Yoga Narasimha, 63
See also Nanjunda

Great Kings of Mysore, The (Maisurina Shriman Maharajajavara Vamshavali)
author of, 62, 70
and Chamaraja's wife Devajammanni, 183–85, 186
and *Chamundi of the Hill*, 63
and goddess Uttanahalli, 41, 74, 182
and identity of goddess, 36, 181
and Krishnaraja Wodeyar III, 62, 69, 70, 183, 187
and location of Chamundi Hill, 181
and marriage, 67–68, 186
migration / conquest in, 74–75
and pilgrimage, 73, 186
as a serial, 206n15
and the two-brother trope, 69, 181–86
and Wodeyar origin story, 35–37, 51, 63–70, 77, 181–87
See also Mysore; Wodeyar, Yaduraya

Hinduism
and animal sacrifice, 118, 119, 120, 200n26
bathing's importance in, 87–88
braminic pantheon of, 59
and commensality, 217n27, 217n28
and convergence of rivers, 87–88
and cremation of the dead, 213n49
and devotional *(bhakti)* traditions, 59, 118
goddess worship in, 121, 191n15
and hierarchy, 118
and "high-caste" Hinduism, 105, 118
and Hindu diaspora communities, 216n12
and Lingayatism, 90, 91–93, 194–95n40, 208n7, 213n49, 217n29, 218n17
and marriage, 86, 90, 105, 219n30, 219n32
material and spiritual fulfillment in, 122
and name of Bhuktimuktipradayini, 121
and pilgrimage, 59–60
and puranas, 59
right-handed practices in, 87
ritual in, 8, 10, 40–41, 118, 119–21
Shaiva Lingayat sect of, 88
and the Sharanas, 90, 91–92, 93, 213n49
and Shiva *puja*, 92
and *sthalapurana* ("sacred geographies"), 59–60
and universal ruler *(manu)*, 122
and Vedic sacrifice, 118
and vegetarianism, 118
See also caste; goddesses; gods; Lingayatism; rituals

Kamsales
and *Bettada Chamundi*, 105, 208n10n
caste of, 91, 105
and cymbals *(kamsale)*, 17–18, 91
as devotees of Shiva, 190n7
home of, 18

Kamsales *(continued)*
  and issue of caste- and ritual-mixing, 107
  and Kamsale Mahadevayya, 17, 21, 25, 95
  and Lingayatism, 18
  as performers, 1, 6, 16–18, 91, 190n7
  and religious and oral histories, 18
  and social change, 18, 105, 106
  and wives Deviri and Somaji, 208–9n11
  See also *Chamundi of the Hill*
Kannada
  and aphorisms called *vachanas*, 18, 21
  and *Bettada Chamundi*, 1, 17, 21, 22–23, 25, 216n23
  and buffalo demon, 30
  and *Chamundi of the Hill*, 1, 27, 51, 106
  and collections of songs, 194n34
  and cowives, 89
  and deity Madeshwara, 18
  and domestication in households, 90
  and folklore studies, 22, 104
  and folk songs, 58
  and Indian calendars, 37
  janapada champu style in, 3
  and Kannada Tammadi, 12
  and *Kodagu*, 47
  literature of, 88
  local songs of, 43
  and marriage, 219n22, 219n24
  and Mysore, India, 16, 29
  and name of village Uttanahalli, 13–14
  narrative of, 218n6
  and Sandalwood, 85, 207n1
  and temple inscriptions, 48
  theater in, 21
  and translation of *betta*, 216n22
  and understanding Mysore, 70
  See also Rajashekhara, P.K.
Karnataka, India
  and blood sacrifices, 215n2
  and brahminic and royal culture, 19–20
  and cult of the seven little mothers, 10
  and discrimination, 25
  domestic life in, 9
  and folk culture, 16, 19–20
  goddess traditions of, 110, 121
  history of, 25, 183
  and Karnataka Prevention of Animal Sacrifices Act, 120
  and king Shuradevaraya, 64, 182–83
  and Lingayatism, 18, 92–93, 210n21
  and local deities, 6, 13
  marriage in, 85, 89, 91
  media reproduction of culture of, 20, 21–22
  and Mysore City, 9–10
  and Mysore kingdom, 60
  and pageant of Kannadiga, 38
  pilgrimage sites of, 10
  and sacred history, 2, 3
  Schedule Castes in, 105
  Shaiva Sharana saints of, 3
  southern region of, 19, 21, 24–25, 27, 43, 60, 85, 89, 90, 91, 92, 107, 109, 110, 121, 122, 195n42, 207n23, 220n38, 221n69, 221n75
  village festivals in, 1
  Virangere, Bandikere, Sunnakere, and Halakere in, 76
  See also caste

Lamar, Kendrick, 114

Index

Lingayatism, 90, 91–93, 94, 100, 101, 103

Mahabaleshwara (Shiva) temple, 10, 11
Mahabharata, 59, 62, 94, 206n10
Malatimadhava (Bhavabhuti), 49
Miranda, Lin-Manuel, 114
Mysore
  and Anglo-Mysore wars, 61
  British colonial history of, 60–61, 62
  and buffalo demon *mahisha*, 53, 71
  castes of, 42
  and Chamaraja's wife Devajammanni, 183–86,
  and Chamundi, 134, 140, 147
  and Chamundi Hill, 50, 53–54, 53 *fig.* 2.6a, 53 *fig.* 2.6b, 63, 71, 73–74, 86, 99, 100, 120, 196–97n2
  and *Chamundi of the Hill*, 52–54, 74–75, 127, 128, 134
  Dasara ("Tenth") festival in, 38, 120
  and devotional and ritual complexes, 119
  and drama *Chama Cheluve*, 16
  as epicenter of divine power, 27, 81
  and festivals, 221n71
  folk tradition of, 21, 28, 48, 57–58, 70–73, 82–83, 85
  histories of, 24, 28, 29, 34–37, 48, 57–58, 60–70, 71, 74–75, 76, 82–83, 85, 206n12
  jasmine of, 144, 150, 156, 168
  Kannambadi in, 100
  kingdom of, 24, 34–35, 60–62, 63, 64, 65, 68–70, 117, 183, 183–87, 191n19, 206n9, 206n12, 207n27
  and Krishnaraja Wodeyar III, 69, 76, 77, 191n19, 207n27
  as land of the buffalo, 29, 30
  and lineage of the Yadus, 62, 65, 181, 183
  literature of, 20, 35, 61, 63–70, 74–75, 181–87, 197n4, 198n10
  and local deities, 24, 27, 29, 34–35, 48, 52, 65, 69–70, 75, 90, 93, 182, 197n4
  and locality, 53, 69–73
  Maramma temple in, 201n26
  and modern media, 21, 57
  and Mysore Hill, 138–39
  and Mysore kings, 12, 28, 30, 34–37, 38, 48, 61–65, 68–70, 77, 89, 90, 182–83, 186–87, 198n10
  Mysore Palace in, 10, 38
  and Mysore Prevention of Animal Sacrifices Act, 120
  and Mysore Radio Broadcasting network, 21
  myths of, 29, 51–54, 60, 70–71, 72, 80
  name of, 29–30, 197n3
  Navaratri ("Nine Nights") festival in, 38, 72
  and oral history, 27, 110
  and Pan-Indian deities, 69–70
  and pilgrimage, 69, 73–74, 82–83
  princely state of, 47, 61
  and Queen Devajammanni, 65–66, 67, 68, 183, 183–85
  religious landscape of, 27, 28, 58, 82–83
  ritual practice in, 115, 191n20, 198n10
  royal history of, 57, 58, 60–70, 82, 181–87, 198n12
  and sacred histories (*sthalapurana*), 27, 69
  and Shri Kanthadatta Narasimharaja Wodeyar, 70
  Shrirangapattana in, 61

Mysore *(continued)*
 Trineshwara temple in, 64
 and the two-brother trope, 62–69, 73, 181–87
 and visions of destruction, 100, 143, 150–52
 Wodeyar foundational narrative about, 62–70, 74–75, 181–87, 198n11
 Wodeyar rulers of, 37, 48, 61, 62–63, 68–69, 70, 76, 77, 187, 191n19, 193n29, 197n3, 198n10, 200n19, 206n11
 and wrath of goddesses, 104
 See also Dasara; Mysore City; Sultan, Tipu
Mysore City
 and Buffalo Point, 30, 32 *fig.* 2.2
 as capital of Mysore, 61
 and Chamundi Hill, 4, 9, 10, 30–31, 32, 36, 37, 38, 40, 50, 109, 191n17
 and "City of Chamunda," 197n4
 Dufferin Clock Tower in, 76–77
 histories of, 181–87
 Kodibhairava shrine of, 65
 and local deities, 2, 5, 30, 33–34, 95, 182
 and location of Nanjangugu, 11–12
 and Mahisha, 31 *fig.* 2.1, 61, 94
 mythic history of, 30–35, 61, 82
 as pilgrimage site, 77, 82–83, 85
 royal history of, 60–65, 77, 82, 182
 Shiva temple in, 64
 and shrines to goddesses, 100
 and slaying of buffalo demon, 85
 and urban histories, 57–58
 Virangere and Sunnakere in, 76
 visions of destruction of, 94
 Wodeyar foundational narrative about, 35–37

Wodeyar rulers of, 60, 185–87

Nanjangudu
 and Chamundi, 81, 87, 105–106, 125, 173–78
 city of, 70, 136, 148, 160, 164, 171
 and devotees of Nanjunda, 78–79, 80, 156–59, 160, 161
 divine power in, 81
 festivals in, 205n55
 and ippe plant, 162, 220–21n59
 and the Kapini River, 134, 147, 176, 208n4
 and local deities, 2, 5, 6, 70–71, 72, 73, 79, 80–81, 89, 137, 153
 location of, 11–12, 14, 40, 63, 77
 Nanjunda in, 139, 173–75
 as pilgrimage site, 69, 73, 74, 113
 and Shiva, 63
 Shri Kantheshwara as resident of, 65, 183
 and wives Deviri and Somaji, 164–66, 174, 178
 See also Nanjunda
Nanjunda, 11 *fig.* 1.2, 139
 and bathing, 136, 171
 and caste hierarchy, 105
 and *Chamundi of the Hill*, 136–39, 191n15
 and the Chola period, 13
 and community, 7
 as deity of Nanjangudu, 2, 5, 11, 65, 70–71, 77–79, 88–89, 101, 104, 105, 136, 137, 148, 153, 156–59, 161–62
 devotion *(bhakti)* to, 4, 54, 78–79, 155, 156–58, 161–63
 festivals of, 12
 and healing traditions, 12–13, 136, 168
 and Kalinga, 13, 167
 and kings of Mysore, 12

and Lingayat identity, 107, 136
as a local deity, 48, 54, 80–81, 90, 149
Madeshwara as brother of, 13, 210n27
and marriage, 220n44
name of, 48
and relationship with Chamundi, 1, 3, 4–5, 6, 13, 14, 16, 24, 31, 42, 54, 58, 69, 70–73, 74, 77–79, 80, 85, 88–90, 93–94, 100, 101–106, 116–17, 137–39, 141, 146, 147–50, 154–72, 176, 214n63, 221n60
and rituals, 105
and Shiva, 4, 12, 13, 92, 210n23
and slaying of demon giant, 208n8
songs about, 18, 35–36, 58, 70–71, 72, 73, 74, 77–79, 80, 116–17, 136–63, 164–70, 171–76
temple of, 12
and wives Deviri and Somaji, 4–5, 13, 54, 71, 72, 78, 80, 89, 93, 101, 103, 104–106, 137, 138, 140, 148–49, 153, 156, 158, 167, 171–76, 192n28, 208–209n11, 214n55, 214n56, 214n57
Navaratri ("Nine Nights") festival, 38, 45, 72, 99, 101, 199n13
See also Dasara

Preface to Morals, A (Lippman), 113, 114

Rajashekhara, P.K., 13, 17, 21, 22–23, 25, 190n6
Ramayana, 59
religion
  and animal sacrifice, 118–20, 200n26, 201n26, 217n35
  and Brahminization, 200n21
  and Christianity, 114, 195n41, 198n6
  and Emile Durkheim, 112, 113
  and folk culture, 113
  and full moon festival, 139, 149
  and goddess traditions, 122
  and hierarchy, 111
  and "high" and "low" culture, 113–15
  and "high" and "low" religion, 114, 115, 123, 216n14
  and indigenous perspectives, 115
  and locality, 190n12, 190n13
  and Mexican Catholic charms, 191n22
  and popular culture, 216n21
  and religious identity, 215n8
  and religious value systems, 122
  and sacred spaces, 112
  and Sharana philosophy, 195n41
  and spaciality, 111–13, 115, 190n11
  See also Buddhism; Christianity; Hinduism; rituals
rituals
  and *agamic* rituals, 12, 49, 119
  and animal sacrifice, 118, 120, 220n43
  and animal slaughter, 5, 15, 110, 120
  and bathing, 76, 86–88, 87
  and blood rituals, 8, 40, 41, 119, 120, 121
  and brahminical ritual, 41, 101, 118, 200n21
  and buffalo sacrifice, 100, 101
  calendars for, 55
  and caste hierarchy, 118
  and caste identity, 18, 102–103, 107
  and Chamunda devotion, 49
  for Chamundi, 11, 35, 37–38, 96, 109–10, 115

rituals *(continued)*
  and Chamundi festival (*utsava*), 99–100
  and connection to sovereignty, 52
  and Dasara rituals, 205n54
  and discrimination, 24, 83, 91
  and festival of Okuli, 79
  and goddess traditions, 25, 36–38, 40, 49–50, 54–55, 94–97, 99–100, 102, 109–10, 111, 118–19, 120, 121, 202n30, 213n45
  and hierarchy, 90
  and "high" and "low" traditions, 111, 121
  in Hinduism, 10, 87
  and human sacrifice, 49–50
  importance of, 113
  and insemination for married couple, 12
  and liberation, 122
  and life-cycle rituals (*samskara*), 76
  and Lingayat identity, 101
  and local communities, 6, 40, 76
  and local deities, 40–41, 54–55, 74, 110
  and "lower castes," 106
  and male king's virility, 52
  and marriage, 93, 100, 210n28
  and meat eating, 122
  of Mysore kings, 28, 35, 38, 40
  and nonagamic rituals, 40, 42, 121
  and the Oddas, 105
  and *puja* ritual, 38, 40, 41, 88
  and purity scale, 91
  and religious tradition, 24, 25, 191n15
  and ritual handbooks, 48, 191n15
  and ritual pollution cleansing, 87–88
  and ritual practice, 8, 28, 38, 40, 41, 48, 87, 88, 96, 105, 110, 115, 116, 117, 118–19
  and ritual professionals, 100
  royal participation in, 37–38, 40
  and Sanskrit rituals, 47–48, 198n10
  and the Sharanas, 101
  and Shivarchakas, 191n20
  for Uttanahalli, 15, 40, 41, 54, 109–10, 115, 200n19
  and vows, 211n39

Sanskrit
  and Brahminization, 47–48
  and buffalo demon *mahisha*, 30
  and Chamunda, 202n29, 212n43
  and the *Devi Mahatmya*, 121
  epics in, 69, 70
  and festivals Navaratri and Dasara, 99
  goddesses' names in, 41, 49
  and goddess traditions, 110, 202–3n36
  and *gramadevate* (goddess of village), 40
  and Great Goddess tradition, 47
  and local deities, 47
  and Mysore, 29, 206n10
  myths in, 28, 42, 43, 94
  and name of Bhuktimuktipradayini, 121
  and Pan-Indic traditions, 43
  and Puranas (ancient mythic stories), 4, 43, 94
  and Sanskrit Hinduism, 47
  and Sanskritic suffixes, 48
  and Sanskritization, 28, 47–48, 198n10, 200n21, 202n36
  and Sanskrit rituals, 47, 198n10
  and slaying of blood-seed demon (Raktabija), 28
  and slaying of buffalo demon Mahisha, 28, 71
  and temple inscriptions, 48

traditions of, 12, 20, 24, 40, 47, 216n24
well known narratives of, 109
Satyanarayana (Vishnu) temple, 10
Sultan, Tipu, 12, 18, 60–61

Uttanahalli, 14 *fig.* 1.3
and Aisu ("Many"), 44, 71
and animal sacrifice, 220n44
and bathing, 144
birth of, 4, 33, 51, 52, 71, 72, 129, 133
and caste, 41, 96, 101–102, 154
and Chamundi Hill, 5, 14, 54, 72, 75, 81, 116
and community, 7
and devotion *(bhakti)*, 4, 14, 54, 72, 119
festivals of, 34, 72, 96, 153
food preparation for, 116
as a "go-between" goddess, 1, 14, 74, 77, 78, 93–94, 102, 103, 117, 146, 155–63, 164
as goddess of Uttanahalli, 2, 4, 13–14, 40–41, 143, 182
and goddess traditions, 40–42, 123, 193n30
identity of, 40–41, 42, 74, 109–10, 119, 193n30
and Jwalamukhi, 15, 64, 182, 198n10, 215n1, 219n28
and Kali, 15
and local deities, 2, 6, 40–42, 48, 54, 72, 81,
and local deities, 119, 198n10
location of, 72, 74, 117
as Mariamma, 40
and myth, 116
name of, 48, 74

offerings to, 15, 133
as pilgrimage site, 69, 74, 113
and ritual practice, 115, 118–19
sacrifices to, 72, 109, 119
as sister of Chamundi, 13, 27, 33, 34, 40, 71–72, 73, 93, 96, 101, 109, 116, 117, 129–30, 131, 133, 142–47, 148, 149, 154, 155, 163, 193n30
and song "Go, Give My Love to Your Brother-in-Law Nanjunda, and Tell Him to Return," 140–54
and song "Sister, Stand on My Tongue and Fight," 129–31, 133
and story of Raktabija, 15, 63–64
temple of, 15, 17, 54–55, 74, 81, 82 *fig.* 3.2, 109–10, 117, 119
and Uttanahalli Shri Pada, 15 *fig.* 1.4
village of, 13–14, 17, 40, 41, 70, 72, 73, 74, 110, 116, 117, 133, 142, 182, 215n2
worship of, 69, 72, 74, 116, 133, 182, 200n19
See also goddesses

Wodeyar, Chamaraja, 34–36, 61, 77, 116, 125, 133
See also Chamundi; *Chamundi of the Hill*
Wodeyar, Kanthirava Narasaraja, 30
Wodeyar, Krishnaraja III, 10, 12, 34, 35, 48, 61
See also Great Kings of Mysore, The (*Maisurina Shriman Maharajajavara Vamshavali*)
Wodeyar, Yaduraya, 34, 36, 37, 63–70, 181–83, 185–87

www.ingramcontent.com/pod-product-compliance
Lightning Source LLC
Chambersburg PA
CBHW020645230426
43665CB00008B/327